THE POLITICAL
PHILOSOPHY OF
COSMOPOLITANISM

EDITED BY

GILLIAN BROCK

University of Auckland

AND

HARRY BRIGHOUSE

University of Wisconsin, Madison

CAMBRIDGE
UNIVERSITY PRESS

CAMBRIDGE UNIVERSITY PRESS
Cambridge, New York, Melbourne, Madrid, Cape Town, Singapore, São Paulo

Cambridge University Press
The Edinburgh Building, Cambridge CB2 2RU, UK

Published in the United States of America by Cambridge University Press, New York

www.cambridge.org
Information on this title: www.cambridge.org/9780521846608

First published 2005
Reprinted 2006

Printed in the United Kingdom at the University Press, Cambridge

A catalogue record for this book is available from the British Library

ISBN-13 978-0-521-84660-8 hardback
ISBN-13 978-0-521-60909-8 paperback
ISBN-10 0-521-84660-9 hardback
ISBN-10 0-521-60909-7 paperback

THE POLITICAL PHILOSOPHY OF COSMOPOLITANISM

In a period of rapid internationalization of trade and increased labor mobility, is it relevant for nations to think about their moral obligations to others? Do national boundaries have fundamental moral significance, or do we have moral obligations to foreigners that are equal to our obligations to our compatriots? The latter position is known as cosmopolitanism, and this volume brings together a number of distinguished political philosophers and theorists to explore cosmopolitanism: what it is, and the positive case which can be made for it. Their essays provide a comprehensive overview of both the current state of the debate and the different visions of cosmopolitanism with which we can move forward, and will interest a wide range of readers in philosophy, political theory, and law.

GILLIAN BROCK is Senior Lecturer in Philosophy at the University of Auckland.

HARRY BRIGHOUSE is Professor of Philosophy and Affiliate Professor of Education Policy Studies at the University of Wisconsin, Madison.

Contents

List of contributors   *page* vii
Preface   ix

1   Introduction   1
    Gillian Brock and Harry Brighouse

2   Principles of cosmopolitan order   10
    David Held

3   Territorial justice and global redistribution   28
    Hillel Steiner

4   International justice and the basic needs principle   39
    David Copp

5   Cosmopolitans, cosmopolitanism, and human flourishing   55
    Christine Sypnowich

6   Global justice, moral development, and democracy   75
    Christopher Bertram

7   A cosmopolitan perspective on the global economic order   92
    Thomas Pogge

8   In the national interest   110
    Allen Buchanan

9   Cosmopolitan respect and patriotic concern   127
    Richard W. Miller

10   Persons' interests, states' duties, and global governance   148
    Darrel Moellendorf

v

11   The demands of justice and national allegiances   164
     Kok-Chor Tan

12   Cosmopolitanism and the compatriot priority principle   180
     Jocelyne Couture and Kai Nielsen

13   Beyond the social contract: capabilities and global justice   196
     Martha Nussbaum

14   Tolerating injustice   219
     Jon Mandle

15   Cosmopolitan hope   234
     Catriona McKinnon

Bibliography   250
Index   260

Contributors

CHRISTOPHER BERTRAM University of Bristol (Philosophy)

HARRY BRIGHOUSE University of Wisconsin, Madison (Philosophy and Education Policy Studies)

GILLIAN BROCK University of Auckland (Philosophy)

ALLEN BUCHANAN Duke University (Philosophy and Public Policy Studies)

DAVID COPP University of Florida (Philosophy)

JOCELYNE COUTURE Université du Québec, Montréal (Philosophy)

DAVID HELD London School of Economics and Political Science (Government)

JON MANDLE SUNY-Albany (Philosophy)

CATRIONA MCKINNON University of Reading (Politics and International Relations)

RICHARD MILLER Cornell University (Philosophy)

DARREL MOELLENDORF San Diego State University (Philosophy)

KAI NIELSEN Concordia University (Philosophy)

MARTHA NUSSBAUM University of Chicago (Philosophy, Law, and Divinity)

THOMAS POGGE Centre for Applied Philosophy and Public Ethics, at the Australian National University

HILLEL STEINER University of Manchester (Government, International Politics, and Philosophy)

CHRISTINE SYPNOWICH Queen's University, Kingston, Ontario (Philosophy)

KOK-CHOR TAN University of Pennsylvania (Philosophy)

Preface

Trade has internationalized rapidly and labor mobility has increased significantly since the end of the Cold War. These developments have sharply raised questions about the moral significance of national boundaries. What obligations do citizens of wealthy countries have toward the citizens of poorer countries? Are they entitled to restrict the entry of immigrant labor, and if so in what ways? Are they entitled to restrict the exit of capital? Do wealthy citizens of wealthy countries owe more to their less advantaged compatriots than to foreigners who are even poorer? Political theorists have started to address these and related issues. They fall into two broad camps: those who consider national boundaries to have fundamental moral significance, and those who consider them to have no, or only derivative, moral significance. We observed that the latter camp, which we think of as committed to cosmopolitanism, had done a great deal of work countering the claims of nationality, but much less work elaborating the detail of, and defending, a distinctively cosmopolitan political theory. So we asked a number of political theorists whose work embodied a cosmopolitan perspective to write essays contributing to the task of defending a positive political philosophy of cosmopolitanism. This anthology is the result.

Most of the contributions were written specifically for this collection. However, in four cases, some material originally appeared elsewhere. The contributions by Hillel Steiner, Allen Buchanan, Richard Miller, and Martha Nussbaum contain previously published work, and we are grateful both to the authors and the publishers of the original pieces for permission to reprint that material here. Hillel Steiner's essay is a revised version of "Liberalism and nationalism" which originally appeared in *Analyse and Kritik*, 17 (1995), pp. 12–20. Allen Buchanan's chapter contains material that was previously published in "Beyond the national interest" *Philosophical Topics*, 30 (2002), pp. 97–131. Richard Miller's chapter, "Cosmopolitan respect and patriotic concern" was originally published in *Philosophy and Public Affairs*, 27 (1998) pp. 202–24. Martha Nussbaum's chapter reproduces and revises material from "Beyond the Social Contract: capabilities and global justice. An Olaf Palme Lecture delivered in Oxford on 19 June 2003" by Martha C. Nussbaum *Oxford Development Studies*, 32 (2004), pp. 3–18. Permission to reprint this last piece has been granted from the original source on condition that we insert a reference to the journal's web site, http://www.tandf.co.uk/journals.

We are very grateful to all the authors, especially for their enthusiasm and energy for the project. Thanks also go to Shanon Daly from the University of Auckland for help in preparing the manuscript for publication. We are especially grateful to Hilary Gaskin of Cambridge University Press for being so supportive of the project, for acting promptly and professionally at every point, and for being so easy to work with. Gillian Dadd, Maureen Leach, Alison Powell, Annette Youngman, and the rest of the production team at Cambridge also deserve special thanks for their excellent work on publishing this book.

CHAPTER I

Introduction

Gillian Brock and Harry Brighouse

GENERAL INTRODUCTION

Nationalism appears to have been on the rise since the mid 1980s. The break up of the former Soviet Union, and the dissolution of the barrier between Western and Eastern Europe triggered the political advance of nationalism in Eastern Europe, as new countries emerged, defining themselves in opposition to the previously existing regimes. Simultaneously, increased immigration from the former communist and from Muslim countries has fuelled nationalist sentiment within Western European states themselves. At its best, the latter development has prompted governments and citizens of those countries to reconsider the meaning of nationality, inducing a more inclusive and multicultural conception of "the nation." At its worst it has provoked xenophobic backlash.

At the same time, the north–south divide between wealthy industrial and post-industrial and poor developing countries has been an increasing object of political concern. Most developing countries are no longer colonies of wealthy ones, but many bear the marks of a history of domination and exploitation. The post-colonial period in Africa in particular has often been brutal, and the extent of responsibility of the former colonial regimes for what followed independence is not clear, and, whatever its extent, rarely acknowledged by the former imperial countries. The US and the former Soviet Union used Africa and the Middle East as focal points for the Cold War, and it is hard to believe that those regions did not suffer politically and economically as a result. While several European countries retain a special interest in their former colonies, that interest is not always helpful, and is rarely accompanied by a willingness to pay back.

Analytical political philosophy of the sort practiced by the contributors to this volume was not, initially, well prepared to deal with the rise of nationalism. The dominant framework for thinking about distributive principles was formulated by John Rawls in *A Theory of Justice* (1971). His

model developed there ignored the problems of thinking about questions
of international distribution, by assuming that the principles of justice are
developed for a closed scheme of social cooperation, which is entered by
birth and exited by death. There is nothing wrong with making such
simplifying assumptions for the sake of developing a theory, but the
assumptions framed the subsequent development of political philosophiz-
ing in such a way that issues of international and multicultural justice
remained at the margins of debate.

The fall-out from the break-up of the Soviet Union coincided with
Rawls's first attempt to consider how his theory might be extended to
cover issues concerning the moral relationships between states (Rawls,
1993a). Rawls's extension was surprisingly conservative. He did not argue
for the universal application of his principles of justice across state
boundaries, but for a respectful relationship between states (as representatives of peoples). He argued that liberal democratic regimes have an
obligation to deal with illiberal decent hierarchical regimes as equals, and
not to endeavor to impose their values; and also that national boundaries place limits on redistributive obligations. While Martha Nussbaum
(amongst many others) is highly critical of Rawls's approach, Jon Mandle's
contribution to this volume offers a sympathetic reconstruction and
reading of Rawls's arguments, claiming that they are in fact better
motivated and less quietistic than some critics have believed.

In the 1990s political philosophers began to address these problems in
earnest. A large and sophisticated literature has developed defending the
legitimacy and intrinsic moral significance of national boundaries; as has
a literature critiquing their legitimacy and significance. Some of this has
taken the form of direct criticisms and defenses of Rawls's positions; but
it has become increasingly independent of Rawls's terms of engagement.
The default position in the debate is, naturally enough, that national
boundaries have significance and legitimacy. Cosmopolitans dispute this
generally by making specific arguments against particular kinds of defenses of nationality. Because the debate has had this character it has been
less clear what the precise content of a positive cosmopolitanism is. It is
somewhat clear what cosmopolitans are against. But what are they for?
And why?

The term "cosmopolitanism" originates with the Stoics, whose idea of
being "a citizen of the world" neatly captures the two main aspects of
cosmopolitanism: that it entails a *thesis about identity* and that it entails a
thesis about responsibility (Scheffler, 1999). As Christine Sypnowich points
out in her contribution, cosmopolitanism, as a thesis about identity,

indicates that one is a person who is marked or influenced by various different cultures. The history of the word "cosmopolitan" has thus come to have both positive and negative connotations, depending on people's attitudes to such an identity. It has had negative connotations, for instance when cosmopolitans were regarded as foreigners to be excluded, such as in the case of Jews or Bolsheviks. It has also had more positive connotations when it is thought to mean that a person is well traveled or worldly, rather than narrow-minded or provincial.

As a thesis about responsibility, cosmopolitanism guides the individual outwards from obvious, local, obligations, and prohibits those obligations from crowding out obligations to distant others. Contrary to a parochial morality of loyalty, cosmopolitanism highlights the obligations we have to those whom we do not know, and with whom we are not intimate, but whose lives touch ours sufficiently that what we do can affect them.

But the precise content of these responsibilities, and the precise weight they have relative to local obligations, are widely disputed among cosmo-politans. The debate about cosmopolitanism is not identical with the debate about impartial and partial morality; cosmopolitans do not (typic-ally) dispute, for example, that we have obligations toward, and preroga-tives relative to, our friends, neighbors, and relatives. The particular focus of cosmopolitan thinking is on the content and weight of obligations beyond national (or, sometimes, state) boundaries, relative to the content and weight of those obligations to which national and state boundaries give rise. We might want to distinguish between *weak* and *strong* cosmo-politanism (as, for example, Scheffler, 1999 and Caney, 2001b, do). Weak cosmopolitanism just says that there are *some* extra-national obligations that have some moral weight. Strong cosmopolitanism, by contrast, claims that, at the most fundamental level, there are no society-wide principles of distributive justice that are not also global principles of distributive justice; and that our fellow nationals not only have no claim on us, but we have no right to use nationality (in contrast with friendship, or familial love) as a trigger for our discretionary behavior. Between these two extremes are a range of views concerning the content and relative weight of obligations and prerogatives relative to compatriots and non-compatriots.

The contributions to this volume suggest that this distinction, though useful, needs a great deal more nuance. For one thing, everyone has to be at least a weak cosmopolitan now if they are to maintain a defensible view, that is to say, it is hard to see how one can reject a view that all societies have *some* global responsibilities. Many theorists who conceive of themselves as anti-cosmopolitan endorse international obligations that are, at least in our real world context, quite demanding. Richard Miller, by contrast, argues in his contribution that certain facts about the structure of actual social institutions support a derivation of quite strong obligations to have special concern for one's compatriots from a cosmopolitan principle of equal respect for all. The contributions here move the debate into the detail of precise questions about the content and weight of the two different kinds of obligation relative to each other. David Held's position "layered cosmopolitanism" described below bridges that divide in an interesting way. Kok-Chor Tan also makes the point that if you have a just global basic structure, it does not seem to matter as much (or at all) if extra attention is then bestowed on compatriots. Strong cosmopolitanism seems to care about something that it is not clear we have to care about. If everyone is adequately positioned to have a good life, why say co-nationals cannot spend excess resources on each other?

Our purpose in commissioning the authors for this volume was to encourage them to work out some of the detail and nuance that a full and viable cosmopolitanism needs to press the debate forward. We approached theorists whose work embodied a cosmopolitan élan, and asked them to think through particular problems that a positive account of cosmopolitanism would have to face, and thus contribute to developing a positive theory of cosmopolitanism. Many of the authors chose to focus on the content of our distributive obligations beyond national boundaries, others on the role of national boundaries in determining the weight of our obligations, others still on the feasibility of cosmopolitan demands that, it is thought, bears on the question of their moral significance.

SOME FURTHER CENTRAL ISSUES DISCUSSED IN THE ANTHOLOGY

A key concern is how precisely to characterize cosmopolitanism. The crux of the idea of moral cosmopolitanism is that each human being has equal moral worth and that equal moral worth generates certain moral responsibilities that have universal scope.[1] Cosmopolitanism's force can well be appreciated by examining what the position excludes. For instance, cosmopolitanism rules out assigning ultimate (rather than derivative) value to collective entities such as nations or states, and it also rules out positions that attach no moral value to some people, or that weight the value people have differentially according to characteristics like ethnicity, race, or nationality. However, when we try to uncover what cosmopolitanism requires, here the view seems less determinate. Part of the indeterminacy is due to there being so many ways to interpret what our equal moral worth entails. Does equal moral worth mean that from the standpoint of a citizen, equal concern is due to all regardless of their citizenship (as, for example, Richard Miller denies)? Are all due equal consideration irrespective of nationality? Does equal moral worth entail ensuring each person has a right to an equal share of the value of all land (as Hillel Steiner maintains)? Should we be trying to equalize resources on the one hand, or our capabilities, or the conditions of human flourishing (as Nussbaum and Sypnowich believe)? Is the equality we should be concerned with different altogether, something like democratic equality (as Christopher Bertram argues)?

Or should we not be concerned with equality at all, but eliminating poverty, or gross insufficiency? Cosmopolitans typically draw attention to vast disparities in the life prospects that people from the poorest and the richest nations face. Such massive inequalities in life chances are typically condemned, but often the concern when investigated is not with inequality *per se*, but rather with the radical insufficiency that some must bear, especially when they are unable to meet basic needs. Whatever the other views to which a cosmopolitan may be committed, there is much agreement that, minimally, all people everywhere should be enabled to meet their basic needs (or some such). David Copp explores how this basic needs principle should apply globally. The contributions of Sypnowich, Nussbaum, Pogge, and Bertram all also bear strongly on the questions of what, precisely, would *constitute* insufficiency and how we would identify it.

Bracketing concerns about insufficiency, though, are there other reasons to be concerned with inequality? Bertram argues that insofar as inequality bears on our capability for democratic citizenship, it should be of concern, but typically, not otherwise. So long as we are all assured of the capability to function as a citizen of a democratic state, inequalities are not *per se* troublesome. Inequalities within a state are likely to be much more problematic than inequalities between states. Political participation in a particular society may require a certain level of wealth. Consider how if most of the population has access to radio, television, and the internet, increasingly collective political deliberations may take place on these media. Those who cannot afford these will be unable to participate politically in an effective manner. In this way inequalities within a state can have an important undermining effect on people's ability to function as equal citizens in a democratic state, and so how within country inequalities might be more damaging than between country inequality, at least with respect to democratic capability.

What else more definite can be said about the positive content of the cosmopolitan position? David Held argues that we can specify a set of interconnected principles that express well the idea of each person's having equal moral significance, and he selects eight of these principles as paramount. These are principles of: "(1) equal worth and dignity; (2) active agency; (3) personal responsibility and accountability; (4) consent; (5) collective decision-making about public matters through voting procedures; (6) inclusiveness and subsidiarity; (7) avoidance of serious harm; and (8) sustainability" (p. 12, below). While the eight principles are universal in scope, how the principles are to be applied or interpreted in local contexts must always take place in situated discussion. This mix of regulative principles combined with interpretive activity, Held terms a "'layered' cosmopolitan perspective" (p. 18, below).

What role is there for the state according to cosmopolitanism? According to some theorists such as Tan, if the cosmopolitan vision of justice is to have any appeal, it must adequately acknowledge "the local attachments and commitments people have that are characteristic of most meaningful and rewarding human lives" (p. 164, below). Tan argues that a way to do this would be to ensure that the global "basic structure" is cosmopolitan – that the global institutions are ones that adequately treat individuals as equals (regardless of their nationality, say). However, once the background global context is just, persons may defensibly favor the interests of their fellow nationals. So cosmopolitan principles should govern the global institutions, but should not directly regulate what choices people may make within the rules of the institutions. Favoring national interests or co-nationals is permissible so long as the background global institutions are just.

Allen Buchanan argues against a popular view (which he terms "The Permissible Exclusivity Thesis") that states may always permissibly decide a state's foreign policy exclusively on the basis of the national interest. This thesis entails the denial of even the weak cosmopolitanism that we earlier claimed could not plausibly be denied. Why is it false? For one thing, if you endorse human rights you cannot also hold the Permissible Exclusivity Thesis, since the commitment to human rights gives at least one important set of concerns that may trump concern with national interest, at least in some cases. If the thesis is so clearly false, what explains its popularity? Perhaps the thought that we have to face what amounts to a false dichotomy: either we may exclusively pursue national interest or we must be committed to a view that embraces some kind of impartial perspective in which no special weight can be given to the national interest. Since the latter option seems so unpalatable, we take up the former position. But, clearly, we have other options: it is not the case that the national interests must either count for nothing or everything. More nuanced positions are available in which we can try to (say) balance concern for human rights of all with any special regard we may show to compatriots or the country's welfare. At any rate, it is only when foreign policy is liberated from its focus on exclusively furthering the national interest that we can begin to ask the right questions.

Darrel Moellendorf also engages with the issue of how to weigh our duties to non-compatriots. He argues that the grounds for duties of justice are best located in our association with one another. Global economic association, which is largely non-voluntary, gives rise to duties of global justice. However, fulfilling duties of global justice is consistent with ignoring or discounting some of the interests of non-compatriots, especially those with whom the citizens are only in weak association. Just global governance requires global institutions that ensure duties of distributive justice are fulfilled and that adequate institutional provisions are made to protect other interests of persons, especially in cases of state failure. Summing up his position then: "states are permitted to ignore all of the time those interests of non-citizens that typically are not protected by the basic structure of states, other interests if and only if they are protected by suitable state or global structures, and that states are permitted to discount all of those duties that its citizens have to those non-citizens with whom they are only weakly associated, although in practice such discounting may be very hard to achieve without prohibitively high moral costs" (p. 161, below).

Many theorists believe there is good reason to include states in prescriptions for a just global order. States may well prove to be a good way to ensure democratic participation and protect certain basic interests and liberties in many cases. Besides, in many cases people are deeply attached to their nations. For many theorists, possibly most, the view is that a unitary world state is undesirable. Rather a federation of states is a more desirable, and in many cases efficient, way to distribute responsibility effectively (Copp and Nussbaum, for instance, maintain such views). But what attitude *should* good cosmopolitan citizens have toward the states they inhabit? None of our contributors endorses a radical view that citizens should be entirely devoid of fellow feeling for their compatriots, though many endorse views consistent with the idea that there is nothing wrong with lacking patriotic sentiment. Couture and Nielsen, however, argue for a *rooted cosmopolitanism* – the idea that patriotic sentiment is not only morally innocent, but can actually be valuable both in under-girding the moral virtues of cosmopolitanism and independently of that function.

Most cosmopolitans believe that there are significant duties of global justice. Many authors focus on issues to do with global distributive justice. Several present arguments why revenues should be collected and placed in a Global Fund of some kind and the proceeds should be disbursed, for instance to ensure that all are positioned to meet their basic needs with dignity, or to protect human rights, or to support unconditional basic income or initial capital stakes. Several arguments locate these duties in the troublesome global economic order that significantly undermines attempts to address global poverty. Moreover, our failure to reform the global economic order deeply implicates us in the misery of those almost 1.5 billion people who live in poverty around the world. Thomas Pogge's work has done much to illuminate the problematic issues.[2] In his contri-bution here he addresses many of his recent critics and responds to their concerns.

Whatever principles of global distributive justice we endorse, and what-ever form we think cosmopolitanism should take in our world, cosmopol-itans must address the issue of whether their project is feasible and whether hope for realizing the cosmopolitan vision is naive or misguided. Though several authors weigh in on this kind of issue throughout the volume, in the final chapter Catriona McKinnon addresses the concern directly, arguing against the view that hope for the cosmopolitan ideal is misplaced, on the grounds that moderate cosmopolitan ideals are in fact feasible.

What direction should research on cosmopolitanism take from this point onward? The essays here carry forward the debates on the meaning and content of cosmopolitan principles. But taken as a whole they do relatively little to address the kinds of concrete reforms of global and local institutions that the principles would demand. We diagnose three reasons for this. First, a global cosmopolitan political movement is still in its infancy, and is working in an ideological environment which makes reform difficult. Second, relatively few philosophers have developed the expertise concerning the institutions of global governance that some of their peers have developed concerning, say, education policy, health care policy, and welfare state design. Some of those who do have this expertise are represented in this collection, but it is striking that there is not the critical mass which exists among philosophers interested in those other policy arenas. This fact is probably connected to another explanation, which is that global governance is conducted at the highest levels of government, where agents are particularly inaccessible and also less inter-ested than policymakers in other arenas in the advice of philosophers. These are reasonable explanations of the lightness of the practical political commentary on institutional reform; but, we suspect that this is the most promising, and the most important, direction that research will begin to take.

NOTES

1 A distinction is sometimes drawn in the literature between *moral* and *institutional* cosmopolitanism. Institutional cosmopolitans maintain that fairly deep insti-tutional changes are needed to the global system in order to realize the cosmopolitan vision adequately. Moral cosmopolitans need not endorse that view, in fact many are against radical institutional transformations. For a good recent account of a strong institutional cosmopolitan account, see Cabrera, 2004.
2 For a good sample of this work, see Pogge, 2002.

CHAPTER 2

Principles of cosmopolitan order

David Held

Cosmopolitanism is concerned to disclose the ethical, cultural, and legal basis of political order in a world where political communities and states matter, but not only and exclusively. In circumstances where the trajectories of each and every country are tightly entwined, the partiality, one-sidedness and limitedness of "reasons of state" need to be recognized. While states are hugely important vehicles to aid the delivery of effective regulation, equal liberty, and social justice, they should not be thought of as ontologically privileged. They can be judged by how far they deliver these public goods and how far they fail; for the history of states is marked, of course, not just by phases of bad leadership and corruption but also by the most brutal episodes. A cosmopolitanism relevant to our global age must take this as a starting point, and build an ethically sound and politically robust conception of the proper basis of political community, and of the relations among communities.

Two accounts of cosmopolitanism bear on its contemporary meaning. The first was set out by the Stoics, who were the first to refer explicitly to themselves as cosmopolitans, seeking to replace the central role of the *polis* in ancient political thought with that of the *cosmos* in which humankind might live together in harmony (Horstmann, 1976). The Stoics developed this thought by emphasizing that we inhabit two worlds – one which is local and assigned to us by birth and another which is "truly great and truly common" (Seneca). Each person lives in a local community and in a wider community of human ideals, aspirations, and argument. The basis of the latter lies in what is fundamental to all – the equal worth of reason and humanity in every person (Nussbaum, 1997b, pp. 30, 43). Allegiance is owed, first and foremost, to the moral realm of all humanity, not to the contingent groupings of nation, ethnicity, and class. Deliberation and problem solving should focus on what is common to all persons as citizens of reason and the world; collective problems can be better dealt with if approached from this perspective, rather than from the point of view of sectional groupings. Such a position does not require that individuals give up local concerns and affiliations to family, friends, and fellow countrymen; it implies, instead, that they must acknowledge these as morally contingent and that their most important duties are to humanity as a whole and its overall developmental requirements.

The second conception of cosmopolitanism was introduced in the eighteenth century when the term *Weltbürger* (world citizen) became one of the key terms of the Enlightenment. The most important contribution to this body of thought can be found in Kant's writings (above all, 1970, pp. 41–53, 54–60 and 93–130). Kant linked the idea of cosmopolitanism to an innovative conception of "the public use of reason," and explored the ways in which this conception of reason can generate a critical vantage point from which to scrutinize civil society (see Schmidt, 1998, pp. 419–27). Building on a definition of enlightenment as the escape from dogma and unvindicated authority, Kant measured its advance in terms of the removal of constraints on "the public use of reason." As one commentator eloquently remarked, Kant grounds reason "in the reputation of principles that preclude the possibility of open-ended interaction and communication . . . The principles of reason are those that can secure the possibility of intersubjectivity" (O'Neill, 1990, p. 194). Kant conceived of participation in a cosmopolitan (*weltbürgerlich*) society as an entitlement – an entitlement to enter the world of open, uncoerced dialogue – and he adapted this idea in his formulation of what he called "cosmopolitan right" (1970, pp. 105–08). Cosmopolitan right meant the capacity to present oneself and be heard within and across political communities; it was the right to enter dialogue without artificial constraint and delimitation.

Contemporary conceptions of cosmopolitanism can be found in the work of Beitz, Pogge, and Barry, among others (see, in particular, Beitz, 1979, 1994, 1998; Pogge, 1989, 1994a, 1994b, and Barry, 1998a, 1999). In certain respects, this work seems to explicate, and offer a compelling elucidation of, the classical conception of belonging to the human community first and foremost, and the Kantian conception of subjecting all beliefs, relations, and practices to the test of whether or not they allow for uncoerced interaction and impartial reasoning. In the sections that follow, I will draw on some of this writing and use it as a basis to set out the outlines of a comprehensive account of the principles of cosmopolitanism – their nature, status, justification, and political implications. I begin by stating the principles and explain how they cluster into three types. I then go on to explore their standing and scope.

COSMOPOLITAN PRINCIPLES

Cosmopolitan values can be expressed formally in terms of a set of principles (see Held, 2002, 2004). These are principles which can be universally shared, and can form the basis for the protection and nurturing of each person's equal significance in "the moral realm of all humanity." Eight principles are paramount. They are the principles of: (1) equal worth and dignity; (2) active agency; (3) personal responsibility and accountability; (4) consent; (5) collective decision-making about public matters through voting procedures; (6) inclusiveness and subsidiarity; (7) avoidance of serious harm; and (8) sustainability. The meaning of these principles needs unpacking in order that their nature and implications can be clarified. While eight principles may seem like a daunting number, they are interrelated and together form the basis of a cosmopolitan orientation.

The first principle is that the ultimate units of moral concern are individual human beings, not states or other particular forms of human association. Humankind belongs to a single moral realm in which each person is regarded as equally worthy of respect and consideration (Beitz, 1994; Pogge, 1994a). To think of people as having equal moral value is to make a general claim about the basic units of the world comprising persons as free and equal beings (see Kuper, 2000). This notion can be referred to as the principle of individualist moral egalitarianism or, simply, egalitarian individualism. To uphold this principle is not to deny the significance of cultural diversity and difference, not at all – but it is to affirm that there are limits to the moral validity of particular communities – limits which recognize, and demand, that we must treat with equal respect the dignity of reason and moral choice in every human being (Nussbaum, 1997b, pp. 42–43). In the post-Holocaust world, these limits have been recognized in the United Nations Charter and, in the human rights regime, among many other legal instruments (see Held, 2004, part 3).

The second principle recognizes that, if principle 1 is to be universally recognized and accepted, then human agency cannot be understood as the mere expression of a given teleology, fortune, or tradition; rather, human agency must be conceived as the ability to act otherwise – the ability not just to accept but to shape human community in the context of the choices of others. Active agency connotes the capacity of human beings to reason self-consciously, to be self-reflective and to be self-determining.[1] It bestows both opportunities and duties – opportunities to act (or not as the case may be), and duties to ensure that independent action does not curtail and infringe upon the life chances and opportunities of others (unless, of course, sanctioned by negotiation or consent: see below). Active agency is a capacity both to make and pursue claims and to have such claims made and pursued in relation to oneself. Each person has an equal interest in active agency or self-determination.

Principles 1 and 2 cannot be grasped fully unless supplemented by principle 3: the principle of personal responsibility and accountability. At its most basic, this principle can be understood to mean that it is inevitable that people will choose different cultural, social, and economic projects and that such differences need to be recognized. People develop their skills and talents differently, and enjoy different forms of ability and specialized competency. That they fare differently, and that many of these differences arise from a voluntary choice on their part, should be wel-comed and accepted (see Barry, 1998a, pp. 147–49). These *prima facie* legitimate differences of choice and outcome have to be distinguished from unacceptable structures of difference which reflect conditions which prevent, or partially prevent, the pursuit by some of their vital needs. Actors have to be aware of, and accountable for, the consequences of actions, direct or indirect, intended or unintended, which may radically restrict or delimit the choices of others. Individuals have both personal responsibility-rights as well as personal responsibility-obligations.[2]

The fourth principle, the principle of consent, recognizes that a com-mitment to equal worth and equal moral value, along with active agency and personal responsibility, requires a non-coercive political process in and through which people can negotiate and pursue their public inter-connections, interdependencies and life chances. Interlocking lives, pro-jects and communities require forms of public reasoning, deliberation, and decision-making which take account of each person's equal standing in such processes. The principle of consent constitutes the basis of non-coercive collective agreement and governance.

Principles 4 and 5 must be interpreted together. For principle 5 acknowledges that while a legitimate public decision is one that results from consent, this needs to be linked with voting at the decisive stage of collective decision-making and with the procedures and mechanisms of majority rule. The consent of all is too strong a requirement of collective decision-making and the basis on which minorities can block or forestall public responses to key issues (see Held, 2002, pp. 26–27). Principle 5 recognizes the importance of inclusiveness in the process of granting consent, while interpreting this to mean that an inclusive process of participation and debate can coalesce with a decision-making procedure which allows outcomes which accrue the greatest support (Dahl, 1989).[3]

The sixth principle, which I earlier referred to as the principle of inclusiveness and subsidiarity, seeks to clarify the fundamental criterion of drawing proper boundaries around units of collective decision-making, and on what grounds. At its simplest, it connotes that those significantly affected by public decisions, issues, or processes, should, *ceteris paribus*, have an equal opportunity, directly or indirectly through elected representatives, to influence and shape them. By significantly affected I mean that people are enmeshed in decisions and forces that impact on their capacity to fulfil their vital needs (see Held, 2004, ch. 6). According to principle 6, collective decision-making is best located when it is closest to and involves those whose life expectancy and life chances are determined by significant social processes and forces. On the other hand, this principle also recognizes that if the decisions at issue are translocal, transnational, or transregional, then political associations need not only to be locally based but also to have a wider scope and framework of operation.

The seventh principle is a leading principle of social justice: the principle of the avoidance of harm and the amelioration of urgent need. This is a principle for allocating priority to the most vital cases of need and, where possible, trumping other, less urgent public priorities until such a time as all human beings, *de facto* and *de jure*, are covered by the first six principles; that is to say, until they enjoy the status of equal moral value and active agency, and have the means to participate in their respective political communities and in the overlapping communities of fate which shape their needs and welfare. A social provision which falls short of the potential for active agency can be referred to as a situation of manifest harm in that the participatory potential of individuals and groups will not have been achieved; that is to say, people would not have adequate access to effectively resourced capacities which they might make use of in their particular circumstances (Sen, 1999). But even this significant short-fall in the realization of human potential should be distinguished from situations of the most pressing levels of vulnerability, defined by the most urgent need. The harm that follows from a failure to meet such needs can be denoted as serious harm, marked as it often is by immediate, life-and-death consequences. Accordingly, if the requirements specified by the principle of avoidance of serious harm are to be met, public policy ought to be focused, in the first instance, on the prevention of such conditions; that is, on the eradication of severe harm inflicted on people "against their will" and "without their consent" (Barry, 1998a, pp. 207, 231).

The eighth and final principle is the principle of sustainability, which specifies that all economic and social development must be consistent with the stewardship of the world's core resources – by which I mean resources which are irreplaceable and non-substitutable (Goodin, 1992, pp. 62–65, 72). Such a principle discriminates against social and economic change which disrupts global ecological balances and unnecessarily damages the choices of future generations. Sustainable development is best understood as a guiding principle, as opposed to a precise formula, since we do not know, for example, how future technological innovation will impact on resource provision and utilization. Yet, without reference to such a principle, public policy would be made without taking account of the finite quality of many of the world's resources and the equally valid claims of future generations to well-being. Because the contemporary economic and military age is the first age to be able to take decisions not just for itself but for all future epochs, its choices must be particularly careful not to pre-empt the equal worth and active agency of future generations.

The eight principles can best be thought of as falling into three clusters. The first cluster (principles 1–3) sets down the fundamental organizational features of the cosmopolitan moral universe. Its crux is that each person is a subject of equal moral concern; that each person is capable of acting autonomously with respect to the range of choices before them; and that, in deciding how to act or which institutions to create, the claims of each person affected should be taken equally into account. Personal responsibility means in this context that actors and agents have to be aware of, and accountable for, the consequences of their actions, direct or indirect, intended or unintended, which may substantially restrict and delimit the opportunities of others. The second cluster (principles 4–6) forms the basis of translating individually initiated activity, or privately determined activities more broadly, into collectively agreed or collectively sanctioned frameworks of action or regulatory regimes. Public power at all levels can be conceived as legitimate to the degree to which principles 4, 5, and 6 are upheld. The final principles (7 and 8) lay down a framework for prioritizing urgent need and resource conservation. By distinguishing vital from non-vital needs, principle 7 creates an unambiguous starting point and guiding orientation for public decisions. While this 'prioritizing commitment' does not, of course, create a decision procedure to resolve all clashes of priority in politics, it clearly creates a moral framework for focusing public policy on those who are most vulnerable. By contrast, principle 8 seeks to set down a prudential orientation to help

ensure that public policy is consistent with global ecological balances and
that it does not destroy irreplaceable and non-substitutable resources.

It could be objected at this point that, given the plurality of interpretive
standpoints in the contemporary world (social, cultural, religious, and so
on), it is unwise to construct a political philosophy which depends upon
overarching principles. For it is doubtful, the objection could continue,
that a bridge can be built between "the many particular wills" and "the
general will" (see McCarthy, 1991, pp. 181–99). In a world marked by a
diversity of value orientations, on what grounds, if any, can we suppose
that all groups or parties could be argumentatively convinced about
fundamental ethical and political principles?

It is important to stress that cosmopolitan philosophy does not deny
the reality and ethical relevance of living in a world of diverse values and
identities – how could it? It does not assume that unanimity is attainable
on all practical–political questions. The elaboration of cosmopolitan
principles is not an exercise in seeking a general and universal understanding on a wide spectrum of issues concerning the broad conditions of life
or diverse ethical matters (for example, abortion, animal rights, or the role
of voluntary euthanasia). This is not how a modern cosmopolitan project
should be understood. Rather, at stake is a more restrictive exercise aimed
at reflecting on the moral status of persons, the conditions of agency, and
collective decision-making. It is important to emphasize that this exercise
is constructed on the assumption that ground rules for communication,
dialogue, and dispute settlement are not only desirable but essential
precisely because all people are of equal moral value and their views on
a wide range of moral–political questions will conflict. The principles of
cosmopolitanism are the conditions of taking cultural diversity seriously
and of building a democratic culture to mediate clashes of the cultural
good. They are, in short, about the conditions of just difference and
democratic dialogue. The aim of modern cosmopolitanism is the concep-
tualization and generation of the necessary background conditions for
a "common" or "basic" structure of individual action and social activity
(cf. Rawls, 1985, pp. 254ff).

Contemporary cosmopolitans, it should be acknowledged, are divided
about the demands that cosmopolitanism lays upon the individual and,
accordingly, upon the appropriate framing of the necessary background
conditions for a "common" structure of individual action and social

activity. Among them there is agreement that in deciding how to act, or which rules or regulations ought to be established, the claims of each person affected should be weighed equally – "no matter where they live, which society they belong to, or how they are connected to us" (Miller, 1998, p. 165). The principle of egalitarian individualism is regarded as axiomatic. But the moral weight granted to this principle depends heavily upon the precise modes of interpretation of other principles.

Two broad positions exist in the literature. There are those for whom membership of humanity at large means that special relationships (including particular moral responsibilities) to family, kin, nation, or religious grouping can never be justified because the people involved have some intrinsic quality which suffices alone to compel special moral attention, or because they are allegedly worth more than other people, or because such affiliations provide sufficient reason for pursuing particular commitments or actions. This does not mean that such relationships cannot be justified – they can, but only in so far as nurturing or honoring such ties is in the cosmopolitan interest; that is, is the best way to achieve the good for humanity overall (Nussbaum, 1996, pp. 135–36; Barry, 1998a). As Scheffler succinctly put it, "special attention to particular people is legitimate only if it can be justified by reference to the interests of all human beings considered as equals" (1999, p. 259).

The second interpretation recognizes that while each person stands in "an ethically significant relation" to all other people, this is only one important "source of reasons and responsibilities among others" (Scheffler, 1999, p. 260). Cosmopolitan principles are, in this context, quite compatible with the recognition of different "spheres" or "layers" of moral reasoning (Walzer, 1983).

In the light of this, it is useful to draw a distinction between "strong" and "weak" cosmopolitanism, or between thick and thin cosmopolitanism as I refer to it. Miller has summarized the distinction well:

According to the strong [thick] version . . . all moral principles must be justified by showing that they give equal weight to the claims of everyone, which means that they must either be directly universal in their scope, or if they apply only to a select group of people they must be secondary principles whose ultimate foundation is universal. The weak [thin] version, by contrast, holds only that morality is cosmopolitan in part: there are some valid principles with a more restricted scope. According to . . . [thin] cosmopolitanism . . . we may owe certain kinds of treatment to all other human beings regardless of any relationship in which we stand to them, while there are other kinds of treatment that we owe only to those to whom we are related in certain ways, with neither sort of obligation being derivative of the other (1998, pp. 166–67).

Whether cosmopolitanism is an overriding frame of reference (trumping all other moral positions) or a distinctive subset of considerations (specifying that there are some substantive global rules, norms, and principles of justice which ought to be balanced with, and take account of, those derived from individual societies or other human groupings) is not a question which will be focused on here at length (cf. Barry, 1998a; Miller, 1998). However, some comment is in order if the rationale and standing of the eight principles are to be satisfactorily illuminated.

I take cosmopolitanism ultimately to denote the ethical and political space occupied by the eight principles. Cosmopolitanism lays down the universal or regulative principles which delimit and govern the range of diversity and difference that ought to be found in public life. It discloses the proper basis or framework for the pursuit of argument, discussion, and negotiation about particular spheres of value, spheres in which local, national, and regional affiliations will inevitably be weighed. In some respects, this is a form of thick cosmopolitanism. However, it should not be concluded from this that the meaning of the eight principles can simply be specified once and for all. For while cosmopolitanism affirms principles which are universal in their scope, it recognizes, in addition, that the precise meaning of these is always fleshed out in situated discussions; in other words, that there is an inescapable hermeneutic complexity in moral and political affairs which will affect how the eight principles are actually interpreted, and the weight granted to special ties and other practical–political issues. I call this mix of regulative principles and interpretative activity neither thick nor thin cosmopolitanism, but, rather, a "layered" cosmopolitan perspective (cf. Tully, 1995). This cosmopolitan point of view builds on principles that all could reasonably assent to, while recognizing the irreducible plurality of forms of life (Habermas, 1996). Thus, on the one hand, the position upholds certain basic egalitarian ideas – those which emphasize equal worth, equal respect, equal consideration and so on – and, on the other, it acknowledges that the elucidation of their meaning cannot be pursued independently of an ongoing dialogue in public life. Hence, there can be no adequate institutionalization of equal rights and duties without a corresponding institutionalization of national and transnational forms of public debate, democratic participation, and accountability (McCarthy, 1999). The institutionalization of regulative cosmopolitan principles requires the entrenchment of democratic public realms.

A layered cosmopolitan perspective of this kind shares a particular commitment with thin cosmopolitanism insofar as it acknowledges a plurality of value sources and a diversity of moral conceptions of the good; it recognizes, accordingly, different spheres of ethical reasoning linked to everyday attempts to resolve matters concerning modes of living and social organization (Böhme, 2001). As such, it seeks to express ethical neutrality with regard to many life questions. But ethical neutrality of this sort should not be confused with political neutrality and its core requirements (see Kuper, 2000, pp. 649f). The point has been succinctly stated by Tan: "a commitment to ethical neutrality entails a particular type of political arrangement, one which, for one, allows for the pursuit of different private conceptions of the good" (1998, p. 283, quoted in Kuper, 2000, p. 649; see Barry, 1995, p. 263). Only polities that acknowledge the equal status of all persons, that seek neutrality or impartiality with respect to personal ends, hopes, and aspirations, and that pursue the public justification of social, economic, and political arrangements can ensure a basic or common structure of political action which allows individuals to pursue their projects – both individual and collective – as free and equal agents. Such a structure is inconsistent with, and, if applied systematically, would need to filter out, those ends and goods, whether public or private, which would erode or undermine the structure itself.[4] For value pluralism and social pluralism to flourish, political associations must be structured or organized in one general way – that is, according to the constituting, legitimizing, and prioritizing principles specified above (cf. Pogge, 1994a, p. 127). Arguments can be had about the exact specification of these; that is, about how these notions are properly formulated. But the eight principles themselves constitute guiding notions or regulative ideals for a polity geared to autonomy, dialogue, and tolerance.

Cosmopolitan justifications

However, while cosmopolitanism must stand by these principles, they are not, of course, self-justifying. Or, to put the point another way, from whence come these principles? From the outset, it is important to distinguish two things too often run together: questions about the origins of principles, and questions about their validity or weight (see Weale, 1998). Both kinds of question are relevant. If the first illuminates the ethical circumstances or motivation for a preference for, or commitment to, a principle or set of principles, the second is the basis for testing their intersubjective validity. In this regard, the justificatory rationale of cosmopolitan principles is dependent on two fundamental metaprinciples or organizing notions of ethical discourse – one cultural and historical,

the other philosophical. These are, respectively, the metaprinciple of
autonomy and the metaprinciple of impartialist reasoning.

The metaprinciple of autonomy (henceforth, the MPA) is at the core of
the democratic project. Its rationale and standing are "political not
metaphysical," to borrow a phrase from Rawls (1985). A basic concept
or idea is political, in this sense, if it represents an articulation of an
understanding latent in public political life and, in particular, if against
the background of the struggle for a democratic culture in the West and
later elsewhere, it builds on the distinctive conception of the person as a
citizen who is, in principle, "free and equal" in a manner "comprehen-
sible" to everyone. In other words, the MPA can be understood as a
notion embedded in the public political culture of democratic societies
and emerging democracies.

The MPA is part of the "deep structure" of ideas which have shaped the
constitution of modern political life. It has roots in the ancient world,
although many elements of its deep structure were not part of classical
thinking, marked as the latter was by a very restricted view of who could
count as a citizen and by a teleological conception of nature and the
cosmos. It was not until the modern world that the MPA became more
firmly entrenched (Held, 1996). It became entrenched in the pursuit of
citizenship, which has always been marked by "an urge," as Marshall put
it, to secure "a fuller measure of autonomy" for each and every person; for
autonomy is the "stuff" of which modern citizenship is made (1973, p.
84). Or, to restate the point in the language used hitherto, it has been
marked by an urge to realize the core elements of an egalitarian conception of the person (with its emphasis upon people as free and equal,
capable of active agency and accountable for their choices), of the democratic regulation of public life (including consent, deliberation, voting,
and inclusiveness) and of the necessity to ensure that, if people's equal
interest in self-determination or self-governance is to be protected, attention must be focused on those who lack the capacity to participate in, and
act within, key sites of power and political institutions (that is, that there
must be a measure of social protection).

Another way to put these points is to say that the MPA is the guiding
political thread of modern democratic societies and that the first seven
cosmopolitan principles, suitably unfolded from a commitment to self-
determination and autonomy, are the basis for specifying more fully the
nature and form of a liberal and democratic order.[5] In short, these
cosmopolitan principles are the principles of democratic public life, but
without one crucial assumption – never fully justified in any case in liberal

democratic thought, classic or contemporary – that these principles can only be enacted effectively within a single, circumscribed, territorially based political community (see Held, 1995). The cosmopolitan principles do not presume, as principle 6 makes clear, that the link between self-determination, accountability, democracy, and sovereignty can be understood simply in territorial terms. Hence, it is possible to have a modern democratic rendition of the Stoic aspiration to multiple forms of affiliation – local, national, and global. The cosmopolitan principles are the core elements of democratic public life, shorn of the contingent link with the borders of nation-states. How these principles should be spliced with organizations, institutions, and borders of political communities is a separate question, to which I will return.

It could be objected that the language of autonomy and self-determination has limited cross-culture validity because of its Western origins. But a distinction must be made between those political terms and discourses which obscure or underpin particular interests and power systems and those which seek to test explicitly the generalizability of claims and interests, and to render power, whether it be political, economic or cultural, accountable. What the language of autonomy and self-determination generates and, in particular, the language of the MPA, is what might be thought of as a commitment or pre-commitment to the idea that all persons should be equally free – that is to say, that they should enjoy equal liberty to pursue their own activities without arbitrary or unwarranted interference. If this notion is shared across cultures it is not because they have acquiesced to modern Western political discourse; it is, rather, that they have come to see that there are certain languages which protect and nurture the notion of equal status and worth, and others which have sought to ignore or suppress it.

To test the generalizability of claims and interests involves "reasoning from the point of view of others" (Benhabib, 1992, pp. 9–10, 121–47). Attempts to focus on this "social point of view" find their clearest contemporary elaboration in Rawls's Original Position, Habermas's ideal speech situation and Barry's formulation of impartialist reasoning (see Rawls, 1971; Habermas, 1973, 1996; Barry, 1989, 1995). These formulations have in common a concern to conceptualize an impartial moral standpoint from which to assess particular forms of practical reasoning. This concern should not be thought of as over-demanding. As one commentator aptly put it: "all the impartiality thesis says is that, if and when one raises questions regarding fundamental moral standards, the court of appeal that one addresses is a court in which no particular individual, group, or country has *special* standing" (Hill, 1987, p. 132, quoted in Barry, 1995, pp. 226–27). Before the court, suggesting "I like it," "it suits me," "it belongs to male prerogatives," "it is in the best interest of my country," does not settle the issue at hand, for principles must be defensible from a larger, human standpoint. This social, open-ended, moral perspective is a device for focusing our thoughts and testing the intersubjective validity of our conceptions of the good. It offers a way of exploring principles, norms, and rules that might reasonably command agreement. I refer to it as the metaprinciple of impartialist reasoning (MPIR).

The MPIR is a moral frame of reference for specifying rules and principles that can be universally shared; and, concomitantly, it rejects as unjust all those practices, rules, and institutions anchored in principles not all could adopt (O'Neill, 1991). At issue is the establishment of principles and rules that nobody, motivated to establish an uncoerced and informed agreement, could reasonably discard (see Barry, 1989; cf. Scanlon, 1998). In order to meet this standard a number of particular tests can be pursued, including an assessment of whether all points of view have been taken into consideration; whether there are individuals in a position to impose on others in such a manner as would be unacceptable to the latter, or to the originator of the action (or inaction), if the roles were reversed; and whether all parties would be equally prepared to accept the outcome as fair and reasonable irrespective of the social positions they might occupy now or in the future (see Barry, 1989, pp. 362–63, 372).

The MPIR cannot produce a simple deductive proof of the ideal set of principles and conditions which can overcome the deficiencies of a political order; nor can it produce a deductive proof of the best or only moral principles that should guide institutional development. Rather, it should be thought of as a heuristic device to test candidate principles of moral worth, democracy, and justice and their forms of justification (Kelly, 1998, pp. 1–8; Barry, 1998b). These tests are concerned with a process of reasonable rejectability, which can always be pursued in a theoretical dialogue open to fresh challenge and new questions and, hence, in a hermeneutic sense, can never be complete (Gadamer, 1975). But to acknowledge this is not to say that theoretical conversation is "toothless" either with respect to principles or the conditions of their entrenchment.

In the first instance, moral impartialism has a crucial critical and debunking role. This position is emphasized most clearly by O'Neill (1991). Impartialist reasoning, in this account, is a basis for disclosing non-generalizable principles, rules, and interests, and of showing how justice is a matter of not basing actions, lives, or institutions on principles that cannot be universally shared. The impartialist vantage point has efficacy *qua* critical stance.

The principles of coercion and deception are among the principles open to serious objection from this perspective. It is impossible for a principle of coercion to be universally shared, for those who are coerced are denied agency and so cannot share their coercer's principle of action. Likewise, it is impossible for a principle of deception to be universally upheld because those who are deceived cannot adopt their deceiver's underlying concerns or share the deceiver's principle of action. (If the deceiver's plan of action was known to all parties, the deception could not, of course, work.) Such arguments do not show "that all coercion or deception is unjust: they show only that actions, institutions and lives which make coercion or deception fundamental are unjust" (O'Neill, 1991, p. 298). Moreover, the same line of reasoning can disclose that human beings cannot construct a just order based on the neglect of need. For a principle of neglecting need will also fail the test of universal adoption. Human beings who sought to adopt such a principle would risk failing to meet their own finite, needy states, let alone those of others. But how, and to what extent, needs should be met remains unspecified in this account.

Impartialist reasoning, thus understood, is a critical device for disclosing non-generalizable principles and unjust institutions, but can it state a more positive position which lays down the underlying principles of a just cosmopolitan order? I believe something more positive can be disclosed in the pursuit of principles and rules that can be universally shared. There is only space here to sketch this thought. In this regard, it is my contention that the eight cosmopolitan principles can all meet the test of impartiality, and form moral and political elements upon which all could act. For they are at the root of the equal consideration and treatment of all human beings, irrespective of where they were born or raised. The impartialist emphasis on taking account of the position of the other, of only treating political outcomes as fair and reasonable if there are good reasons for holding that they would be equally acceptable to all parties, and of only treating the position of some socioeconomic groups as legitimate if they are acceptable to all people irrespective of where they come in the social hierarchy, is consistent with the eight principles and does not provide grounds on which they can be reasonably rejected. The principles of equal moral status, equal public engagement, and the public justification of

collective institutional arrangements are robust enough not to fall foul of
these considerations (see Held, 2006).

Within this theoretical framework, it can be argued that individual or
collective social arrangements generating serious harm (urgent unmet
need) cannot be justified by reference to a special social standing, cultural
identity, ethnic background, or nationality – in fact by reference to any
particular grouping – if the latter sanctions closure or exclusion in relation
to the core conditions of human autonomy, development, and welfare
(see Caney, 2001a). To the extent that a domain of activity operates to
structure and delimit life expectancy and life-chances, deficits are disclosed in the structure of action of a political association. These deficits
can, furthermore, be regarded as illegitimate to the extent to which they
would be rejected under the conditions of the MPIR. If people did not
know their future social location and political identity, they would not
find the self-interested defense of specific exclusionary processes and
mechanisms convincing. These justificatory structures cannot easily be
generalized and are, thus, weak in the face of the test of impartiality.
Unless exceptional arguments are available to the contrary, social mechanisms and processes generating serious harm for certain groups and
categories of people fall to the requirement of impartiality (see Barry,
1995, 1998a).

Impartialist reasoning is a basis for thinking about the problems posed
by asymmetries of power, unevenness of resource distribution, and stark
prejudices. It provides the means for asking about the rules, laws, and
policies people might think right, justified, or worthy of respect. It allows
a distinction to be made between legitimacy as acquiescence to existing
socioeconomic arrangements, and legitimacy as "rightness" or "correct-
ness" – the worthiness of a political order to be recognized because it is the
order people would accept as a result of impartialist reasoning. The latter
can be conceived not as an optional element of a political and legal
understanding, but as a requirement of any attempt to grasp the nature
of the support and legitimacy enjoyed by particular social forces and
relations; for without this form of reasoning, the distinction between
legitimacy as "acceptance" and legitimacy as "rightness" could not be
drawn.

It should be emphasized that the pursuit of impartial reasoning is a social
activity – not a solitary theoretical exercise. For as Arendt has written:

The power of judgement rests on a potential agreement with others, and the
thinking process which is active in judging something is not . . . a dialogue

between me and myself, but finds itself always and primarily, even if I am quite alone in making up my mind, in an anticipated communication with others with whom I know I must finally come to some agreement . . . And this enlarged way of thinking . . . cannot function in strict isolation or solitude; it needs the presence of others "in whose place" it must think, whose perspective it must take into consideration, and without whom it never has the opportunity to operate at all. (1961, pp. 220–21, as cited by Benhabib, 1992, pp. 9–10)

The aim of a "theoretical conversation" about impartiality is an antici- pated agreement with all those whose diverse circumstances affect the realization of people's equal interest in self-determination and autonomy. Of course, as an "anticipated agreement" it is a hypothetical ascription of an intersubjective or collective understanding. As such, the ultimate test of its validity must depend in contemporary life on the extension of the conversation to all those whom it seeks to encompass. Only under the latter circumstances can an analytically proposed interpretation become an actual understanding or agreement among others (Habermas, 1988). Critical reflection must conjoin with public debate and democratic politics.

Together the MPA and MPIR provide the grounds of cosmopolitan thought. The MPA lays down the conceptual space in which impartialist reasoning can take place. For it generates a preoccupation with each person as a subject of equal moral concern; with each person's capacity to act autonomously with respect to the range of choices before them; and with each person's equal status with respect to the basic institutions of political communities, that is, with an entitlement to claim and be claimed upon (see Rawls, 1971, pp. 544–45; Barry, 1989, p. 200). It provides motives, reasons and constraining considerations to help estab- lish agreement on reasonable terms. The MPIR is the basis for pursuing this agreement. It is a device of argument that is designed to abstract from power relations in order to disclose the fundamental enabling conditions of active agency, rightful authority, and social justice. Of course, as a device of argument it can be resisted by those who reject the language of autonomy and self-determination; but then we must be clear that this is precisely what they are doing.

FROM COSMOPOLITAN PRINCIPLES TO COSMOPOLITAN LAW

Cosmopolitan law refers to a domain of law different in kind from the law of states and the law made between one state and another for the mutual enhancement of their geopolitical interests. Kant, the leading interpreter of the idea of such a law, interpreted it as the basis for articulating the equal moral status of persons in the "universal community" (1970, p. 108). For him, cosmopolitan law is neither a fantastic nor a utopian way of conceiving law, but a "necessary complement" to the codes of national and international law, and a means to transform them into a public law of humanity (see Held, 1995, ch. 10). While Kant limited the form and scope of cosmopolitan law to the conditions of universal hospitality – the right to present oneself and be heard within and across communities – I understand it more broadly as the appropriate mode of representing the equal moral standing of all human beings, and their entitlement to equal liberty and to forms of governance founded on deliberation and consent. In other words, cosmopolitan law is the form of law which best articulates and entrenches the eight principles of cosmopolitan order. If these principles were to be systematically entrenched as the foundation of law, the conditions of the cosmopolitan regulation of public life could initially be set down.

Within the framework of cosmopolitan law, the idea of rightful authority, which has been so often connected to the state and particular geographical domains, has to be reconceived and recast. Rightful authority or sovereignty can be stripped away from the idea of fixed borders and territories and thought of as, in principle, an attribute of basic cosmopolitan democratic law which can be drawn upon and enacted in diverse realms, from local associations and cities to states and wider global networks. Cosmopolitan law demands the subordination of regional, national, and local "sovereignties" to an overarching legal framework, but within this framework associations can be self-governing at diverse levels (Held, 1995, p. 234).

In this conception, the nation-state "withers away," to borrow an old Marxist phrase. But this is not to suggest that states and national democratic polities become redundant. Rather, states would no longer be regarded as the sole centers of legitimate power within their borders, as is already the case in many places (Held, McGrew, Goldblatt and Perraton, 1999, the conclusion). States need to be articulated with, and relocated within, an overarching cosmopolitan framework. Within this framework, the laws and rules of the nation–state would become but one focus for legal development, political reflection, and mobilization. Under these conditions, people would come, in principle, to enjoy multiple citizenships – political membership, that is, in the diverse communities which significantly affect them. In a world of overlapping communities of fate, individuals would be citizens of their immediate political communities, and of the wider regional and global networks which impacted upon their lives. This overlapping cosmopolitan polity would be one that in form and substance reflected and embraced the diverse forms of power and authority that already operate within and across borders. In this sense, cosmopolitanism constitutes the political basis and political philosophy of living in a global age (see Held, 2004).

NOTES

I would like to thank Gillian Brock for inviting me to prepare this paper. The section on cosmopolitan principles draws on earlier work of mine (Held, 2002, 2004) but seeks to elaborate and extend this material in an argument about the scope and status of cosmopolitanism today. I would also like to thank the Leverhulme Trust for supporting the work of which this essay is a part.

1 The principle of active agency does not make any assumption about the extent of self-knowledge or reflexivity. Clearly, this varies and can be shaped by both unacknowledged conditions and unintended consequences of action (see Giddens, 1984). It does, however, assume that the course of agency is a course that includes choice and that agency itself is, in essence, defined by the capacity to act otherwise.

2 The obligations taken on in this context cannot, of course, all be fulfilled with the same types of initiative (personal, social, or political) or at the same level (local, national, or global). But whatever their mode of realization, all such efforts can be related to one common denominator: the concern to discharge obligations we take on by virtue of the claims we make for the recognition of personal responsibility-rights (cf. Raz, 1986, chs. 14–15).

3 Minorities clearly need to be protected in this process. The rights and obligations entailed by principles 4 and 5 have to be compatible with the protection of each person's equal interest in principles 1, 2 and 3 – an interest which follows from each person's recognition as being of equal worth, with an equal capacity to act and to account for their actions. Majorities ought not to be able to impose themselves arbitrarily upon others. Principles 4 and 5 have to be understood against the background specified by the first three principles; the latter frame the basis of their operation.

4 As Miller aptly wrote, "an institution or practice is neutral when, as far as can reasonably be foreseen, it does not favor any particular conception of the good at the expense of others" (1989, p. 7; see pp. 72–81).

5 I say "first seven cosmopolitan principles" because the eighth, sustainability, has traditionally not been a core element of democratic thinking, although it ought to be (see Held, 2006).

CHAPTER 3

Territorial justice and global redistribution

Hillel Steiner

It is a commonplace of political history that, at some times in some places, liberalism and nationalism have *not* been incompatible. More than that, they have been good friends – lending each other vital support, rejoicing in one another's triumphs, holding a shared view of who is the enemy and so forth. Nor, according to Onora O'Neill, has this affinity been merely coincidental.

In a pre-liberal world, [a person's] social identity might be given by tribe or kin, it might not depend on those who share a sense of identity being collected in a single or an exclusive territory. Because liberal principles undercut reliance on pedigree and origin as the basis for recognizing who count as our own, and who as outsiders, liberalism had to find some alternative basis for identifying who counts. Pre-eminent among these ways are the differential rights with respect to a given state that citizenship confers. (O'Neill, 1992, p. 118)

Liberalism, she seems to be suggesting, has actually *needed* nationalism. Why? Well, because its hallowed subjects – namely individual persons, each of whom it lavishly adorns with all manner of rights and liberties – find themselves badly in need of some salient form of social identity when they emerge from their various imperial subjugations, ancient and modern. For whatever severe oppression and disempowerment they for so long endured under those subjugations, one thing they did *not* thereby lack was a strong sense of social identity: a sense of identity underwritten by their being officially and principally regarded as members of this family or that clan. That particular form of strong social identity being lost to them in the emancipatory world of liberalism, its only plausible replacement is said to consist in their recognition as citizens, as persons possessing significant and fully fledged membership in a national group. And nationalism is the celebration of that membership.

So what we have here is essentially a psychological hypothesis with strong political implications. People are said to have a vital need to be socially identified – to be thought of as members of groups – and, moreover, groups whose membership is neither open-endedly inclusive nor primarily elective. Marx (Groucho, that is) once famously remarked that he wouldn't want to be a member of any club that would have him in it. On the present hypothesis, while I might *want* to be a member of a club that would have me in it, what I *need* is to be a member of one that has no choice in the matter.

Now it is certainly beyond my competence to assess either the authenticity of that need or its weight or the grounds for claiming that its incidence has been as widespread as O'Neill suggests. Nor do I intend to dwell on the quite serious degree of practical indeterminacy attending the suggestion that significant membership in a national group is the favored, perhaps now the *only*, way of satisfying it. That indeterminacy is, these days, the unmistakable message of many recent events in the former Yugoslavia, the former Soviet Union, and several other places around the globe. Just which national membership will bestow on a person the social identity he or she needs is a matter being decided, in those places, by repeated resort to distinctly illiberal means.

And this, of course, is the problem about the relationship between liberalism and nationalism. For whatever historical affinities they have shared, whatever services they may have rendered to each other along the way to the modern world, the tensions between them are, and arguably always have been, transparently obvious. Neil MacCormick, the liberal legal philosopher, speaks for many when he rather despondently records that

Whether "nation" and "nationalism" are antithetical to or compatible with "individual" and "individualism" is a question of acute personal concern for me. I have been for a good many years a member of the Scottish National Party, and yet remain in some perplexity about the justiciability of any nationalistic case within the terms set for me by the other principles to which I adhere. (MacCormick, 1981, pp. 247–48)

More trenchantly, Ernest Gellner describes these tensions as "a tug of war between reason and passion" (Gellner, 1971, p. 149). Why? What's the problem here? Wasn't Hume surely correct to insist that reason is the slave of the passions and that conflict between them is therefore impossible?

We do not, I think, need to disagree with Hume in order to see what Gellner and MacCormick are getting at. Nationalism is associated with passion because its imperatives are inherently particularistic. "This measure is necessary," the nationalist will say, "because it best serves the interests of *my* nation. My nation (or as in earlier times, my tribe or my family) is what matters most. Its wellbeing is far more intimately connected to my own wellbeing and to my sense of who I am than are the sundry other considerations with which it may, and often does, conflict."

Liberalism, in contrast, is associated with reason because its imperatives are universalistic. It indiscriminately assigns rights to everyone. And it adamantly rejects any proposed differentiation of these assignments that invokes bottom-line premises which unavoidably include terms like "me" and "mine."[1] "That this policy would be good for me and mine" cuts no *moral* ice with liberals, because moral judgements – judgements about what *should* be done – have to be drawn from bottom-line premises devoid of any proper name or particular reference. Premises containing such terms may well furnish reasons for *my* doing or having certain things, but they cannot – logically cannot – furnish reasons for *others* to let me do or have them. They cannot serve those others as justifications for measures which require their (passive or active) cooperation: cooperation which would therefore be non-rational.

Not, of course, that liberalism forbids the pursuit of self-interest, whether by individuals or groups. Indeed, the very wide scope it allows for such pursuits has, historically, been a primary target of its fiercest critics, among whom nationalists of one stripe or another have figured quite prominently. But what liberalism does forbid are those pursuits of self-interest that cross the boundaries demarcating other persons' moral rights. And the liberal's problem with many nationalisms, past and present, is that they have engaged in just such boundary-crossings on a truly massive scale, especially though not exclusively in relation to members of other nations.

Is this at all avoidable? Can nationalisms be reconciled? And can they be reconciled in such a way as to render the many diverse values, which they severally embody, compatible with one another's and, ultimately, with individuals' moral rights? To ask these questions is to ask whether those rights are sufficient to yield a set of national and international norms which at once allow scope for nations to enact their respective value-sets *and* entail clear limits on how far those enactments may extend. And to answer this question we need first to take a look at what those rights are.

In a fairly recent book on rights, I have argued that at least a necessary condition for any set of rights to be a *possible* set – that is, to be realisable – is that all the rights in it are mutually consistent, or what I there call *compossible* (Steiner, 1994, especially ch. 3). The duties corresponding to those rights have to be ones which are jointly fulfillable and not mutually obstructive. By means of a rather extended chain of reasoning, which I certainly will not bore the reader with here, I try to show that this condition is satisfied only by a set of rights, each of which is (or is reducible to) a discrete property right – one which can be fully differentiated from every other right in that set and which therefore does not (in the language of set theory) *intersect* with any of them.[2] I further argue that, for a set of rights to be like this, it has to have a certain historical structure whereby each current right is one derived from the exercise of an antecedent right. The upshot of all this is that sets of mutually consistent rights are jointly and exhaustively constituted by a subset of ultimately antecedent or *foundational* rights and by the subset consisting of all the rights successively derived from those foundational rights.

Now let us apply these conceptual truths about rights in general to the specific case of liberalism. At the core of liberalism are three normative claims – claims which are not always as carefully distinguished from each other as they should be. The first and, in a way, least exceptionable of these is that foundational or non-derivative moral rights are held by *all* individuals. The second claim, hardly more controversial, is that these rights are the *same* for everyone. Of course, there are several liberalisms and, correspondingly, several competing conceptions of what these rights are. What I have tried to show in my book is that only one foundational right, the right to equal negative freedom, can generate a set of rights that satisfies the compossibility condition I have just described.

It is liberalism's third claim that expresses what is most distinctive about it and that brings it into sharpest contrast with many other moral and political doctrines. And this is that no moral right may be permissibly overridden, regardless of how much social benefit might be achieved by doing so. There are numerous ways of characterizing this inviolable status which liberalism assigns to rights: Ronald Dworkin says that *rights are trumps* (Dworkin, 1981b); Robert Nozick sees them as *side-constraints*, that is, as restrictions on how we may permissibly go about pursuing our other values (Nozick, 1974, pp. 28–33); John Rawls assigns them *lexical primacy*, by which he means that all their demands, even otherwise trivial ones, must be satisfied prior to the satisfaction of any other demands, however weighty these others might be (Rawls, 1972, pp. 42ff). Yet another way of characterizing the liberal status of rights is to see them simply as *personal vetoes*. Whichever characterization we prefer, they all point to the same thing: namely, that each person has a set of claims on the conduct of other persons

– a set of claims that must not be traded off by political decision-makers and must therefore be honored irrespective of the cost of doing so.[3]

I suggested above that the foundation of these claims, the basic moral right from which all our other moral rights are derived, is a right to equal freedom. In my book, I argue that this right immediately entails two other near-foundational rights which are construed, in a quasi-Lockean way, as rights to self-ownership and to an equal share of the value of natural resources. In effect, it is exercises of these two rights that then serially generate all the various other moral rights we can have or, more precisely, all the mutually consistent moral rights we do have.

And it is not hard to see that many of the types of right implied by these two have a pretty direct bearing on some of the more salient aspects of nationalism. For it is from the underlying right of self-ownership that liberalism infers such more familiar rights as those against murder and assault as well as rights to freedom of contract and association. And it is the right to natural resources that not only forms part of the basis of legitimate territorial claims but also, and interestingly, generates related requirements for international distributive justice, about which I will have more to say below.

Because our main focus here is on territorial claims, I am not going to dwell for long on the ways in which the liberal right of self-ownership constrains the permissible pursuit of national interests. Most of these ways are well enough known already. Rights against murder and assault have immediate restrictive implications for the conduct of nations' military activities, many of which implications have long been enshrined in various international conventions. Rights to freedom of contract pretty straighforwardly underwrite free trade and proscribe all manner of restrictions on it. Rights to freedom of association crucially entail rights to freedom of *dis*sociation: that is, they prohibit the kind of conscription implicit in Berlin Walls. And just as they allow free emigration, they symmetrically prohibit national restrictions on immigration since, whatever social benefits are thought to be secured by such restrictions, they amount to violations of the rights of those citizens who are willing to take outsiders in. So in all these cases, political decision-makers – even *democratic* ones – are morally disempowered from enacting such measures by virtue of the fundamental rights liberalism assigns to each person: rights which it construes as enjoying constitutional status in any legitimate legal system.

Which brings us to territorial claims. I think it is fair to say that territorial claims, though not the *sole* objects of nationalist preoccupation, have probably excited more of its passion than any other type of issue.

To be sure, even if nations' territorial claims had everywhere and always been compossible, there would still be lots of other things for nationalists to be exercised about: the preservation of their language and culture, the prosperity of their economy, and so forth. And many kinds of measure designed to advance these concerns are, as I have just indicated, not permitted under liberal principles. But perhaps the simplest and most encompassing measure deployed on behalf of these and other national concerns is, and always has been, the assertion of exclusive claims to territory, to portions of the earth's surface along with the supra- and subterranean spaces adjacent to them. Indeed, the assertion of such claims, if not always their recognition by others, is one of the essential criteria for distinguishing nations from other types of social group. And liberal principles have a very direct bearing on these claims.

The first and most important feature of this bearing is that, for liberalism, all legitimate group claims must be aggregations of – must be reducible without remainder to – the legitimate claims of individual persons. This means that a group's legitimate territorial claims can extend no further than the legitimate territorial holdings of its members or their agents. How do persons acquire legitimate titles to territory? Basically, there are two ways. First, by those titles being transferred to them voluntarily by the previous legitimate title-holders. But second and more fundamentally, by their staking claims to land which is not already claimed by others.

Now, readers of Locke and the voluminous literature exploring these Lockean arguments will be intimately acquainted with all the complexities implicit in that second stipulation. Locke himself explores the possibility of deriving claim-stakers' entitlements *solely* from their rights of self-ownership, suggesting that claim-staking consists in their investing some of their self-owned labour in portions of as-yet-unowned land. But even he acknowledges that this "first come, first served rule" cannot be the whole story on establishing legitimate land titles. (I will return to this problem below.)

Yet for him, for liberals generally and perhaps for many others as well, it remains an important *part* of that story. So any piece of land currently rightfully belongs to whomever it has been transmitted by an unbroken series of voluntary transfers originating in the person who first staked a claim to it. Any interruption of that pedigree, say by unredressed acts of conquest or expropriation, invalidates that current title no matter how innocently its current holder may have acquired it. And needless to say, in our slowly liberalizing world of today, much applied philosophy literature and much litigation in American, East European, Australasian, and other courts are deeply immersed in trying to figure out which current persons or groups are and are not in possession of legitimate titles to the land they claim on this basis. But however complex many of these enquiries have already proven to be – requiring, as they often do, massive amounts of historically remote data – those liberal principles do yield two rather concrete and highly topical inferences concerning nations' territorial entitlements.

The first of these is the endorsement of a right of *secession*. For although Locke himself (for reasons which remain mysterious) balked at embracing this conclusion (Locke, 1967, p. 364), it is very clearly implied by his principles. That is, precisely because a nation's territory is legitimately composed of the real estate of its members, the decision of any of them to resign that membership and, as it were, to take their real estate with them, is a decision which must be respected. Emigrants are not, under liberal principles, necessarily condemned to leave with only the shirts on their backs and whatever they can cram into their suitcases. Of course, nations may, if they choose, expel members, engage in certain forms of "ethnic cleansing," etc. But what they may not do is expropriate legitimate landowners or evict their tenants. Jurisdiction over land, like jurisdiction over persons, is a purely voluntary affair for liberals and it is thus predicated on the agreement of all the parties concerned.

The second inference about national territorial entitlements, and the one which I personally find the more interesting of the two, engages issues of *international distributive justice*. More interesting because, historically at least, liberalism has had conspicuously little to offer by way of a systematic account – one firmly anchored in its own basic premises – of what wealth transfers some nations owe to others. Indeed it is a notorious feature of political theorizing in general that the questions it tends to address are posed at the level of polities taken separately, as if these were hermetically sealed units, with only occasional genuflections in the inter-national direction when it comes to matters of trade and migration and war and peace. But the logical reach of basic liberal rights, although it certainly encompasses these matters as we have just seen, also extends well beyond them. Why? How?

I said above that, even for Locke, the "first come, first served rule" is not the whole story on persons acquiring legitimate titles to as-yet-unowned land. This rule, you will recall, is derived by him from our near-foundational right of self-ownership. But that right is itself only one of the two types of right immediately implied by our most fundamental right, the right to equal freedom. The other one is a right to an equal share of natural resource values. Rights to equal freedom imply *both* of these rights, rather than only the first, in order to prohibit claim-stakers from engrossing too much and thereby leaving others with little or no freedom at all. Locke himself says that claim-stakers, in appropriating a piece of land, must leave "enough and as good" land for others (Locke, 1967, pp. 306, 309, 310).[4] But as many writers in the Lockean tradition have long appreciated, this "enough and as good" restriction is badly in need of some amplification if it is to sustain the freedom entitlements of countless persons who are generationally differentiated.

Accordingly, and again for reasons which would take too long to detail here, some of these writers have interpreted this restriction as a requirement that each person's entitlement, rather than being one in kind – an entitlement to literally an equal portion of land – is one to cash: that is, to an equal share of the *value* of land.[5] This interpretation neatly accommodates the problem of generational differentiation and also takes account of the fact that, for a host of reasons, land values vary over time. The idea, then, is that landowners thereby owe, to each other person, an equal slice of the current site value of their property: that is, the gross value of that property *minus* the value of whatever labour-embodying improvements they and their predecessors may have made to it.[6] Hence the validity of their titles to that land vitally depends upon their payment of that debt.

This has immediate implications for what some nations justly owe to others. Liberalism's basic individual rights being ones of universal incidence, the equality of each person's land-value entitlement is necessarily *global* in scope. Everyone everywhere has a right to an equal share of the value of all land. To respect people's basic liberal rights, whether here or abroad, not only do we have to refrain from murdering or assaulting them, but also we must not withhold payment of their land-value entitlements.

Just what those entitlements amount to is obviously going to depend on how many people there are and what the current aggregate global value of land is. Neither of these magnitudes poses insuperable computational problems. We pretty much know, or can do, how numerous various populations are. And people who own or purchase pieces of real estate usually have a fairly shrewd idea of what those sites are worth. Evidently the ownership of an acre in the Sahara Desert is of a different value, and consequently attracts a different payment liability, than the ownership of an acre in downtown Manhattan or the heart of Tokyo. Similar things can be said about real estate in the Saudi oilfields, the Amazon rainforests, the Arctic tundra, the Iowa cornbelt, the Bangladeshi coast, and the City of

London. No doubt the values of these sites tend to vary with such factors as technological change, population shifts, and changing consumption patterns, as well as depletions of extractable resources and discoveries of new ones. But whatever relative variation there might be among these values, there is every good reason to suppose that their aggregate secular trend is unlikely to be downwards. Mark Twain was not giving his nephew unsound advice when he said: "Buy land, son; they're not making it any more."

Since nations' territories are aggregations of their members' real-estate holdings, the validity of their territorial claims rests on the validity of those land titles. So nations wishing to sustain the legitimacy of their jurisdiction over these bits of real estate have to ensure that those titles retain their validity. And since states claim exclusive entitlement to the use of force in their societies, including the enforcement of debt-payments, it falls to them to ensure that those land-value payment liabilities are met. To put it in a nutshell, liberal principles demand that *states pay rates*.

In my book, I describe the total revenue yielded by such payments as a *Global Fund*.[7] Each nation therefore has an equal *per capita* claim on this fund. That national claim is simply the aggregation of the individual claims that vest in each resident of the territory over which that nation exercises jurisdiction. Accordingly, each person – regardless of where on the globe he or she resides – is owed that equal amount. Its payment might well take the form of what is currently termed an *unconditional basic income*[8] or, alternatively, an *initial capital stake*.[9] Whatever form it takes, though, it must be equal for all.[10]

The operation of this *Global Fund*, we might reasonably speculate, would serve to establish a variety of benign incentive structures informing relations both within and between nations. So I will conclude by briefly mentioning three of them.[11]

First, the global impact of such a fund is bound to be strongly redistributive since the differential incidence of its levies, in conjunction with the *per capita* parity of its disbursements, pretty much guarantee a substantial reduction in international (as well as national) economic inequalities. These international inequalities have always played a not unimportant role in generating high levels of demand for emigration among poorer nations. Under the regime of the *Global Fund*, poorer nations, being its net beneficiaries, would find fewer of their members leaving to seek their fortunes abroad. Second, the operation of such a fund might be expected to foster greater willingness to compromise in international boundary disputes (over land whose legitimate title-holders are difficult to identify), inasmuch as it attaches a price-tag to any instance of territorial acquisition or retention. And third, the existence of such a fund would give nations stronger *dis*incentives to engage in such odious practices as ethnic cleansing and forced expatriation, since their society's receipts from the fund would thereby decline with their loss of those members, whereas the *Global Fund*'s territorially based levy on them would remain the same. Indeed, nations might well come to cherish each of their members all the more – to provide them each with a strong sense of social identity – for being sources of guaranteed income!

In short, the whole world might become a bit more liberal, both domestically and internationally. Now, wouldn't that be a *Good Thing*?

NOTES

This essay is a revised version of a paper, entitled "Liberalism and nationalism," which appeared in *Analyse & Kritik*, 17 (1995), pp. 12–20. I am grateful to the editors of that journal for permission to reproduce parts of it here, and to Simon Caney and Tim Gray for their comments on it.

1 "Unavoidably," in the sense that the only unconditional objection that the nationalist can offer to any counter-proposal (for a reversed differentiation, or none at all) is that it is contrary to *his/her* particular nation's interest.

2 That is, the set of physical components (spatio-temporal locations, material objects) involved in performing the obligatory action correlatively entailed by any right does not intersect with a corresponding set entailed by any other right. I describe this compossibility requirement as implying that all rights are *funded.*

3 These claims may, of course, be traded off by the persons vested with them: right-holders can *waive* their rights, thereby extinguishing the duties correlatively entailed by them.

4 That is, the individual right involved is the *negative* one, that no one else appropriate more than an equal portion of natural resources. Waldron, however denies that Locke actually intended this "enough and as good" formula as a restriction on just appropriation (Waldron, 1988, pp. 209–18).

5 In a fully appropriated world – whether appropriated by individuals or groups – this cash entitlement is readily construed as a redress payment for the violation of negative rights to others' forbearance from over-appropriating, i.e. engrossing more than would leave enough and as good for each person.

6 These values are conceived as periodized ones, that is, as the current *rental* value of the assets involved. The value of labor-embodying improvements is excluded from the calculation of this liability because persons' rights of self-ownership imply unencumbered rights to the fruits of their labor, i.e. provided landowners' liabilities have been met.

7 For reasons not germane to the concerns of this essay, the sources of the revenues constituting this *Global Fund* consist of *more* factors than only land values; specifically, they also include decedents' estates (cf. Steiner, 1994, ch. 8).

8 Cf. Van Parijs (1995) for a prominent statement of the argument that a liberal conception of distributive justice vests all individuals with a right to an unconditional basic income.

9 Cf. Ackerman and Alstott (1999), and Dowding, De Wispelaere and White (eds.) (2003), for arguments that justice vests individuals with a right to an initial capital stake. Arguably, such a stake is a more liberal – because less *paternalistic* – instantiation of the underlying entitlement involved.

10 Cf. Steiner (2003), for reasons why Van Parijs is wrong to suggest that the required equality of individual entitlements can be justly restricted to one's compatriots.

11 Cf. Tideman (1991) for a more extended discussion of some of these incentive structures.

CHAPTER 4

International justice and the basic needs principle

David Copp

There are striking and disturbing differences in the life prospects of people living in different countries. Most alarming is the fact that many people in many countries are unable to meet their basic needs.[1] In some cases basic physical needs are going unfilled. People lack a source of clean water, adequate medical care, a healthy diet, and so on. In other cases, the needs going unfulfilled are psycho-social needs. Many people do not receive a basic education. There is a moral gravity to situations in which people are unable to meet their basic needs. It is widely agreed that the better off have a duty of charity to assist those living in poverty. I believe, however, that there are duties that go beyond charity. Some differences in life prospects between people in different countries are to be expected, even in a fully just international order. But I believe, with qualifications, that there is injustice in the fact that some countries do not have the resources to enable their people to meet their basic needs while other countries have resources that are surplus to their people's basic needs.

In this essay, I work with a principle I have proposed before, according to which justice requires a state in favorable circumstances to enable its members to meet their basic needs throughout a normal lifespan (Copp, 1992 and 1998). I call this the "basic needs principle." My goal is to investigate the extension of this principle to the international situation, and to argue that issues of global distributive justice could arise even in a benign world in which every state is internally just. I shall maintain that, if there were a global state, it would have a duty (*ceteris paribus*) to ensure the ability of each subordinate state to enable its members to meet their basic needs. In the present situation, existing states have a duty (*ceteris paribus*) to work to create a global state or system of institutions that could discharge the global society's duty to enable people to meet their basic needs. I shall not attempt to argue for the basic needs principle, although I will point to a number of strategies one might use in arguing for it. Near the end of the essay I will respond to objections.

INTERNATIONAL DISTRIBUTIVE JUSTICE AND
THE BENIGN WORLD

International distributive justice concerns justice among the various countries of the world and their peoples. The injustices that concern me consist in or supervene on relevant differences in life prospects, where such differences are due to inequality in the distribution of resources among the countries in the world. They are *international* injustices in two respects. First, in principle, they could be corrected by a redistribution of resources among the countries of the world. And second, they would not exist (as injustices) if the different countries of the world were isolated from one another on different planets in the cosmos.

In some cases, injustices of the relevant kind are due to prior unjust actions, such as the unjust appropriation of territory. In some cases of this kind there are two injustices, the injustice of the prior action, and the injustice that consists in or supervenes on the differences in life prospects. I am concerned with injustices of the latter kind.

Let us perform a thought experiment. Imagine that the world is divided into states in the familiar way and that each of these states is well-ordered and internally just. Basic human rights are respected, for example, and the requirements of distributive justice, whatever they might be, are met in each country. Moreover, governments are well intentioned. There have been no acts of injustice between the countries. Call this the "Benign World." By focusing on what justice would require in this world, we focus on "ideal theory," to use John Rawls's term, and put aside problems of noncompliance (Rawls, 1999b, pp. 4–5). I hold that, despite our assumptions about the Benign World, there might still be injustice in it that consists in or supervenes on relevant differences in life prospects, where such differences are due to inequality in the distribution of resources.

Rawls seems to disagree. Let me use the term "resources" very broadly to cover both "natural resources" and "cultural resources," where the latter include such things as a society's political culture, its level of technical knowledge, its people's industriousness and capacity for innovation, and so on.[2] In these terms, Rawls's view is that, in addition to population policy, "cultural resources" are more important to the wealth of a society than its control of natural resources (Rawls, 1999a, pp. 108–10). He holds that, because of this, "the arbitrariness of the distribution of natural resources" does not ground a requirement to redistribute resources (Rawls, 1999a, p. 117). Rawls *does* hold that well-ordered societies have a duty to assist societies that are in "unfavorable circumstances" to become well-ordered and thereby "to sustain a liberal or decent society."[3] But he views this as a transitional duty that would cease to require assistance if all societies were internally just (Rawls, 1999a, pp. 106, 118). I shall contend to the contrary that justice might require the redistribution of resources even in the Benign World.

THE BASIC NEEDS PRINCIPLE

According to the basic needs principle, justice requires a state in favorable circumstances to enable its members to meet their basic needs throughout a normal lifespan. This formulation conceals some complexities that I need to discuss. I have addressed them more fully in Copp, 1992 and 1998.

Taken by itself, the principle permits a great deal of inequality in life prospects. But it is not the only principle of justice. Justice also requires equality of opportunity and the basic liberties, for example, and inequalities in life prospects may threaten equality of opportunity or democracy (Copp, 2000 and Brighouse, 1996). The principle is compatible with these points as well as with more demanding egalitarian views.

In practice, the principle would demand significant redistribution of resources. The details depend on a variety of factors, including our understanding of the idea of a basic need. But on any plausible understanding, even if we leave aside special needs that would be enormously expensive to meet, the principle would make significant demands. It requires a society to ensure to the extent possible that its members have access to such things as high-quality medical care, a sound basic education, decent housing, clean water, a nutritious diet, and so on. The principle might therefore demand significant intervention in the economy. Given that there are special needs, the demands on the economy can be even more significant.

The requirement to enable people to meet their basic needs is limited to a "normal lifespan." I have in mind a lifespan sufficient to enable a person to experience the stages we expect to see in a worthwhile life, including childhood, maturation, adulthood that permits achievements including child rearing, and a period of retreat leading to completion (see Slote, 1990). These notions are vague, and the details depend on variable cultural factors. The point is that justice does not demand that we enable a person to stay alive no matter what. There are two restrictions. First is the restriction to a normal lifespan, and second is the restriction that I explain next.

The things for which we have basic needs are requirements of autonomous agency. I cannot spend any time in this essay investigating the concept of autonomy and its relation to the basic needs. For the most part we can work with an intuitive understanding of what is at stake. But I have argued elsewhere that the requirements of autonomous agency include the needs that would standardly be listed as basic, including both physical needs and psycho-social needs of the kinds I mentioned above (Copp, 1992, 1998, and 1995, pp. 172–77). If I am correct about this, then, to simplify matters for present purposes, we can stipulate that, in this essay, the term "basic need" refers to the requirements of autonomous agency. Given this stipulation, we can see why the basic needs have normative significance. We can also see why the basic needs principle is compelling as a principle of justice.[4]

Moreover, since the point of enabling people to meet their needs is to support their autonomous agency, the principle should be understood to require enabling people to meet their needs provided that they are capable of autonomous agency. This is the second restriction.

In attempting to *enable* people to meet their needs, a society is required only to do the best it can, given what reasonable people would find acceptable. For example, a society would count as having enabled a person to meet her medical needs if she has had the best medical care that could be given her. And a state may qualify as having enabled people to meet their need for security if it has reduced the risk of crime to a level that reasonable people would find acceptable. There are complications I cannot address here, including complexities about insurance.

One might question whether justice requires *continuing* to enable people to meet their needs even if they have wasted resources. This is a complex issue that raises questions about responsibility and fairness. It also raises worries about moral hazard and issues of institutional design. I doubt that justice requires continuing to help people who squander resources, but I do not want to argue the point here (see Fleurbaey, 1995).

Let me now turn to the idea of *favorable circumstances* that figures in the basic needs principle. A state is in relevantly favorable circumstances if and only if it has the following two properties. First, it is economically in a position to enable its members to meet their basic needs, and second, it is able to do so by permissible means. It is able to do so without violating any moral constraints of greater importance than the requirement concerning basic needs.

States that are *not* in favorable circumstances are subject to two important requirements. First, justice requires that they strive to get themselves into favorable circumstances so that they will be able to meet their members' needs. Second, it requires that they do as well as they can to enable as many of their members as they can to meet their needs, beginning with those who are least able to meet the most important needs. There may be trade-offs between these two requirements. Because of this, one might propose a principle, similar to Rawls's difference principle, according to which, if a state is not in favorable circumstances, justice permits some people to have resources surplus to their basic needs only if either (a) such inequalities work to the advantage of those who are worst off with respect to their ability to meet their basic needs, by enhancing their ability to meet their needs, or (b) the inequalities enhance the likelihood that future generations will be able to meet their needs (see Rawls, 1971). Call this the "difference principle of basic needs." Unfortunately, I will have to set it aside. For my purposes, the chief question raised by states that are not in favorable circumstances is whether other states have a duty in justice to assist them. This question will be the major focus of attention as I proceed.

STATE, QUASI-STATE, AND SOCIETY

I believe that a state of affairs is not *unjust*, unless either there is an agent with a duty to correct it, or there was an agent who violated a duty in bringing it about or permitting it to come about. Recall Robert Nozick's thought experiment in which ten Robinson Crusoes live alone on isolated islands, unable to communicate or trade (Nozick, 1974, pp. 185–86). If some of the Crusoes have surplus resources while others are unable to meet their needs, the situation is perhaps tragic, but I submit that it is not *unjust* because, I assume, no one violated any duty in bringing it about, and no one has a duty to correct it. There are unhappy states of affairs that *would* be matters of injustice if they had been wrongly brought about or wrongly allowed to continue, and one could *call* them unjust. The term is not of any importance. But I work with a conception of an injustice as a state of affairs that is something to be *corrected*, and that is some agent's *responsibility*, in that either the agent brought it about and is responsible for doing so, or the agent can correct it and ought to correct it and will otherwise be responsible.

The basic needs principle postulates a duty regarding basic needs. It says there is injustice when, in a state in favorable circumstances, there are people who are unable to meet their basic needs. We need to ask which agent or agents are responsible for correcting this injustice. I hold that only the state, or the society acting through the state as its agent, is appropriately held responsible for discharging the duty regarding basic needs.[5]

First, given "ought" implies "can," we need to identify an agent or agents with the ability to enable everyone to meet their needs. If a society is not organized into a state, then perhaps no agent has this ability unless a state can be created. No person or small group has the ability, except perhaps if they can create a state or similarly powerful organization, or unless they already occupy roles in institutions that accord them significant power. When a society *is* organized into a state, the state is in the position of having the ability, if any agent does, to fulfill the duty regarding basic needs. Moreover, second, this duty requires achieving a condition of the society as a whole; hence it is appropriate that an agent of the society be held responsible for bringing it about. Discharging the duty would require so organizing the society that everyone is able to meet their needs, and we have seen that this might require an extensive redistribution of resources and a reorganization of society's institutions. It would not be appropriate to hold any individual or small group within the society responsible for achieving this unless they have assumed the responsibility by accepting a relevant institutional role within the state. Typically it is only the state that is in a position to act as agent of the society in the first instance. Hence, it seems, it is the society, or the state acting as its agent, that has the duty regarding basic needs (see Murphy, 1993, and Goodin, 1988).

To be sure, in principle there can be situations in which, although there is not a state, there is an institutional structure or a set of organizations that approximate a state in having the ability to act on behalf of the society. A quasi-state of this kind might be able to discharge the society's duties. For simplicity, I will largely ignore this point.

I assume that when a collective entity has a duty, the members of that entity have derivative duties (*ceteris paribus*) to perform actions that, taken together with the similarly required actions of other members, would constitute the entity's carrying out its duty. Given this, my view is that the state has the primary responsibility to fulfill the duty regarding the basic needs – or the society does, with the state acting as its agent. Individuals may, however, have derivative duties to do their parts in the society's project of carrying out this duty.

One might object that there can be situations of natural abundance and restraint in which everyone would be able to meet their needs throughout a normal lifetime without there being any special kind of institutional setting. But in typical modern circumstances, an institutional setting and an appropriate mix of public policies are required. For instance, there needs to be a legal framework to create secure conditions for productive activity and trade, and such a framework exists only where there is a state. Hence, if a society is in a "state of nature," then unless it is in conditions of natural abundance and restraint, it is likely to be unable to discharge the duty regarding basic needs. I think that a society in this kind of situation would have a duty to establish a state in order to gain the ability to discharge its duty – assuming that the state would then be sufficiently likely to discharge the duty. The duty to establish a state surely would be implied by any plausible rationale for the basic needs principle. If there is such a duty, then the members of the society have a derivative duty, *ceteris paribus*, to do their parts in establishing a state.

Now the people in a state of nature situation might be so isolated from one another that they do not constitute a society. And even if they do constitute a society, they might not be able to create a state. This is why, in a state of nature situation, there may be no agent with the duty regarding the basic needs. And it may be that no person has a duty, everything considered, to attempt to create a state. People may be too isolated from one another to have a realistic prospect of success.

One might think that, in situations in which basic needs are unmet, people would have a direct duty, and not merely a derivative duty, to work to enable others in society to meet their basic needs. I agree. There are various kinds of circumstances in which individuals are required to help others to meet their needs. Parents have duties to their children. We have duties in rescue situations and duties to help victims of famine. These duties have rationales independent of the duty regarding the basic needs, but, like that duty, they can be supported by the moral gravity of the basic needs. The main point is that the basic needs principle does not merely require the provision of assistance to those in need. It requires achieving a condition of the society as a whole. It requires structuring the basic institutions of society so that its members are able to meet their needs throughout a normal lifespan. This duty is not plausibly viewed as falling on individuals, except derivatively, as I have argued.

Given all of this, I think it is plausible that the duty of justice under the basic needs principle falls in the first instance on the society, or on the state viewed as its agent. In state of nature situations, the rationale that supports the principle suggests that people have a qualified duty (*ceteris paribus*) to work to create a state.

RATIONALES FOR THE BASIC NEEDS PRINCIPLE

The basic needs principle can be supported in a variety of ways. I can only sketch a few arguments. (For another argument, see Copp, 1995, pp. 201–03.)

Earlier I suggested that the principle can be grounded in the moral importance of autonomous agency, given that, as I stipulated, the basic needs are the requirements of autonomous agency. Autonomy is arguably of basic moral value. If we hold in addition that autonomous agents are equally deserving of respect, it is appropriate that people be equally enabled to meet their basic needs.

The principle can also be supported by a Rawlsian argument. Rawls's difference principle requires maximizing the control over "primary social goods" enjoyed by people in the worst-off position in society (Rawls, 1971). As Amartya Sen has pointed out, however, people differ in the resources they need in order to meet their basic needs (Sen, 1987, pp. 14–16). Because of this, even if a society satisfies the difference principle, it is possible that many of its members – including some of its better-off members – are unable to meet their basic needs.[6] Given this, it is arguable that the people in Rawls's original position would choose a "difference principle of basic needs" instead of the difference principle (see above; Copp, 1992, 1998; Shue, 1980, p. 128; Sterba, 1978, pp. 115–21; compare Moellendorf, 2002, pp. 81–83). Such a principle would say roughly that inequalities must benefit those who are worst off in respect of their ability to meet their basic needs by providing them with resources that enhance their ability to meet their basic needs. In societies in favorable circumstances, this principle on its intended interpretation would be extensionally equivalent to the basic needs principle.

Some philosophers have argued that justice requires sufficiency rather than equality (Frankfurt, 1987), or that it requires giving priority to the worst off (Parfit, 1995). Since the basic needs principle establishes a minimum floor, one might see it as defining an appropriate conception of sufficiency, or an appropriate conception of the priority of the worst off.

Robert Nozick has proposed that justice in the acquisition of property is subject to a "Lockean proviso" (Nozick, 1974, pp. 174–82, 150–55). I think that the plausibility of the proviso reflects the deeper plausibility of the moral importance of providing for needs. The reason there is a presumption against anyone's acquiring exclusive property rights over the last waterhole in the desert, for example, is surely that everyone *needs* water. There would not be a similar presumption against acquiring exclusive property rights over the only pink rock in the desert. Nozick suggests that a just system of property must satisfy the proviso. I suggest that to reflect the moral importance of providing for needs, a just system of property must satisfy the basic needs principle.[7]

INJUSTICES IN THE BENIGN WORLD

The basic needs principle applies to the situation in the world as a whole, assuming there is a global society. I think it is plausible, moreover, that there *is* a global society (Copp, 1995, pp. 139–40; also Moellendorf, 2002, pp. 36–38). There are global economic institutions and trade. There are global political institutions, including the United Nations. The communities in the world are not isolated from one another in the way that Nozick's Crusoes are isolated. So I assume there is a global society. Given this, the central point is that even if every country in the world satisfies the basic needs principle, it is possible that the global society as a whole does not satisfy the principle.

To see this, return to the Benign World. Assume that every country in the Benign World satisfies the basic needs principle. Assume that some countries are in favorable circumstances and that others are not. In countries that are in favorable circumstances, everyone is able to meet their basic needs throughout a normal lifespan. Matters are different in countries that are not in favorable circumstances. Given our stipulations about the Benign World, these countries are doing the best they can by permissible means to bring themselves into favorable circumstances, while also striving to enable their members to meet their basic needs. But some people are unable to meet their needs. Is this situation unjust?

The situation is not necessarily unjust. There are two issues. First is an issue of feasibility. Is the global society in favorable circumstances for enabling everyone in the world to meet their needs? Second is an issue of agency. Is there a global state? If not, is the international community organized in such a way that it could implement a permissible set of policies that would bring it about that everyone is able to meet their needs?

Let us organize the discussion around these issues. Begin with a situation in which there is a global state and consider, first, cases in which it is in favorable circumstances, and second, cases in which it is not. Turn then to a situation in which there is not a global state. Distinguish, first, cases in which the global society could act to meet the duty regarding basic needs, and second, cases in which it could not do this, but in which the states in the world could work together to create a global state or entity capable of dealing with injustice. I begin with cases in which there is a global state.

What are we supposing, in imagining a global state? A state corresponds to the legal system that is in force in a territory. A state is the system of institutions – together with the people who occupy the offices and roles of the institutions – that governs a territory (and its residents) in which a legal system is in force, and that administers and enforces the legal system and carries out the programs of government (Copp, 1999). In order for a global state to exist, there would have to be a global legal system, at least in a minimal sense, and there would have to be institutions to administer it.

Beyond this, there are various possibilities. A global state could be a unitary entity, or it could be a federation of states, each of which is subordinate to the global state. I will assume that we are dealing with a federation. A global federation could be so weak that it is unable to rule without the consent of the constituent states. Or, it could be strong enough to have reduced the subordinate states to the status of mere administrative units. We can abstract from many of these complexities. The substantive issue is whether the global state has sufficient power and administrative capabilities that it could implement a permissible set of policies that would bring it about that everyone in the world is able to meet their needs. For simplicity, I will assume that it does.

There are different ways to extend the basic needs principle to the case of a global federation. First, we could think of the global state as having the same duty with respect to enabling people to meet their needs that the individual subordinate states would have with respect to their members if the global state did not exist. On this view, in effect, the subordinate states are morally transparent. The global state's duty is to deal directly with the needs of individual people, just as if the subordinate states did not exist. Call this the "transparency view." Second, we might think that the individual subordinate states have the primary responsibility to ensure that their residents are able to meet their needs. We might think that the global state is required only to ensure that the subordinate states have sufficient resources to be able to meet this primary responsibility. Call this the "divided responsibility view."

The divided responsibility view is surely the more natural and sensible, at least in any world with a history similar to our own. On the transparency view, the existence of the global state in effect absolves the subordinate states of their duties regarding basic needs. I see no reason to suppose that this is so, especially in the Benign World, given that, by hypothesis, each of the subordinate countries in that world is just. It is more natural to think that the duty of the global state is to work to bring it about that every subordinate state is in favorable circumstances, rather than to deal directly with the needs of individual persons.

On the divided responsibility view, subordinate states have a role in relation to their members that is analogous in important ways to the role of parents in relation to their children. Parents have the primary responsibility to ensure the welfare of their children but the state ought to provide backup. The state can step in, in circumstances in which parents are not doing what they ought. Similarly, it seems plausible that subordinate states under a global federation would have the primary responsibility for enabling their members to meet their needs although the global state ought to assist states that are not in favorable circumstances. Moreover the global state might be required to step in, if a subordinate state is not doing what it ought.

The divided responsibility view may be the more sensible and natural in our world and in the Benign World, but in different circumstances it might not be. Certainly, if the global state had a unitary rather than a federalist constitution, the duty regarding the basic needs would fall primarily on the global state. The underlying question is presumably how best to write the constitution of a global state given the various kinds of circumstances it might be in.

If the Benign World is organized into a global state, the main issue that remains is whether it is in favorable circumstances. Is there a permissible and feasible set of policies that would bring it about either that every subordinate state is in favorable circumstances or that everyone in the world is able to meet their needs? If the answer is negative, then the global state would be required in justice to attempt to bring it about that it is in favorable circumstances or that it comes to be in nearly favorable circumstances. If the answer is affirmative, then presumably the subordinate states that are in favorable circumstances have either physical or cultural resources that could be transferred to the less well-off states to bring them into favorable circumstances. In this case, I propose that the global state has a duty in justice to organize a fair system for the transfer of resources from the more wealthy countries to the less well-off countries to ensure that every country comes to be in favorable circumstances. The subordinate countries have a duty to do their parts in implementing this system.

One might have various pragmatic objections to this proposal, such as that there is no guarantee that the less well-off states will use the resources appropriately. In the Benign World, however, these objections are not well-founded since, by hypothesis, agents in the Benign World do what they are required to do as a matter of justice. In the Benign World, the global state would do what it could to bring about justice, and the subsidiary states and their officials would play their parts to enable the global state to carry out its duty.

INTERNATIONAL JUSTICE IN THE ABSENCE OF A GLOBAL STATE

Suppose now that the Benign World is not organized into a global state. Even so, the global society might be organized in a way that makes it capable of joint action. There could be a quasi-state, as I mentioned before. In this case, there would be an entity capable of acting on behalf of the global society, although not perhaps with the effectiveness of a state. Situations of this kind would be sufficiently similar to the cases in which the world is organized into a state that we can set them aside and turn directly to situations in which the problem of agency is central.

Imagine, then, that states are in a situation analogous to the situation of persons in the domestic state of nature. Following our reasoning about the latter situation, if some states in the global state of nature are not in favorable circumstances, then all states would have a duty (*ceteris paribus*) to work together to create a global state – assuming that this state would be sufficiently likely to discharge the duty regarding basic needs. A duty of this kind surely would be implied by any plausible rationale for the basic needs principle – it would be derivative from the duty regarding basic needs that is incumbent on the global society. It would only hold other things being equal – on the assumption that enough other states are willing to do their parts – but this is so, *ex hypothesi*, in the Benign World. It is plausible, then, that the states in a global state of nature in the Benign World would have a duty to work together to create a global state (or quasi-state) that could discharge the global society's duty.

It might seem that individual states in the global state of nature would have non-derivative duties to assist states that are not in favorable circumstances. An analogous issue arose in connection with the domestic state of nature. Again, I agree. There can be rescue cases and famine cases. But we do not need to invoke the basic needs principle to support the idea that better-off states can be obligated to assist less well-off states in such cases.

Moreover, the basic needs principle does not merely impose a duty of assistance. In a global state of nature – at least in the Benign World where, *ex hypothesi*, a global state would be a force for justice – the principle (or its underlying rationale) imposes a duty on existing states to work together to create a global state (or quasi-state) that would be able to discharge the duty regarding basic needs. And assuming that the global society would then be in favorable circumstances, the global state (or quasi-state) would have a duty to so structure the basic institutions of the world that the subordinate states are able to ensure the ability of their members to meet their basic needs. This duty is not merely a duty to assist the less well off.

OBJECTIONS

I cannot here address objections to the basic needs principle as such, but I do need briefly to address skepticism directed specifically at the idea of *international* distributive justice. I can see four lines of objection.

First is the objection that the global society is not "thick" enough to sustain duties of justice. Brian Barry argues that a system of justice must be such that "all the parties stand prospectively to benefit from the scheme," and he argues that the conditions for prospective benefit do not exist in the world as a whole (Barry, 1982, p. 233). Michael Walzer argues that there are requirements of distributive justice within a group only if the group shares a culture or set of "common meanings" (Walzer, 1983, ch. 3; see Moellendorf, 2002, pp. 72–74, 76–78). Walzer seems to think that the global population does not have a relevant set of common meanings. I do not find these views plausible, but even if they are correct, the most that follows is that there are conditions under which there would not be requirements of global justice. And I agree that the basic needs principle would not apply to the global population if that population did not constitute a society. I agree, then, that it is a contingent matter whether there are requirements of global justice.

The second objection is driven by the worry that a global state would not be viable, or that it would not be a force for justice. Thomas Nagel says that "the world is not a plausible candidate for a single state" (Nagel, 1991, pp. 174–79). Rawls agrees with Kant that a global state would likely become either a despotism or a fragile empire torn by civil strife as various groups tried to secede from it.[8] Such pessimism might be appropriate if directed at the idea of a unitary global state. But my argument requires only the viability of a global federation or system of institutions with the ability to discharge the duty regarding basic needs. Indeed, Rawls seems to agree with Kant that a "federative union" of states might be conducive to world peace (Rawls, 1999a, p. 70).

The third objection rests on the idea of a division of moral responsibility. It sees each state as responsible for achieving justice within its borders, and so – assuming there has been no unjust interference – it denies that other states have any responsibility for whether justice is achieved within a state. This position actually implies that a global state *would* be responsible for achieving global justice. The interesting question is whether there can be a reason of justice to create a global state when there is not one. Suppose, then, that some states in the Benign World are in unfavorable circumstances. Suppose that the explanation for this is that they began by being very poorly endowed with resources. Suppose that they are not at all responsible for their difficulty. In this case, given the rationale for the basic needs principle, it would be difficult to deny, merely on the basis of an abstract idea of the division of responsibility, that the better-off states have a duty to create institutions to help the less well-off states.

The final objection is based in a kind of optimism about politics. Rawls thinks that people's basic needs would be met in any well-ordered society, and he conjectures that, leaving aside "marginal cases," any society could become well-ordered, "were it reasonably and rationally organized and governed" (Rawls, 1999a, pp. 108–10, and pp. 38, 119. See below, note 6). It appears to follow that, except for marginal cases, the only thing preventing societies from escaping poverty is their political organization. Given this, one might argue, virtually every society actually *can* enable its members to meet their needs. Leaving aside emergency situations and marginal cases, one might conclude, there is no need for a global state or quasi-state to assist societies that are mired in poverty. I think that such an argument would be mistaken. A well-ordered society that lacked relevant technology – or that faced an HIV epidemic or desertification – might not be able to enable its people to meet their needs. Issues of global justice might arise even if every state were well governed.

Rawls is correct about the importance of good government. In some cases, governments have used resources unwisely or for corrupt purposes. In some cases, population policy creates difficulty. One might argue that, in such cases, wealthier societies have no obligation to help. But this view is not plausible where the problem rests with past governments, or where the government is despotic. In any event, in the Benign World, *ex hypothesi*, every state does its best to enable its people to meet their needs.

The wealthier states in that world cannot argue that societies in unfavorable circumstances are responsible for their own difficulties; hence they cannot use this ground for denying that they have duties to redistribute resources.

CONCLUSION

My goal in this essay has been to investigate the extension of the basic needs principle from the domestic situation to the international situation and to argue that issues of global distributive justice could arise even in a world in which every state is internally just. I argued that a global state would have a duty to ensure that each subordinate state can enable its members to meet their basic needs. Plausible rationales for the basic needs principle imply as well that states in a global state of nature would have a duty (*ceteris paribus*) to work to create a global state or system of institutions that could discharge the global society's duty regarding basic needs.

I restricted my discussion largely to the imaginary Benign World so that I could set aside worries about compliance with justice. In the Benign World, each country is stipulated to be doing the best it can to achieve justice. In the actual world, however, countries have seized resources from others, and this supports a requirement of redistribution over and above the duties implied by the basic needs principle. In the actual world, moreover, corruption, lack of concern, and simple inefficiency mean that governments cannot in general be trusted to use resources as required by the basic needs principle. Even if a global state were created in the real world, it would be vulnerable to corruption, and many countries would be unwilling to cooperate with it. For these reasons, we must be pessimistic about the likelihood of achieving justice in the real world. And because of this, even if the basic needs principle is correct, it is not clear what justice requires states to do, all things considered, in order to achieve a just international order.

NOTES

Versions of this paper were presented in 2002 to the Conference on International Justice, University of St. Andrews, to the 2003 meetings of the Central Division of the American Philosophical Association, and to the Philosophy Departments at the University of Illinois, Urbana-Champaign, the University of Illinois, Chicago, and the University of Virginia. For helpful discussion, I am grateful to these audiences, and especially to John Simmons and John Skorupski.

1 For information on global poverty, see: http://www.worldbank.org/poverty/mission.

2 Here I follow Dworkin, 1981b and Roemer, 1996.

3 Rawls defines a "decent" society as a "nonliberal society" that meets "certain specified conditions of political right and justice." (Rawls, 1999a, pp. 3, fn. 2, 67, 88.)

4 The ability to meet a basic need presumably counts as a "capability," as Amartya Sen uses the term. My approach gives priority to a subset of "capabilities," perhaps the subset Sen calls "basic" capabilities. (See Sen, 1987, p. 16; Copp, 1992.)

5 But see below. For the concept of a state, see Copp, 1999. For the concept of a society, see Copp, 1995, ch. 7.

6 Rawls seems to disagree (Rawls, 1999a, pp. 38, 119, also pp. 67, 88; Rawls, 2001, p. 44). Yet in one place he suggests supplementing his principles of justice with a requirement much like the basic needs principle (Rawls, 2001, p. 44, note). It is important nevertheless that he does not share my conception of basic needs. He explains that by "basic needs" he means the needs that must be met in order for people "to take advantage of the rights, liberties, and opportunities of their society" (Rawls, 1999a, p. 38, fn. 47).

7 For a similar view, see Mack, 1995. Nozick says that the proviso will protect access to things "necessary for life" (Nozick, 1974, pp. 178–79). He would deny that the mere fact that some are unable to meet their needs implies that the proviso has been violated (p. 181).

8 Rawls, 1999a, p. 36.

CHAPTER 5

Cosmopolitans, cosmopolitanism, and human flourishing

Christine Sypnowich

Debates about equality tend to take as their context the relations among citizens in a single society. Yet problems of inequality obviously go beyond a particular territory or country. The greatest equality gaps are no longer, as they were a hundred years ago, between rich and poor persons within a country, but between rich and poor peoples: problems of inequality are most egregious between the haves and have-nots in the international context. And yet we lack the capacity to redress global injustice: institutional resources, human motivation and the concepts of political philosophy all presume the predominance of the nation-state paradigm and obligations among citizens. As one prominent commentator puts it, "liberal goals are achieved in a liberalized societal culture or nation" (Kymlicka, 2001, p. 216). Thus perhaps the toughest test of an egalitarian theory is what it can contribute to the promotion of equality, not among citizens, but around the globe. In this essay I argue that problems of international justice are illuminated by a theory of egalitarianism that is committed to equalizing the conditions of human flourishing. If we are to make human beings in the world more equal, then we must consider how cultural practices affect human flourishing. My argument casts doubt on the coherence of neutralist concepts of justice that, in either local or global applications, avoid any commitment on matters of value.

Few egalitarians would dispute that richer peoples have duties of redistribution to poorer peoples. The question is how extensive are these duties of global justice, particularly in comparison to the duties of domestic justice. For some, claims of nationality are such that our duties to the disadvantaged within our country should take priority. Moreover, the policy of looking out for one's own is bolstered by the view that the distant disadvantaged are better served if they are left to help themselves, which respects their capacity for self-determination. Others argue that nationality is arbitrary and that there is no reason why an adequate egalitarian theory should not be global in scope, with no regard for borders or territory. In the face of this difficult tension, I argue that focusing on equalizing the conditions of human flourishing will enable us to find a middle course, which affirms our cosmopolitan duties whilst recognizing the inevitable and valuable role of a culture of self-determining citizenship.

COSMOPOLITANISM VERSUS COSMOPOLITANS

Political philosophers are increasingly concerned with the extent to which individuals and nations have obligations of justice to non-nationals. The idea of such obligations has been dubbed "cosmopolitanism." The history of this word suggests, however, that it is a curious choice of term. In the past, to be cosmopolitan was to be a certain kind of person marked by diverse cultural influences. The term could imply either praise or denigration. On the one hand, cosmopolitanism was a form of privilege, connoting the well traveled and culturally sophisticated, contrasted with the provincial and naive; cosmopolitanism was an admirable but perhaps elite aesthetic. On the other hand, the cosmopolitan was also the target of xenophobia, disrespect, suspicion, and mistrust. Cosmopolitans were regarded as foreign, "dirty," and decadent, associated with Jews or "Bolsheviks," whom bigots sought to exclude.[1]

The cosmopolitanism of global justice, in contrast, is an ethical perspective. The current usage of cosmopolitanism builds on the word's etymology, kosmos, meaning world, and polis, meaning state, conjoined to refer to a global state that would institutionalize an international moral order. This kind of cosmopolitanism has a certain political cast, affirming a concern for the well being of persons outside one's milieu in a spirit of indifference toward their particular cultural practices. Prejudice has no part of contemporary cosmopolitanism, but nor does enthusiasm for the exotic. As Charles Jones puts it, cosmopolitanism is a moral perspective that is impartial, universal, individualist, and egalitarian, the fundamental idea of which is that "every human being has a right to have her or his vital interest met, regardless of nationality or citizenship" (Jones, 1999, pp. 15–17).

This is a contrast between what might be dubbed cultural worldliness and moral worldliness, the former interested in the distinctive contributions of different cultures, the latter interested in moral duties to persons irrespective of cultures. The two are often muddled in current debates among political philosophers, however, since defenses of cosmopolitanism often refer both to the aesthetic ideal of a "citizen of the world" who savors cultural diversity, and the moral ideal of international obligations. Thus in a critique of nationalism, Jeremy Waldron appeals to "the cosmopolitan self" who lives a "freewheeling cosmopolitan life" in which he or she

learns Spanish, eats Chinese, wears clothes made in Korea, listens to arias by Verdi sung by a Maori princess on Japanese equipment, follows Ukrainian politics, and practices Buddhist meditation techniques. (Waldron, 1999, p. 95)

For Waldron, such a conception of the person is better able to respect the autonomy of the individual who can choose and revise how to live, irrespective of ethnicity or nationality. But not just personal freedom is at stake; Waldron also implies a cosmopolitan ethic is an antidote to the "cultural exclusiveness" and "ethnic sectarianism" which have produced global injustice (Waldron, 1999, p. 113). Elsewhere, liberal political philosophers have drawn on this ideal of the cosmopolitan self to make an argument for international justice. Thus Anthony Appiah refers to the "cosmopolitan patriot" who is both attached to home, but takes "pleasure from the presence of other, different, places that are home to other, different people." Such a perspective also produces a commitment to the "equal dignity of all persons" and "the notion of human rights – rights possessed by human beings as such" (Appiah, 1996, pp. 22, 25).

There are some genuine tensions, however, between the cosmopolitan aesthetic and cosmopolitan ethics, or cultural worldliness and moral worldliness. First, the beautiful and the moral are not the same thing, and indeed there is always the potential for a conflict between the two. Beautiful things can be the result of unjust arrangements, and thus the values of cultural worldliness will sometimes be at odds with those of moral worldliness. (Consider the child labor that produces splendid oriental carpets.) The cosmopolitan person's enthusiasm for cultural creations might involve a certain indifference to the circumstances of their origin. Cosmopolitan ethics, in contrast, insists on the priority of justice, regardless of aesthetic considerations, and perhaps at their cost.

A second difference is thus the attitude to difference itself. Whereas neither perspective is one of loyalty to one's own, the cosmopolitan aesthete enjoys diversity; the cosmopolitan ethicist, on the other hand, calls for a universal standard. Finally, a third difference is each position's relation to inequality. It might be noted that the cosmopolitan is typically a privileged person, who has access to foreign travel, some knowledge of art and the means for enjoying it, who possesses sophisticated tastes and a cultivated, open mind. This is evident in the enthusiastic endorsement of cultural worldliness on the part of what must be admitted are relatively privileged persons, usually from relatively privileged societies: e.g. academics, who have opportunities for the cosmopolitan way of life that most people lack. And those who express mistrust of cosmopolitanism, however bigoted and pernicious their views, might well be giving expression to a resentment of cultural inequality that is spawned by material inequality.

The cosmopolitan mode of life thus seems awkwardly paired with cosmopolitan justice. Moral worldliness seeks the mitigation, if not elimination, of disparities of wealth; instead of being the fruit of disadvantage, it seeks to be its antidote. The fact that people in wealthy parts of the world enjoy a high standard of living whilst people in poor parts of the world can barely survive is denounced as without any moral justification. And thus those of us who lead cosmopolitan lives are in some sense targeted as obligated to share our wealth with those parts of the world we have been able to experience aesthetically. In light of all this, global justice is perhaps poorly described as a "cosmopolitan" position, given the long association the term has with positions of privilege.

Might, however, the morally worldly need some kind of cultural worldliness? That is, does the pursuit of global justice require a focus on the constituents of human flourishing, constituents that involve precisely those matters of cultural value emphasized by the culturally worldly cosmopolitan? I believe that the current usage of cosmopolitanism as a moral perspective in fact requires some recourse to the original, non-pejorative idea of cosmopolitanism as a mode of life; global justice involves some idea of cultural evaluation. In what follows I will argue that current arguments for moral worldliness must in fact resort to cultural worldliness.

GLOBAL EGALITARIANISM

Rawls's theory of justice has been an important inspiration for theories of global equality. Recall that *A Theory of Justice* argues for the redistribution of wealth in light of the arbitrariness of circumstances that determine one's level of advantage. This is captured with the thought experiment of the original position, where behind a "Veil of Ignorance," I do not know what kind of person I will be in the society I am designing, and thus self-interest dictates I come up with principles of justice that protect the worst off. The idea that levels of wealth and resources are the result of arbitrary and undeserved factors seems ideal for capturing the contingency of being born with one citizenship or another, and the consequent impact this can have on one's material position (Rawls, 1971).

It might be suggested that Rawls's theory works best on the international stage. After all, in the context of a single, affluent national polity, the idea that my ability to be wealthy or poor is the unmerited by-product of a "natural lottery" is vulnerable to a variety of objections derived from concepts of free will, desert, and responsibility. But to be born in a poorly governed, drought-stricken country as opposed to an affluent liberal democracy truly does seem to be a matter of plum bad luck. As Harry Brighouse puts it: "National membership is for the most part morally arbitrary. We did not choose our nationality from a range of serious options any more than we chose our race or sex, or the class position of our parents" (Brighouse, 1998, p. 379). Thomas Pogge notes that the years since 1945 have

culminated in unprecedented economic inequality between the most affluent tenth of humankind and the poorest fifth. What makes this huge and steadily growing inequality a monstrosity, morally, is the fact that the global poor are also so incredibly poor in absolute terms. They lack secure access to food, safe water, clothing, shelter, basic education and they are also highly vulnerable to being deprived of the objects of their civil and political human rights by their governments as well as by private agents. Some 18 million of them die prematurely every year. (Pogge, 1998a, p. 185)

Thus many theorists of international justice have applied Rawls's arguments to the problem of global inequality. Some global egalitarians go so far as to defend a "global difference principle" where inequalities between human beings across the globe are only justified if the worst off benefit, thus calling for a dramatic redistribution of wealth from the haves to the have-nots (Beitz, 1979, pp. 143–53; Pogge, 1989, ch. 6).

Rawls himself, however, resists such radical global interpretations of his argument. In *The Law of Peoples*, Rawls contrasts his position with that of cosmopolitans who take national boundaries to have no mitigating effect on efforts at distributive justice. Rawls counsels respect for national diversity: societies, their institutions, values, and policies, are various and not all societies can reasonably be expected to accept any liberal principle of distributive justice. Rawls insists that in the global context, our measure should not be a "global egalitarian principle" but rather a mere "duty of assistance"; our target is not to engineer equality but rather to "assist burdened countries to become full members of the Society of Peoples and to be able to determine the path of their own future for themselves." The duty of humanitarian assistance is restricted as a "principle of transition" that takes as its aim improvements in the management of the disadvantaged country's economy (Rawls, 1999a, p. 118).

These three principles: a duty of assistance rather than strict egalitarian principle; aid toward full membership in a global community rather than global equality; and a posture of transition rather than longstanding commitment, have attracted considerable controversy. For many egalitarians, Rawls's global principles betray the ideals of his original theory of justice. Kok-Chor Tan laments that whereas Rawls finds an individual's lot arbitrary in the domestic arena, in international politics, Rawls assumes a communal unit of analysis, forcing individuals to shoulder the burden of their country's lot. In effect, individuals are held accountable for their country's inadequate domestic policies, whether or not they played a role in formulating them (Tan, 2000, p. 179). Rawls thus ends up retracting his egalitarianism, lowering his sights in the global context and leaving intact inequality within societies other than his own as well as the inequality between his society and others (Tan, 2000, p. 165).

There are some obvious obstacles to exporting Rawls's principles of justice to other disadvantaged peoples. One difficulty is the identity of the relevant parties. Are the "haves" and "have-nots" individuals or nations? Given that some have-not nations possess pockets of great affluence, affluence that in some cases surpasses that of the well off in have nations, it is uncertain who should contribute to whom. Thus Rawls's concern that nations pull themselves up by their own bootstraps responds in part to the problem of internal maldistribution. Holding countries responsible for their own distributive woes is a way of dealing with the complexity of who to target in trying to equalize global wealth. Moreover, remedy for the maldistribution of wealth within a country is a burden that may be unfeasible for third parties to shoulder; it is perhaps also unfair to expect them to do so. Nonetheless, Rawls's argument has the paradoxical upshot that individuals in poor countries who are far worse off than the relatively privileged worst off in Rawls's own country are entitled to less, not more, amelioration.

How might we resolve this stalemate about the ambitions of global justice? The root of the difficulty is Rawls's metric of primary goods. Rawls's difference principle seeks to attend to the worst off's share of primary goods that include such things as wealth, income, and property. On the one hand, this metric is mobile and easily redistributed globally. Hence radical global Rawlsians have no difficulty envisaging ambitious reallocations of resources from the rich to the poor. On the other hand, there is great uncertainty about the effect of such redistributions. It may be that Rawls is reluctant to throw generous stores of goods to the far-off disadvantaged precisely because of the lack of clarity of his own measure. After all, people's ability to live well depends on more than just access to goods. How they acquire the goods and what they do with them are also crucial in determining how well they live. There are cultural factors here that the cosmopolitan person's more strongly evaluative, cultural approach can help identify.

The extent to which someone lives well is often termed a matter of their well being; I will use this term and the term, human flourishing, interchangeably to denote what we seek to foster by egalitarian policies. Focusing only on the distribution of goods, I will argue, is an inadequate answer to the "equality of what" question, particularly once it is asked in the global context. A better standard is the conditions of human flourishing, which can also enable a more perspicuous debate about the extent of egalitarian obligations on a global scale. In short, once we provide a better answer to what it is we seek to make more equal, we are better able to determine the stringency of our egalitarian obligations to non-nationals.

EQUALITY OF WHAT? HOW MUCH EQUALITY?

We have seen that there are two issues pertaining to the problem of how we should conceive of equality in the international arena. The first is what is the metric for measuring inequality and its amelioration. This is the problem of "equality of what," which is acutely difficult to answer in the global context, where people vary so much in their circumstances and interests. Another tough issue is the extent of equality; that is, how far should our equalizing policies extend, or how ambitious should be their grasp. Here again we confront a challenge that is all the greater when situated in the international arena, where the disparities are so overwhelming and the task of remedy seeming almost infinite. Let us first address the question of what to equalize.

It is instructive that Amartya Sen's call for a shift in focus in egalitarian argument to the criterion of capabilities was launched in the context of impoverished societies outside the Western liberal democratic and capitalist framework (Sen, 1999). One rival approach, equality of welfare, which centers on experiential states or the satisfaction of preferences, has the advantage of focusing on the subjective impact of redistribution. How the person fares with their allocation of goods, their level of satisfaction or contentment, certainly seems a relevant consideration in the matter of equality. However, welfarism suffers from taking people's ambitions at face value. People's preferences and plans of life can take the shape that they do precisely because of the distorting effects of unequal distribution. Desire fulfillment can give a misleading measure of well being because of the problem of "entrenched deprivation," where the disadvantaged person adjusts his or her expectations, goals, and desires. "The extent of a person's deprivation, then, may not at all show up in the metric of desire-fulfillment, even though he or she may be quite unable to be adequately nourished, decently clothed, minimally educated and properly sheltered" (Sen, 1992, pp. 42, 54–55). One can become accustomed to disadvantage, and thus be cheery in the face of the objective reality of an inadequate standard of living. Or one can take for granted a relatively privileged position and feel discontented and yearn for more.

This problem is manifest in attitudinal comparisons between the materially advantaged in a society of hyper-consumerism, alienation, and neurosis, which can indicate a shortfall in welfare, compared to the materially disadvantaged in the close-knit and protective community who are happy with little (Sen, 1999, pp. 62–63). It is a poor theory of global equality that simply reinforces the effects of an unequal distribution and concludes that the demands of equality are met simply because the poor are undemanding.

On the other hand, a resources or goods approach, though it has the advantage of seeking a fair distribution of wealth regardless of people's preferences, suffers from an inability to attend to the particularities of the source and effect of inequality. Focusing on equitable shares of goods fails to take account that "what goods do for people" will be subject to enormous variation because of differing circumstances in how people live. These circumstances are personal, social, and environmental. They include nutritional needs, disease, and disability; location and the attendant physical factors of climate, famine, and natural disasters; as well as the cultural impact of location in the form of norms, customs, and expectations; gender relations, family structure, etc. (Sen, 1999, pp. 70–71, 88–89).

It should be apparent that these considerations are particularly relevant when comparing the position of persons globally. An interpersonal comparison of capabilities that allows for contextual factors has a paradoxical effect on the demands of redistribution in the international context. On the one hand there are grounds for making significant redistributions in order to take account of the serious shortfall in capabilities that result from the particular circumstances of deprived persons in underdeveloped countries. Yet on the other hand it is true that the underdeveloped context might have a more modest minimum to achieve the same level of capabilities. Sen notes when considering the effect of "social exclusion" on human capabilities:

The need to take part in the life of a community may induce demands for modern equipment (televisions, videocassette recorders, automobiles and so on) in a country where such facilities are more or less universal (unlike what would be needed in less affluent countries), and thus imposes a strain on a relatively poor person in a rich country even when that person is at a much higher level of income compared with people in less opulent countries. (Sen, 1999, pp. 89–90)

Sen stresses how, compared to a goods approach, his metric of capabilities can pinpoint precisely what is at issue when diverse people are poor.

Sen does not, however, tackle the root of the problem of alternative approaches, which is their agnosticism about value. Rawls's schema is inadequate not just because of its "goods fetishism" that fails to take account of the impact of goods on persons. The neutralism of egalitarian positions such as that of Rawls is also a serious defect. Primary goods are inadequate as an egalitarian measure because of their lack of commitment to the question of what counts as doing well, an assessment of the purposes to which goods are put. For it is apparent that poverty is significant because of the impoverishment of well being that it produces. We need to identify the universal constituents of human flourishing, particularly in cases of global justice, in order to understand our global obligations to those leading lesser lives.

These constituents can be grouped into three categories. First, there is being able to choose how to live since a non-autonomous life falls short as a flourishing existence. A second constituent of well being that involves self-mastery and objectively worthwhile pursuits, for there are better and worse ways of living and even the freely chosen pursuit can be defective. Finally, personal contentment is an important feature of flourishing, since freely chosen objective pursuits are insufficient if the person derives no pleasure or fulfillment from them. Well being must be understood ambitiously to involve more than just subsistence. People need food, shelter, and health, but also education, friendship, and love, participation in public life, play, and sport, the experience of nature, culture, and opportunities for intellectual reflection in order to enjoy well being. Indeed, it may be that improvements in the latter constituents of well being are more important than improvements to the former, for example health, at some point. To get a handle on the "real stuff of well being" requires that we go "deeper than basic needs" to other objective values and their realization (Griffin, 1986, pp. 52–53).

Human flourishing itself cannot be equalized, of course. Whether one person is flourishing or not will depend on the conditions in which they live – adequate provision of material resources, health, education, access to culture, nature, and leisure. Some conditions, though vital to living well, can only be fostered by political measures, not provided by them. For example, it is probably fair to say that the most important factor in determining whether or not a person flourishes, besides having enough to eat, is the presence of friendship and love in one's life. But this is hardly something that can be guaranteed by state policy.[2] Public policy can, perhaps, address a culture of anomie or alienation that breeds loneliness; support for a rich and diverse public culture of clubs, festivals, and concerts, drop-in centers, nature walks, libraries, and swimming pools can provide opportunities for social interaction and community. And public policy can provide support for families to help raise children who are loved and lovable. Nonetheless, the important matter of having love in one's life cannot be a matter of adequate social provision; we can live under ideal conditions for flourishing and still fail to flourish. One's lack of human relationships might just be the inevitable result of a certain kind of character. Some of us are like the character Eeyore in A. A. Milne's children's story *Winnie-the-Pooh*: determined to take a grim look on life. Others of us resemble the lazy aristocrat Oblomov in Ivan Aleksandrovich Goncharov's novel of the same name: slothful persons who do not make the most of our potential. These characters may be the result of environmental factors – family background, schooling, class position, or deprivation, but it seems safe to assume that no society, however successful its policies, can wholly eliminate glumness or sloth. A flourishing approach must therefore accept shortfalls in flourishing that derive from personalities. Yet though flourishing itself cannot be equalized, we must attend to the levels of flourishing of individuals to determine whether shortfalls in flourishing are the result of conditions that can and ought to be improved by public policy. And we should have a demanding set of expectations as well as an imaginative preparedness to see the environmental roots of deficits in well being.

Another legitimate kind of variation in flourishing is cultural. Here we should deploy the culturally worldly cosmopolitan's criteria of value, both sensitive to cultural difference yet convinced of universal norms that can be applied to the artifacts of different cultures. The attention to context is to be distinguished from a relativism that eschews the possibility of an objective understanding of flourishing in the first place. One should defer to local standards where they pose a genuine framework for well being, but the ideal of well being or flourishing nonetheless involves certain objective features. The idea of universal constituents of human flourishing means that we will not simply acquiesce to the local in all matters, since it may be that local practices contribute to shortfalls in flourishing. The focus on women's development projects among agencies such as Oxfam, where women are trained in new skills and acquire new capacities of self-determination is an illustration of how the ideal of flourishing can serve to elevate or extend the local understanding, rather than be cowed by it. Thus although the actualization of flourishing will be shaped by the practices of a particular community, the constituents of flourishing are universal. The concept of flourishing thus must both have recourse to local norms as well as being prepared to transcend them.

We are thus concerned to ensure, as much as possible, that people actually exercise their capabilities in our understanding of flourishing. It is the equalization of the conditions of flourishing that is the proper aim of an egalitarian policy, but the extent to which this aim is realized will be assessed according to, in considerable part, whether people actually flourish. Thus we cannot be content with an account that supplies people with the wherewithal without attending to its results; it is not just potential but its actualization that counts as flourishing. Although we must distinguish flourishing per se from the social conditions of flourishing, since it is the latter that is amenable to principles of justice, flourishing and its conditions must be kept connected since the latter must be designed with the former in mind, and the former will help regulate the latter.

It is unclear whether Sen's approach takes adequate account of the relation between the conditions and achievement of flourishing, or what he terms capabilities and functioning. For Sen, functioning, which involves the exercise of a capability, should be jettisoned in favor of mere capability, which gives scope for choosing not to exercise a possibility that is nonetheless available (Sen, 1992, pp. 51–53). Here he is responding to an objection by G. A. Cohen, who faulted Sen's earlier version of the capabilities concept for "athleticism." As Cohen emphasizes, "What goods do for people is not identical with what people are able to do with them," and it is only the latter that is properly the province of justice (Cohen, 1993). In acceding to Cohen, Sen noted that capability, rather than functioning, has the advantage of providing scope for choice. Capability allows us to see that x, y, and z are accessible to a person, even if he or she opted only for x. Not just doing x, but choosing to do x and doing it, might be the best measure of well being (Sen, 1992, pp. 51–53).

The difficulty with this more modest approach is that it seems to absent itself from the matter of how people in fact live, content with the presence of mere opportunities for flourishing, which the agent is free to choose or not to choose to seize. Freedom is an aspect of well being, but well being per se nonetheless involves a matter of actual achievement. And achievement is our only evidence for capability; in order to determine whether or not people have the capability to flourish, we must make substantive judgements about whether or not they actually are flourishing in virtue of the exercise of these capabilities. As Sen admits, "practical difficulties of data availability" would indicate that functionings or actual flourishing remain central to our analysis of the presence of capabilities. The situation is analogous to the contrast drawn between equality of opportunity and equality of outcome; whether or not there is genuine equality of opportunity cannot be determined without reference to the extent to which outcomes are in fact equal (Sypnowich, 2003).

In the global context, where a history of deprivation can condition one's choices, egalitarians should be wary of lowering their sights to the mere availability of possibilities for human flourishing, rather than human flourishing per se. Even if conditions are improved, the effects of disadvantage can be long lasting. A culture of fatalism and low expectations can be transmitted across generations long after the original disadvantaging conditions have been ameliorated. Cultural conditions can build upon material conditions so that remedy of the latter, the original source of disadvantage, might not be sufficient for improving disadvantaged persons' levels of flourishing.[3] We need to attend to the lack of flourishing per se and seek to improve it, even if it is only the conditions of flourishing that we can address in doing so. It is important that we appeal to flourishing itself to ensure that there are not additional measures that must be taken to encourage people to take advantage of conditions that are conducive to flourishing.

In any case, "athleticism" seems an integral aspect of a well-developed account of human flourishing. There are two relevant senses of athleticism at work here. One is the idea that an agent actually exercising a capability is an inappropriately "athletic" conception, as charged by Cohen and Sen. This argument does not refer to the content of the capability, but rather the agent's relation to it, and I have offered grounds for affirming such an "athletic" account. A second sense of athleticism is a normative understanding of the capabilities themselves, which emphasizes how capabilities should consist of not only subsistence but also activity and participation. These two senses are nonetheless related; avoiding athleticism in the first sense might risk forgoing the second. After all, achieving flourishing involves persons engaging with their capabilities, participating in the conditions of flourishing and there is a risk that focusing exclusively on access to flourishing will not only fail to take account of actual flourishing, but it will also have too thin an understanding of what counts as flourishing. In particular, it may reduce our egalitarian criterion to the simple satisfaction of basic needs. The ideal of active engagement with the world, creative labor, and fellowship, as conceived by socialists such as William Morris, are vital aspects of well being even if mere survival does not depend on them.

FLOURISHING PROVIDERS

The emphasis on human flourishing is also an important corrective to the welfare and resources metrics from the point of view of those who are giving aid to the disadvantaged in far-flung corners of the globe. Merely handing over resources is going to be an unsatisfactory method of meeting one's global egalitarian obligations. Donors will want to see the effects of their contributions on the well being of disadvantaged persons. From the point of view of outsiders concerned about the effect of aid, the standard of satisfying preferences will be of interest only if preferences are directed to the realization of objective goods. Egalitarians rely on an ideal of community, where justice requires individuals being prepared to contribute for the sake of the satisfaction of needs other than their own. This is only intelligible if understood in terms of individuals who care not just about who has what, but how they are doing with their respective shares, whether they are able to derive flourishing from their share of resources.[4]

The problem of the global donor thus provides an additional motivation for the flourishing approach. That many international charities take pains to inform their donors of the effects of their donations bears out the importance of the flourishing perspective. It might be objected that the donor's perspective is relevant on strategic or pragmatic grounds, since satisfied donors are more likely to be generous donors, but that the satisfaction of the well off is hardly a criterion for a normative theory of global equality. Why, the objection goes, should the matter of the redistribution of global wealth be held hostage by the views of the globally advantaged?

I think, however, that it is not just an illegitimate intrusion of realpolitik in the domain of political philosophy to consider the perspective of advantaged persons who seek to contribute to the improvement of the globally worst off. For the idea of global justice depends on a concept of reciprocity where in virtue of our common humanity we have obligations of redistribution to those, not only as in the case of citizens, we have never met, but also who are culturally remote. So it is important that the connection between donors and recipients of global egalitarianism is well forged. Moreover, there is a particular respect in which the interests of such persons are in fact a way of calibrating the success of the egalitarian enterprise. People who part with their money to help others will want to know that their efforts are effective. To that extent, their concerns are in harmony with the egalitarian enterprise, and indeed can contribute to a high bar of achievement, rather than posing a constraint on the ideals of egalitarianism or their realization.

Nonetheless, we should attend to the perspective of the global donor with some caution. The decision to make charitable donations can be determined by the sympathies of the moment; made conditional on paternalistic proselytizing; skewed by the distractions of other causes and the temptations of self-interest. Thus the perspective of the global donor can be no more than a supplementary consideration in matters of international obligations to remedy inequality. However, insofar as the practical world of global redistribution requires an appeal to the well off to contribute to the less well off, a flourishing perspective promises to be more effective than others.

All this suggests the importance of thinking about global flourishing not just in terms of interstate transfers, as Rawls's laws of peoples proposes. Such a strategy makes the pursuit of global justice a rather abstract, bureaucratic affair, which can be summarily discharged. This is not to say that states do not play a vital role in the redistribution of wealth. Rather, the global policies of states should be viewed in terms of the discharging of obligations of particular persons, citizens of one country who also understand themselves as part of a global humanity to whom they owe obligations and whose obligations merit successful realization rather than token gestures (Sen, 2002, p. 40). Thus thinking of particular persons whose interests are bound up with the pursuit of global justice, and whose own flourishing depends on the successful deployment of the capability to be just, directs us to consider how global justice must be accountable, its efforts scrutinized and its results tested and subjected to improvement and revision.

How stringent should the demands be on the highly flourishing in one country to contribute to those who fail to flourish in another country?

The moral worldliness of political cosmopolitanism would suggest an almost limitless obligation. If human flourishing is the primary value, it is difficult to provide grounds for why the flourishing of one's country-men or women matters more than the flourishing of persons far away. Thus a human flourishing concept of moral worldliness seems to confirm the imperative to provide aid wherever it is needed, regardless of borders or territory. Moreover, insofar as we are concerned that people flourish not just in terms of bodily health, but also in the cosmopolitan's criterion of cultural well being, with scope for human interaction, music, art, and enjoyment of nature, it would seem that the bar for global redistribution is very high indeed.

This understanding of egalitarianism in terms of the conditions of flourishing will be cautious about grand universal standards whose ambitions are difficult to realize. However, at the same time the focus on flourishing, which takes account of how successful a redistribution of resources turns out to be when it comes to actualizing greater equality of flourishing, is prepared to be more ambitious than other metrics. Once we seek the genuine improvement of the lives people live, we find ourselves raising the bar of equality, undertaking far-reaching aid projects and global redistributions in order to further human flourishing. Does this mean that national territory is irrelevant in matters of global justice? It seems to have no place in terms of minimizing the obligations of affluent people to provide aid to deprived non-nationals. Does it have any role, however, for the deprived non-nationals themselves? Here we will find that cultural worldliness gives us a more complex picture.

SELF-DETERMINATION AND UNIVERSAL FLOURISHING

Thus far the idea of cultural worldliness has figured in our argument for global egalitarianism insofar as our measure is the conditions which cause people to have impoverished lives, a measure that necessitates cultural criteria, not just the criteria of income and goods. The ethics of international justice thus requires a culturally attuned approach. The resulting idea of egalitarian flourishing, even if it focuses on the particular conditions that impede flourishing, rather than goods and resources per se, nonetheless indicates a massive transfer of such goods and resources between different parts of the world, regardless of nationality.

The marriage of moral and cultural worldliness, however, involves two aspects of human flourishing that bring nationality back into the picture: self-government and cultural diversity. First, let us consider the problem of self-government, or the relation between human flourishing and responsibility. In discussions of egalitarianism in a local context, it is often argued that redistribution should be conditional on the blamelessness of the have-nots. That is, only inequality that is the result of bad luck, as opposed to bad choices, should be ameliorated. The lazy, the irresponsible, the foolish or self-indulgent do not merit the aid of their fellow citizens. This hard line on the problem of "welfare bums" conceptualizes it as a trade-off between human need on the one hand and the virtues of responsibility on the other.

A flourishing approach, however, is able to offer a more unified strategy. Enabling personal responsibility is part and parcel of improving the situation of the worst off. That is, personal responsibility is among the things we are trying to improve, rather than a countervailing principle that checks or mitigates egalitarian improvement. Simply joining the queue for social assistance does little for a person's capacities, resourcefulness, or initiative, let alone self-respect or dignity. The advantage of the flourishing approach is that it recognizes the importance of more amorphous measures of not living well. This is no less applicable to problems of global poverty. Aid policies should be tied to measures that enable self-improvement, not to "punish" poorly administered peoples, but rather to enable them to improve their institutions and policies and thereby improve their flourishing, both in the form of effective self-government, and in the form of the superior outcomes such government produces.

Our efforts to remedy inequality, in taking a flourishing approach, will aim to enable people to improve their own lot. This does not mean taking no interest in how a people run their economic, social, and political affairs, as Rawls's standoffish law of peoples indicates. Faced with the real political difficulty involved in helping needy people with whom one has no substantive relationship, not even the abstract one of citizenship, it is tempting to beat a hasty retreat to a minimalist position such as that of Rawls. Giving aid in a way that avoids violating self-determination yet succeeds in genuinely improving human flourishing is a real dilemma. But rather than simply dispatching parcels of aid, however generous or paltry, and turning our backs, those of us fortunate to live in the "have" regions of the world must actively contribute to flourishing in part by recognizing the role the "have-nots" must have in improving themselves. We cannot remedy global inequality just by throwing money at the problem; we need to understand, work with, and improve the local institutions, practices, and policies that will be the vehicle for remedying disadvantage. With technological support, resources, training and guidance, people will achieve both the flourishing of self-governance as well as other constituents of flourishing – high levels of education, better nutrition, etc. – that such governance aims to achieve.

This brings us back to the point about cultural variation of the objective constituents of flourishing. Given cultural diversity, it is important that communities have some autonomy in the administration of aid from abroad. A given community is likely to understand the particulars of their case, the specific needs and challenges that hinder the flourishing of their people. Local problems will need local solutions, in some fundamental sense. So it is important on grounds of an egalitarian conception that encompasses local culture and self-determination as features of human flourishing, as well as practical effectiveness, that disadvantaged people have a role in determining their own fates. And the culturally worldly cosmopolitan who insists on the value of the variety of cultures in the world will be the first to point out that the stuff of one culture cannot be easily supplied by another.

One of the features of global inequality is the cost it imposes on cultural diversity. The economic dominance of America, for example, not only means that the world's wealth is unevenly distributed, but also that the cultural practices of underdeveloped countries are vulnerable to the behemoth of Western consumerism. As Tan warns, "not only are the cultures of poorer countries not regarded highly by the richer ones, but the cultures of the latter are threatening to drive out the culture of the poor even in their own countries" (Tan, 2000, p. 120). Thus in our understanding of global egalitarianism as seeking to improve people's flourishing, we are better able to appreciate the cultural shortfall imposed by economic disparities. All this means that although advantaged peoples are not entitled to put the interests of their fellow citizens first, disadvantaged peoples are not best helped by unconditional largesse on the part of the advantaged: self determination, self-help, and cultural autonomy are important features of human flourishing that limit foreign aid to policies and projects that seek to enable self-improvement on the part of disadvantaged persons.

This emphasis on self-direction might seem to suggest a relativist position. That is, if we want to let people shape their own destinies as part of the process of improving flourishing, then perhaps we are committed to a hands-off approach to cultural practices, abstaining from judging the merits of one culture in light of our own. This brings us to another concern about the role of culture and morality in cosmopolitanism, that is, how much we want to address internally imposed violations of human flourishing, such as violations of universal criteria like the fundamental human right to not be tortured or maimed, the principle of equality between the sexes, the importance of scope for personal choice about how to live, freedom of expression, and opportunities for political participation. Attending to flourishing requires that we be sensitive to the nuances of a different context, not just to accommodate cultural diversity, but also, when it comes to fundamental aspects of human flourishing, to take a critical stance on cultures. This follows from our earlier discussion of how flourishing has objective constituents, even if it admits of cultural or subjective variation.

Global justice cannot be a no-strings-attached shuffling of resources. If we want to raise the level of flourishing in economically impoverished parts of the world, we will also attend to how different parts of the world are impoverished in democratic or liberal terms. Of course, the commitment to the role of democratic participation as a constituent of human flourishing means that First-World democrats cannot simply march into the Third World with a new "white man's burden" of cultural imperialism, this time liberal democracy rather than Christianity. As Tan argues, such a stance must remain committed to the principle of self-governance: "the motivation for change must be internal and outside involvement must aim primarily to realize the aspirations of oppressed individuals" (Tan, 2000, p. 137). In sum, there is an egalitarian obligation on the part of citizens of the world to defend the fundamental interests of vulnerable people, wherever they are, in light of universal criteria, yet with some accommodation of principles of self-help and local knowledge.

CONCLUSION

In this essay I have sought to apply the concept of egalitarian flourishing to the vexing problem of global injustice. I have argued that such an approach attends to the global scope of what is dubbed "cosmopolitanism" in contemporary political philosophy, whilst appreciating the cultural interests of the "citizen of the world," the cosmopolitan. This marriage of ethical principles and an appreciation for modes of living, or what I have called moral worldliness and cultural worldliness, gives us a number of advantages over neutralist approaches to egalitarianism.

First, such an approach can better understand the dimensions of inequality in distant parts of the world, which have particular circumstances, needs, and challenges that cannot be conceived or addressed in monetary terms. Thus flourishing is what is unequal and it is flourishing that we seek to improve in our global egalitarianism as we target the unequal conditions that produce unequal well being. Flourishing is an objective measure, insofar as we can set out universal constituents such as health, education, political participation, friendship, and family. But how these constituents are to be understood and realized will depend enormously on the particular context and subjective situations of the people involved. Second, the concept of flourishing enables us properly to expound the relation between the haves and have-nots. The redistribution of global resources requires a sense of reciprocity wherein donors can understand the impact of their contributions and assess their effectiveness, as well as involve themselves to the extent that they can facilitate the development of worst-off peoples.

Third, flourishing helps to stipulate the extent of global redistribution. The well-off are obligated to contribute to the worse-off not to equalize wealth; given human diversity it is unclear what that means, let alone what purpose it serves. Rather, lack of flourishing, and in the first instance, severe shortfalls of flourishing, are the target of our redistributive policies. Connected with this is a fourth consideration that concerns the stringency of the obligation to redistribute global wealth. The flourishing perspective emphasizes the role of self-governance and self-help in attending to disadvantage in countries other than our own. This is a principle that emerges from the idea of equalizing social conditions in order to improve well being, since policies that impart skills and further local institutions enable the self-direction that is essential to living well.

Fifth, human flourishing is affected, of course, not just by lack of resources or opportunities, but also by oppression. And thus the global egalitarian finds the flourishing approach useful in its insistence that we seek not just the redistribution of wealth but also the furtherance of fundamental human rights, in order to improve the human flourishing of people in societies other than our own. Again the self-help idea is important here, since our strategy should not be a kind of "moral imperialism" that bulldozes its way through sovereign territories to fix human rights, but rather a strategy of enabling the internal movements that seek social change.

Finally, the argument of this paper presents a challenge to theories of equality, offering a radical and ambitious conception of what it is we are seeking to equalize in the form of the conditions of human flourishing. However, such a conception must also be offered with a more modest view of the role of egalitarian political philosophy. Human flourishing may be a demanding measure for equality, but it is hardly a straightforward one; it does not supply us with a simple formula or yardstick. Ultimately, the task of rich peoples providing aid to poor peoples is political, a task to which philosophy can only offer a framework for understanding. I hope to have clarified egalitarianism in this essay by providing a demanding yet nuanced project of equalizing the conditions of human flourishing; how to effect egalitarianism globally remains a matter of will and action in light of particular circumstances.

We live in a world characterized by enormous disparities of wealth and property, of health, self-respect, and the development of human potential. The moral worldliness of contemporary arguments for cosmopolitanism must be paired with cultural worldliness to give scope to the non-material aspects of human flourishing and sensitivity to the diversity that culture presents. It is an unequally flourishing world and it is by focusing our theory and practice on the social conditions that impede the flourishing of persons that we will better achieve the global justice that, for all the successes of egalitarian movements in certain, privileged parts of the world, continues so desperately to elude us.

NOTES

I am indebted to a number of people for incisive and helpful comments on earlier drafts: David Bakhurst, my challenging students in a seminar I taught on equality, members of the Queen's Political Philosophy Group, particularly Rob Lawson, Will Kymlicka, Alistair Macleod, Margaret Moore, Nancy Salway, and Mick Smith.

1 Paradoxically, "cosmopolitan" was also a Bolshevik term of abuse connoting disloyalty to Russia, bourgeois class origins, or dilettantish tastes.
2 Although it is interesting to note how socialist utopians have sought to address inequality in romantic success: the nineteenth-century French socialist Charles Fourier argued that the young should provide sexual services to the old; the Bolshevik Alexandra Kollontai proposed a more encompassing idea of love with "winged eros"; in contemporary debate Philippe Van Parijs has suggested financial compensation for bad luck in the marriage market (see Fourier, 1972; Kollontai, 1992 and Van Parijs, 1995).
3 Glenn Loury's idea of "racial stigma" in the case of black Americans captures this phenomenon. See Loury (2002).
4 Cohen (1994) emphasizes the role of relations of community for redistribution.

CHAPTER 6

Global justice, moral development, and democracy

Christopher Bertram

Of all the unlucky things that can happen to a person, being born into the wrong state has to be one of the worst. Someone who is born to become the citizen of a wealthy country enjoys life prospects far better than those unfortunate enough to be born in a poor one. According to a common view, the goal of distributive justice is to nullify the effects of brute luck on a person's life and to make their success or failure a function not of their circumstances but of their choices.[1] Such a conception, once projected onto a global scale, becomes awesomely demanding in its apparent redistributive implications. Moreover, since there will always be new people born into circumstances not of their choosing, but, rather, determined by the prior choices of their forbears, such a view suggests an almost permanent regime of correction and transfer.

This essay argues that in order to secure individuals' access to an important set of goods and some morally significant capacities, we ought to favor political arrangements that severely limit the scope for such luck-compensatory transfers. The goods in question are those associated with being a functioning citizen of a democratic community and the capacities are the Rawlsian ones of being able to form, pursue, and revise one's conception of the good and of a sense of justice. Access to such goods and capacities – indeed, their formation and sustenance – requires the decentralized political arrangements characteristic of a plurality of states in the world and the possibility for citizens to shape their lives through a combination of individual and collective choices and efforts.

The inequalities that characterize the actual world are the product of centuries of both choice and effort on the one hand, and exploitation and oppression on the other. There is nothing that could justify such extensive inequalities, which leave some without enough to sustain their most basic capacity for life, whilst others enjoy almost unimaginable luxury. But were we to start with a plurality of democratic states operating against a

75

background of fair initial distribution of resources, it is foreseeable, as a consequence of reasonable choices, that some nations, states, or peoples would become wealthier than others. This essay contends that, subject to some qualifications, this predictable consequence is unobjectionable just so long as all are assured of the capability to function as citizens of democratic states.

In what follows I first argue that certain types of political arrangement are propitious for the development of moral capacities – such as the sense of justice – and also give individuals access to important dimensions of human flourishing. I then say a little about what the preconditions (in terms of resources, institutions, social structure, and culture) for those political arrangements might be. I then argue that the extensive decision-making autonomy associated with such arrangements makes a measure of inequality practically inevitable and that this should not be a matter of moral concern. Finally, I reply to some possible objections, entering necessary caveats and qualifications.

PSYCHOLOGY AND STABILITY

A complete theory of justice should contain an account of how people come to acquire and retain a commitment to its principles. Arguably, a theory that simply postulates universal principles without showing how they might be realized and maintained is otiose. Prominent among theories that do seek to marry the ideal to a sensitivity to the limitations of human nature and the practicalities of moral education and formation is that of John Rawls (1999b). For Rawls, one of the principal desiderata of just social arrangements is that they should generate positive feedback to strengthen themselves over time. If an institutional setup fosters a sense of alienation in those who work within it, or decreases their motivation to play their part, it is unlikely to persist over many generations. This requirement finds expression in Rawls's emphasis on stability.

In Rawls's own theory of justice for the domestic case, an important characteristic of the well-ordered society is that it have this self-reinforcing quality. Within the wider society, particular institutions, such as the family, play a vital role in fostering the moral attitudes and dispositions necessary to sustain justice at the societal level and the scope given to family autonomy is partly justified by this role. Although Rawls's own view of the family and its actual configuration has rightly been criticized as being altogether too benign, the example is important for my argument here. The promotion and assurance of justice may require institutional arrangements which, if they are to retain integrity, themselves in turn place pressure on what may be done to promote justice.[2]

It is, then, a strong objection to a conception of justice that its institutional embodiment will fail to generate its own support. One way in which this failure might happen is if citizens systematically disidentify with the decisions taken within the structures that constitute that institutional embodiment. For example, if citizens do not see its decisions and processes as being their own but rather as being imposed upon them by technocratic or bureaucratic elites. I shall argue that political and legal structures where decisions that are fateful for citizens are not subject to their control but are rather taken by such elites will indeed fail to generate the necessary support. Specifically, that the institutional framework that the fostering of moral agency requires is one in which citizens enjoy considerable discretion about how to conduct their own lives (and those of their families) and where such restrictions as they impose on their conduct for mutual benefit are genuinely subject to their democratic control.

So what characteristics must institutions have if they are, first, to foster the development and sustain the possession of the capacity of people to formulate their plans and aims in life and to subject those plans to something like the right degree of critical scrutiny and revision, and second to have due regard for the personhood and agency of others and to their right to pursue their plans and aims? Two things seem especially important, even if they do not constitute the whole story about the formative capacity of just institutions.[3] These two properties are first, that of supporting an appropriate connection between a person's actions and what we may call, for want of a better word, their fate. Second, that of sustaining the possibility of each person achieving or securing the recognition by others of their own significance in a way that is non-self-defeating. The first claim is that the development of autonomy and of a sense of self-respect is usually dependent on a person's fate being connected to their actions in an appropriate kind of way (see Rawls, 1999b, §67). By this I mean simply that insofar as my actions in the world have, and are reasonably expected to have certain consequences for my well-being, for my attainment of my objectives, insofar as it matters what I do, then my sense of self-respect and of myself as being a presence in the world will be enhanced. By contrast, if my fate seems wholly disconnected from how I act, I will come to lose self-respect and a sense of myself as having significance. The key notion is that it is generally desirable that things are such that I can take responsibility for and recognize myself in the way in which things turn out for me.

Notoriously many features of the world conspire to deprive people of a sense that their actions make a difference to their fate. Poverty traps are one example; involuntary unemployment another. In the case of poverty traps it is hard for individuals to act to improve their situation. To work seems pointless, since they will lose in benefits what they gain in wages. People are condemned to a life of passivity and dependency, and, particularly, dependency on the will of bureaucrats and politicians. Similarly, people who have worked all their lives in some industry may find that due to market conditions they suddenly lose both their liveli- hood and the activity which gave meaning to their lives. This deprivation is experienced like a deprivation due to an act of God or nature: the individual's fate is placed outside their control and put in the hands of others.

The second important psychological dimension is *recognition* (see Dent, 1988). The important thought here is that, normally, for human beings to enjoy the sense of self-respect that is necessary for them both to function as effective pursuers of their own ends and to be reasonable in their dealings with others, they must be granted by others an unforced recognition of their moral status. While this can take a number of forms – including love relationships and relations of care and nurturing among family members – it must involve individuals being recognized by others as having sufficient standing in the world to give them a right to the reasonable pursuit of their interests and that their most critical interests have at least a *prima facie* claim to be met.

There is a fairly straightforward connection between these sorts of psychological considerations and Rawls's two moral powers (1993b, lec- ture 2). A person who lacks a sense of themselves as a significant presence in the world and therefore of their own agency, will hardly be able to form, revise, and pursue a conception of the good. Insofar as they can do something similar, they are likely to adapt their aims to what is possible in an excessively restricted and unambitious way. Similarly, someone lacking a sense of themselves as acting autonomously in the world will be less receptive to the correlative claim of others to act similarly and hence will fail to develop or to exercise a sense of justice. Instead, their attitude to others may become marked by resentment and jealousy.

THE CAPABILITY FOR DEMOCRATIC CITIZENSHIP

One recent attempt to articulate an alternative to "luck egalitarian" theories of distributive justice, and that focuses instead on the types of relationships that individuals might enjoy together in a democratic society, is Elizabeth Anderson's essay "What is the point of equality?" (1999). Anderson's positive ideal rests on a vision of society as a set of relations among equals, relations of respect and non-domination.[4] She argues that egalitarians, in pursuit of this ideal, should pursue the distributive aim of securing for each member of society the capability for democratic citizenship. She thereby adapts and extends Amartya Sen's capability approach to justice (see, e.g. Sen, 1992), to argue that we should enable all citizens to achieve a range of functionings associated with becoming a fully participating member of a democratic community.

On Anderson's view the position she calls "democratic equality" has both positive and negative objectives.

Negatively, people are entitled to whatever capabilities are necessary to enable them to avoid or escape entanglements in oppressive social relationships. Positively, they are entitled to the capabilities necessary for functioning as an equal citizen in a democratic state. (Anderson, 1999, p. 316)

These twin aims occupy a space somewhere between the merely formal egalitarianism of rights of classical liberalism and the comprehensive social ambition of some other conceptions of egalitarianism. Democratic equality selects for its focus those capabilities that are relevant to the needs citizens have to stand as equals to one another in a democratic society. Clearly some deficits in capability space matter to our achieving this status and others do not. The capability to perform a graceful pirouette in ballet or the capability to bend a free kick like Roberto Carlos, though both valuable to their possessors, are not relevant to their standing as co-citizens with others.

Anderson suggests that if people are to stand in such relations to one another, they need both the capability of political agency and to play their part within the wider civil society of which they are members. The first of these requires that they have formal freedoms such as the right to vote as well as protections for their right to political speech and assembly. The second requires protection against exclusion from, or demeaning segregation within, social institutions and spaces such as parks, streets, firms, schools, hospitals, and so on. In both cases, such high-level capabilities presuppose and draw upon other broader capabilities, such as the capability to function as a human being and as someone who participates in a "system of co-operative production." In order to achieve these more basic, grounding capabilities, people need to be assured of adequate nutrition and shelter. They also need to have the opportunity for sufficient education to permit them to deliberate effectively together. Additionally, they need to have sufficient opportunities to access the means of production, to be rewarded fairly and to achieve proper recognition for their performance within the general cooperative scheme.

As with other variants of the capability approach, democratic equality does not aim to ensure that people will achieve actual functionings at any particular level, merely that they will have access to such levels. This means that people have to be sufficiently motivated if they are to take advantage of their capabilities. Someone may enjoy a capability without achieving the related functionings if they are lazy and live the life of a couch potato or because they value other activities more. Moreover, while it is important that all persons have the capability to access *some* relevant functionings at an equal level, for other functions it is only important that all achieve a threshold level. For example, everyone should have the right to vote, but whilst everyone should be enabled to read and write, democratic equality does not require that everyone should achieve the same level of competence in obscure foreign languages.

Finally, democratic equality is not a starting gate theory that provides us all with a range of initial (relevant) capabilities and then allows us to get on with life. Sometimes people lose capabilities as a result of their voluntary choices. When this happens, "luck egalitarians" will permit people to fall below a capability threshold. But the democratic egalitarian approach is different: if a relevant capability must be restored to a person for them to stand in a relationship of equals to others, and it can be within reasonable limits of cost and difficulty,[5] it should be, notwithstanding the fact that a person's capability loss was, to put things bluntly and crudely, their own fault.

PRECONDITIONS FOR DEMOCRATIC EQUALITY

What is necessary for people to enjoy the capability for democratic citizenship, the capability to stand as equals with others in a democratic community? A full treatment of this is beyond the scope of this paper, but it should be possible to delineate some types of precondition. First, citizens will need access to sufficient resources to assure them of access to adequate levels of nutrition, education, housing, health care, and so on. Second, they need access to the right types of institutions: such as democratic assemblies, systems of local government and administration, and a free and reasonably diverse media. Third, the distribution of wealth and income must not be so unequal as to undermine the equal standing of citizens or their access to political decision-making mechanisms. Fourth, cultural background conditions must be propitious for democratic citizenship: even given formal equality of rights and adequate material resources for everyone, a society where attitudes are such that a subordinate status is assigned to women or to members of some ethnic groups, will not realize democratic equality. In this section I attend to these conditions, paying special attention to how they might be secured in the global rather than the domestic sphere.

Absolute resource preconditions

The absolute resource preconditions for someone to function as a citizen of a democratic society are probably rather modest (see Rawls, 1999b, p. 107). Clearly, to function as such, people need to be assured over most of their lifespan of adequate levels of nutrition and access to health care, and they also need access to a certain level of education. The temptation for those who think of themselves as liberal egalitarians (in a broad sense of those words) will be to set the bar too high, out of an understandable concern for the world's poor. There are very many people in the world today whose access to resources is such that they cannot function as citizens of their societies. But we need to distinguish between the level of absolute poverty that would rule a person out of effective participation in *any* democratic society and the level that excludes them from being effective participants in particular societies given the wealth, income, and resources of that society and the distribution of those goods within the society.

That the absolute resource preconditions are modest can be seen both from historical and contemporary examples. Historically, our ancestors in various countries often achieved levels of functioning as participants in political life that are comparable to or surpass those that we enjoy today. Yet they did this at a much lower level of economic development than we now have in North America or Europe. Indeed, it is possible that the absolute resource preconditions for democratic participation by all have been met in some countries for well over a century. In today's world, we should beware of insisting that democratic capability is out of reach of many of the poor, lest we devalue the continuing achievements of many such people in continuing to participate effectively in political life, often at levels surpassing those of wealthy countries.

Institutional preconditions

The second set of prerequisites for democratic citizenship are institutional. The point here is partly the very prosaic one that you cannot have a functioning democracy and be a voter without elections.[6] But we can go beyond this to say that for citizens to function as such and to play various associated political roles, they need not only elections, but also representative institutions of some kind, political parties, perhaps machinery of local government, and guarantees of basic liberties such as freedom of association, assembly, and speech. And the "public forum" needs to be arranged so that all citizens can secure a reasonable degree of access to it and so that it functions properly as an arena for the exchange of ideas and the negotiation of interests.

To focus just on the formal satisfaction of these requirements would not be enough. Democratic institutions may exist but yet not be vehicles through which citizens can hope to exercise effective influence over the matters that are most significant for them. The causes of democratic failure are many and varied. They include the excessive influence of money over the political process, and redistricting and gerrymandering that disenfranchises large numbers of voters. I shall discuss the money problem in a moment. Here I should like to emphasize one particular source of trouble: the preemption of citizen decision-making by elites. The problem here is that there is very little scope for decision-making in practice, because all the decisions that matter have already been taken by someone else, somewhere else. If, for example, people nominally have a say in governing their school but in practice their decisions are completely constrained by budgetary or policy decisions taken in an education ministry, they will not have the capacity to exercise their democratic agency in relation to school government. If British or Danish electors are unable to change some policy or other because of prior decisions by a supra-national body like the European Union, a similar difficulty arises. Again, if the International Monetary Fund imposes a structural adjustment plan on some indebted Third World nation, the actual deliberations of the citizens of that country may be deprived of all significance.

I have deliberately selected my examples in the paragraph above so that some of them pander to the prejudices of the right, and others to the left. The point is not to say that decisions should never be preempted by higher bodies, Supreme Courts, or international agencies. Sometimes this has to happen because the nature of the problem is such that it can only be addressed by some such body. But at other times the level at which a matter is settled may have nothing to do with the merits of having it settled in this particular forum or that one, and everything to do with the desire of lobbyists, non-governmental organizations, lawyers, industries and so on to achieve their preferred result where they can. When this happens, something of value is diminished or lost: namely the capacity of citizens to exercise their democratic agency. It is easy to see that global institutions charged with implementing some distributive pattern or other, would have especially disempowering effects on the democratic agency of individual citizens.

Social preconditions

The main social obstacle to citizens enjoying democratic capability is inequality. The ways in which inequality can undermine their co-equal status are several. I discussed above the fact that the absolute resource preconditions for democratic citizenship are modest, but they are modest in abstraction from consideration of what others have within a society and how access to the means of political participation may require a particular level of wealth in a particular society. So, for example, if a society becomes wealthier and most of the population gain access to radio, or television, or the internet, collective political deliberation will increasingly take place on the assumption that people can listen to the radio, watch TV, or surf the net. Those who cannot afford such things used to participate with others in the public forum, but increasing wealth and inequality means that they can no longer do so. Their relative disadvantage in the space of resources has turned into an absolute disadvantage in the space of democratic capability (for discussion see Sen, 1983).

Second, large inequalities in wealth may translate directly into political influence for the wealthy in ways that are directly undermining of political equality. So, for example, if a society permits excessive concentration of media ownership or fails to restrict the financing of political campaigns, the political system will become unresponsive to the needs and voices of the many. Third, there is the familiar point that, in a society characterized by great inequality, the rich and poor do not enjoy genuine equality before the law. Laws will often impact differently on people, depending on their wealth and income, and whilst the rich will have the services of talented teams of lawyers to defend their interests, the poor will not.

There is no need to labor these familiar issues. Some mitigation of these effects of material inequality on the equal status of citizens may be possible through reforms designed to insulate political decision-making from the power of money (although there is room for skepticism about the effectiveness of such insulation in many cases). The interesting point concerning *global* distributive justice is the fact that within-country inequality may be more damaging to individuals' access to democratic capability than between-country inequality will be. The economic inequality that we find within states can have a dramatic effect on whether people have the capability to function as democratic citizens. The wealthiest citizens of the United States have, as a result of their wealth, a political influence that far outstrips that of their poorest compatriots. The wealth and income enjoyed by the richest Americans threatens the democratic capability of the poorest Americans far more directly than it threatens the ability of poor Indians to participate in the political life of *their* country. To be sure, the capacity of those poor Indians is damaged or undermined by the rich of India, the point here is, however, that within-country differences are usually more significant for access to this important capability than between-country differences are.

This should not be taken as a denial that between-country differences can be important for democratic agency. I mentioned earlier as one possible example of preemption of democratic decision-making, the possibility that an organization like the International Monetary Fund may evacuate the democratic processes of a country of their significance. When, and insofar as, events like this are a consequence of between-country inequalities, those inequalities also damage citizens' access to democratic capability.

Cultural preconditions

Even where people have adequate resources and suitable institutions there may also be cultural obstacles to many of them attaining the capability for democratic citizenship. For example, in societies which assign a subordinate status to women it will not be possible for women to stand as co-equal citizens with men whatever the formal rights they may be given by constitutional or other laws. And clearly, a parallel point can be made about members of oppressed racial or ethnic minorities within a society. The Roma of Slovakia, for example, may be equal in the eyes of the law, but they cannot function as citizens of Slovakian society on the same basis as other Slovakians because of the pervasive discrimination against them.

IS DEMOCRATIC EQUALITY AN EGALITARIAN PRINCIPLE?

Securing the capability for democratic citizenship for all in a plurality of different polities looks like an attractive goal. Individuals achieve the capability to function in an important domain of human life, together with the achievement of other functionings that sustain that higher-level capability. What is more, the closeness of the dealings that citizens have with one another and the degree of control they can exercise over their lives together should be a good environment for the fostering of the virtue of justice and senses of reciprocity and responsibility. Moreover, since, in a well-ordered society, co-citizens all enjoy their status fully rather than as a matter of degree, there is an important sense in which this conception is an egalitarian one. Although it involves a sufficiency threshold, it is a threshold that, once met, secures certain important goods for all, equally.

It may be, then, that the achievement of equality in this capability space is compatible with some, and perhaps considerable, inequality in the space of wealth and income. It might therefore be tempting to say, if we allocate sufficient importance to the bundle of capabilities associated with democratic citizenship, that egalitarians should be satisfied just so long as everyone (at their different levels of wealth and income and in their different states) has sufficient to cross the threshold where those capabilities are assured. But this would be to move too quickly, as a straightforward example should make clear.

Imagine three parties engaged in mutually beneficial cooperation that takes them all above a relevant capability threshold. Let us further imagine that their cooperation may be governed by an ensemble of rules that distribute the benefits and burdens of working together and that these rules are the object of choice and negotiation. We can imagine for simplicity that there is a limited number of such possible ensembles. Imagine further two scenarios. Under one, two of the parties insist on an ensemble of rules that guarantees all three parties of their capability threshold but under which the benefits of growth above the threshold-securing level flow overwhelmingly to themselves. Under the other, a different ensemble of rules ensures that such benefits are more or less evenly distributed among the three parties. Other things being equal, I think we should want to say that the more even distribution is better from the point of view of justice than the less even one and that the parties who work together to insist on terms of trade that enrich themselves whilst the third party languishes just above the sufficiency threshold are thereby acting unjustly. To make this more concrete, we could even grant names to the parties involved. We

could call them Third World, EU and NAFTA. It would be a great
achievement to get Third World above the sufficiency threshold, but even
if this were secured there would still be objectionable injustice if EU and
NAFTA conspired to maintain trade rules that ensured their own further
enrichment but little or no additional benefit to Third World. The lesson
that we should take from this is that securing the capability for functioning
at a certain level cannot provide a *complete* account of distributive justice
because there are some circumstances where sufficiency is assured and yet
where it seems wrong to think of the outcome as just.

We can also imagine circumstances where we are forced to choose
between securing a sufficiency threshold for some and responding to the
urgency of the demands of others. Here we need to be careful to distinguish between two problems: the problem of what principles of justice we
ought to adopt at a fundamental level and the problem of what our policy
goals should be. If we set up an abstract example, involving two equally
numerous groups of people, one of whom faces immediate death through
starvation if they do not receive our aid, the other of whom risks falling
below a threshold where the capability for democratic citizenship is
possible, then it seems right that the urgency of the first group's claim
should trump the demands of the second group. This tells us that, at least
sometimes, we should give priority to the least advantaged rather than
aiming at securing a capability threshold at a certain level. But it certainly
does not tell us that we should not, if we are interested in justice, pursue
the capability for democratic citizenship as a primary goal. This is because
that goal is not just of value in itself but should also be valued instrumentally to the satisfaction of individuals' most urgent interests (see Sen, 1999,
ch. 6). As Amartya Sen's work on famines has shown, the fact that people
have a political voice via democratic institutions is vital if policy-makers
are not to neglect their most vital needs. Indeed, the sensitivity of
democratic institutions to such needs is a vital protection for the most
vulnerable, not just against the indifferent and greedy, but also against
high-minded bureaucrats and theorists who would use political power to
further their own view of what justice requires in the face of the "short
term" interests of those who are actually poor.

A PLURALITY OF NATIONS GENERATES INEQUALITY IN THE SPACE OF WEALTH AND INCOME

If citizens are to exercise their capacity for democratic decision-making
together with one another and to identify with the collective making the

decisions, then it is foreseeable that many decisions that are important and fateful for individuals' lives will be taken at national or subnational level. And this is as it should be if citizens are to have the possibility of enjoying the goods associated with having significant control over their lives, getting ahead by their own efforts, and so on. Citizens of some countries will opt for more of a market economy than citizens of others, some national legislatures will set the working week at thirty-five hours, and others will not. And, partly because of policy and partly because of individual choices, some societies will have higher labor-force participation rates than others, and so on for a range of different possible decisions.

Even if we were to start with a perfectly equal endowment of resources among nations,[7] we would expect the wealth and income available to nations to vary over time. Would this be objectionable from the point of view of democratic equality? No, or at least, not as such. If a country became so poor that its citizens' capacity to function as citizens or to stand as equals to one another were undermined, then that would be a matter of concern. Although it seems unlikely that a genuinely democratic nation would thus impoverish itself by poor decision-making, one cannot completely rule out the possibility.

The case of democratic nations co-existing together and starting from a baseline of equality is a highly idealized one. It is instructive, though, in that it throws up a contrast with luck-egalitarian views (see Rawls, 1999b, pp. 117–18 and Blake, 2002). According to those views, individual citizens of poor nations who had opposed decisions that resulted in relative disadvantage to their nation or who were not responsible for a decision in virtue of having been born after it was made, would be owed compensation. Presumably, this compensation would come, if it came from anywhere, from transfers from the relatively advantaged citizens of wealthier nations. By contrast, on the view defended here, so long as citizens remain capable of exercising the capability for democratic citizenship alongside their (perhaps imprudent) compatriots, they suffer no deficit in the relevant space and are therefore not candidates for such transfers.

Democratic equality therefore sets a limit on what justice demands by way of compensatory transfer: it is less demanding than luck egalitarianism. But the question naturally arises of what should be done about those societies with citizens who fall below the resource threshold where the capability for democratic citizenship can be exercised. One way this might happen is if a country is so poor that, however resources are distributed within the country, some people are going to have insufficient to get them over the capability threshold. But another, and perhaps more likely, problem is where internal maldistribution of resources is such that some people fall below that threshold even though they would not do so with a more egalitarian distribution.

The worry here is this: that we have focused our attention on supplying the conditions under which citizens can take collective responsibility for their own fate. Here we have the possibility that they may, by their own decision, undermine the conditions for that democratic responsibility. We might draw an analogy with the case of an individual who chooses a path in life that undermines the possibility of them exercising responsible choice in the future. An individual who becomes dependent on drugs or alcohol would be an example of this.

One way in which we might start to think about this problem, would be to draw an analogy with families. Families share some significant and relevant features with nations: they involve more than one person, decision-making rights are not equally distributed among generations at any one time, but decisions taken by members of one generation can be significantly fateful for members of another. First, let us consider the hypothetical case of two families, the Smiths and the Joneses – we can call this the Two Caring Families case. The Smith and Jones family are, at a given time, identical in all important respects. The two parents in each family enjoy the same levels of skill as the two in the other family, have identical job prospects, and so on. Similarly, each family has the same number of children, of the same sexes and ages. In each family, father and mother discuss whether it would be best to maximize their income and use paid care to look after the children whilst the parents are at work or, rather, for one parent to work and the other to remain at home with the children. The Smiths choose for both parents to work and in the Jones family the mother pursues her career whilst the father stays at home with the kids. After many years it becomes clear that the children who grow up in one family have been relatively advantaged compared to the ones who grew up in the other family (perhaps the increased wealth of the Smith household makes the difference, or the more nurturing environment of the Jones household). So we have a pattern of unchosen individual disadvantage that results from responsible collective choice. Should we sanction a compensatory transfer payment from the relatively advantaged children to the disadvantaged ones in this case? My instinct, which falls short of being an argument, is to say no, just so long as the disadvantaged children remain above a certain threshold. To say otherwise is to disincentivize responsible choice ("The kids will be just as well off whichever way we choose, honey, so we may as well do whatever suits *us* best").

Imagine now a similar case, which we can call the Caring and the Uncaring households. In the Caring household, the parents choose whichever of the household models from the Two Caring Families case that you, the reader, thinks best. In the Uncaring household, the parents are alcoholics or heroin addicts who fail to make responsible choices (in fact progressively lose the capacity for responsible choice) and whose children consequently suffer significant disadvantage. Here we may consider intervening and arranging for the children to be brought up in another household altogether, or, if this does not happen, we may consider that the disadvantaged children have a right to support in order to overcome a disadvantage that is not only not chosen by them, but, indeed, not really chosen by anyone.

The analogy between the Caring and Uncaring households with the case where some states are failed states should be easy to see. But as Tolstoy said, every unhappy family is unhappy in its own way, and, likewise, failed states fail for many and varied reasons. It would be nice to come out with a categorical statement of a duty of assistance to cover the case of failed states. Starting from the capability perspective defended in this paper, the obvious thing to say would be that citizens of functioning democratic states have a collective duty of assistance that would aim to assure that citizens of failed states regain the capability for democratic citizenship. Such a duty might require direct intervention in the affairs of failed states or the provision of substantial material aid to their members. But, naturally, questions will arise about how extensive and demanding that duty will turn out to be, questions to which I cannot provide a complete and satisfactory answer in this essay.[8] Relevant considerations will include the impact of assistance on the assisting society. So, for example, it would not be reasonable to have a duty so demanding that it would undermine the possibility of citizens in the assisting country themselves enjoying the capability for democratic citizenship. And there we should also apply a test of reasonable prospect of success to justify either intervention or assistance. Just as a heroin addict may be entitled to our assistance as she first attempts via rehab to regain the capability to stand as a co-equal citizen with others, but we may reasonably deny such assistance to the addict who has lapsed after twenty such attempts, it is entirely possible that there are societies where the prospect of success is so remote that we may reasonably deny our assistance.[9]

CONCLUSION

If democratic equality, that is to say the provision to each person of the capability for democratic citizenship, is an important goal for egalitarian justice, then if we are to provide that capability to each we must give both people and peoples a substantial degree of control over their own affairs. If peoples are genuinely to exercise such control via democratic institutions then it is foreseeable that some nations will end up richer than others in the space of wealth and income. Within nations it is plausible to suppose that income inequalities are very important for the maintenance of political equality. If there is a massive gap between rich and poor then the poor will be pushed below the capability threshold where they can exercise the capacity for democratic citizenship. Between nations, though, there is much less reason to suppose that income and wealth inequalities are significant in this way.

This essay has argued that significant inequalities in the space of wealth and income are both compatible with and a plausible effect of pursuing one attractive conception of what egalitarians value. But it would be wrong to conclude without pointing out that very many of our fellow humans suffer significant deficits not just in the space of democratic capability, but also in that their very ability to function as human beings is endangered by war, famine, drought and so on. My focus on democratic equality for the sphere of global justice should not be taken to suggest that their claims on us are not of the greatest urgency.

NOTES

Earlier versions of this chapter were given at the Université Catholique de Louvain, during a period as a Hoover Fellow there in 2002, and at the Universities of Sheffield, Cardiff, and Oxford. I am grateful to Philippe Van Parijs, Axel Gosseries, Yannick Vanderborght, Hervé Pourtois, Andrew Williams, Paul Bou-Habib, Robert Stern, David Bell, Jon Mandle, Catriona McKinnon, Harry Brighouse, and Alessandra Tanesini for comments or conversation.

1 Advocates of such views include Ronald Dworkin, Richard Arneson, G. A. Cohen, and Eric Rakowski.

2 These remarks, which partly draw on Rawls's discussion of the sense of justice (1999b, ch. 8), are not meant to do more than indicate a relevant parallel. Rawls's over-benign and uncritical attitude to actual family structures was rightly criticized by Susan Moller Okin (1989). For recent discussion on the delicate relationship between family autonomy and justice see Swift (2003).

3 No doubt explicit education and facts about parenting and family life are also relevant.

4 We can see that Anderson's vision is focused on the same issues of securing for all the institutional conditions which can enable each person to be an effective presence in the world and thereby secure their allegiance to a just society, that were the subject of the previous section.

5 Naturally, more could be said about what those limits of cost and difficulty ought to be or, at least, how we should go about determining them.

6 I leave to one side the possible counterexample of direct democracy.

7 It will be controversial how to measure this. For the sake of argument the reader can insert his or her preferred answer to this question.

8 In focusing on the threshold needed to realize the capability for democratic citizenship, it looks like the duty of assistance proposed here will be more demanding than that advanced by Rawls (1999a).

9 I ignore here the qualification that nations should not manipulate the international order so that an excessive proportion of the benefits of growth above that needed to secure the capability threshold flow to themselves.

CHAPTER 7

A cosmopolitan perspective on the global economic order

Thomas Pogge

In a recent book (Pogge, 2002), I have claimed that we – the more advantaged citizens of the affluent countries – are actively responsible for most of the life-threatening poverty in the world. The book focuses on the fifteen years since the end of the Cold War. In this period, billions of people have suffered greatly from poverty-related causes: from hunger and malnutrition, from child labor and trafficking, from lack of access to basic health care and safe drinking water, from lack of shelter, basic sanitation, electricity, and elementary education.[1] Some 18 million people have died prematurely each year from poverty-related causes, accounting for fully one third of all human deaths. This fifteen-year death toll of 270 million is considerably larger than the 200-million death toll from all the wars, civil wars, genocides, and other government repression of the entire twentieth century combined.[2]

Some critics maintain that these problems are peanuts compared to the bad old days when a large majority of humankind was poor.[3] In 1820, they tell us, 75 percent of humankind was living below the World Bank's "$1/day" poverty line, while today this percentage is only 20 percent. (This poverty line is defined in terms of the purchasing power that a monthly income of $32.74 had in the year 1993 [Chen and Ravallion, 2001, p. 285]. In 2004, this line corresponds to the purchasing power of $500 *per year* in the United States.[4]) According to these critics, what is remarkable about world poverty is how very little of it there still is today.

I disagree. For one thing, it is quite inappropriate to use percentages for the comparison. The killing of a given number of people does not become morally less troubling the more the world population increases. What matters morally is the *number* of people in extreme poverty. In 1820, this number was about 750 million (75 percent of about one billion.)[5] In 1998, this number was nearly 1,200 million (Chen and Ravallion, 2001, p. 290).[6] Since 1820, the number of extremely poor people has thus increased by over 50 percent, while the number of people living below the World

Bank's more reasonable "$2/day" poverty line has tripled.[7] Moreover, severe poverty was quite hard to avoid in 1820, because even the average purchasing power of incomes worldwide barely reached the World Bank's higher poverty line. Today, by contrast, the average purchasing power of incomes worldwide is well over ten times that level, and severe poverty is entirely avoidable. We are not avoiding it only because of the fantastic increase in inequality.[8]

My main claim is then that, by shaping and enforcing the social conditions that, foreseeably and avoidably, cause the monumental suffering of global poverty, we are *harming* the global poor – or, to put it more descriptively, we are active participants in the largest, though not the gravest, crime against humanity ever committed. Hitler and Stalin were vastly more evil than our political leaders, but in terms of killing and harming people they never came anywhere near causing 18 millions deaths per year.

Most of my readers believe that this claim is obviously mistaken, if not preposterous. Perhaps for this reason, they pay little attention to the structure and details of the case I am building. Instead, they present various general conjectures about what my mistake may be. They suggest that I am making *conceptual* mistakes by re-labeling as harm what are really failures to aid and protect.[9] They suggest that I am *factually* wrong about the causal explanation of severe poverty or confused about the counterfactuals to which I compare the world as it is.[10] They suggest that I am *morally* wrong by presenting as minimal certain moral requirements that are actually excessively demanding.[11] These criticisms are worth addressing, and I will address many of them in the context of explaining the main lines of argument in *World Poverty and Human Rights*.

POSITIVE DUTIES

Before doing this, I should dispose of one misunderstanding. My book seeks to show how existing world poverty manifests a violation of our *negative* duties, our duties not to harm. To show this, I leave positive duties aside. I do not assert that there are no positive duties, or that such duties are feeble. Rather, I avoid claims about positive duties so as to make clear that my case does not depend on such claims. My focus is solely on duties not to harm as well as on duties to avert harms that one's own past conduct may cause in the future.

Duties of this last kind – to avert harms that one's past conduct may cause in the future – do not fit well into the conventional dichotomy of positive and negative duties. They are positive insofar as they require the agent to do something and also negative insofar as this requirement is continuous with the duty to avoid causing harm to others. One might call them intermediate duties, in recognition also of their intermediate stringency. My focus is exclusively on negative and intermediate duties, and thus on harm we are materially involved in causing rather than on all the harm people suffer.

This focus is motivated by the belief that negative and intermediate moral duties are more stringent than positive ones. For example, the duty not to assault people is more stringent than the duty to prevent such assaults by others. And, having assaulted another, the attacker has more reason to ensure that his victim's injuries are treated than a bystander would. Suggesting these views in the book, I do assume something about positive duties after all. But this is meant to be a very weak assumption, accepted not merely by libertarians but by pretty much all except act-consequentialists. I do *not* assume that any negative or intermediate duty is more stringent than all positive duties. Rather, I assume that negative and intermediate duties are more stringent than positive duties *when what is at stake for all concerned is held constant* (Pogge, 2002, p. 132). I go to some length to stress that I do *not* believe the absurdity some critics[12] have attributed to me: namely that *any* negative duty, including the duty to refrain from doing some small harm, is more stringent than *every* positive duty, including the duty to rescue thousands of children.[13]

Now if negative duties (not to harm) and intermediate duties (to avert harms that one's past conduct may cause in the future) are indeed more stringent than positive duties, then it could be misleading to appeal only to positive duties when duties of the other two kinds are also in play. Consider a corporation polluting a river with dire consequences for the health of many. One might ask this corporation, along with other businesses in the region, to help reduce that problem through donations toward purchasing pollution control equipment and toward paying for medical treatment of those sickened by the pollution. This sort of request may be politically opportune. But it also misleadingly suggests that the polluting corporation is morally in the same boat as the other potential donors: helping out for a good cause, pursuant to an imperfect positive duty of occasional charity. In fact, these two points are related. What makes such a plea in the positive-duty idiom politically opportune (when it is so) typically is precisely the misleading suggestion that its addressees have no negative and intermediate duties to forestall the harm they are being asked to help mitigate.

One may well think that being misleading is a very small price to pay for political success against the catastrophic problem of world poverty. But, for better or worse, it does not seem that we are actually facing this choice. The appeal to positive duties has been well presented by Peter Singer, Henry Shue, Peter Unger, and others (Singer, 1972; Shue, 1980; Unger, 1999). If citizens in the affluent countries were minimally decent and humane, they would respond to these appeals and would do their bit to eradicate world poverty. If they did this, my argument would be of much less interest and importance, and I might not see the need to elaborate it at such length. As it is, I see it as my best chance to contribute to ending or reducing the immense deprivations we affluent are now inflicting upon the global poor.

I also see my argument as essential to an accurate portrayal of how we affluent citizens of the rich countries are morally related to those deprivations. Yes, we are able to alleviate them, and, seeing how cheaply this can be done, we surely have positive duties to do so. But because we are also implicated, with many others, in shaping and enforcing the social institutions that produce these deprivations, and are moreover benefiting from the enormous inequalities these unjust institutions reproduce, we have much more stringent duties to seek to reform these social institutions and to do our fair share toward mitigating the harms they cause.

AN ECUMENICAL APPROACH TO DEMONSTRATING HARM

Let us now look at the arguments of my book. The case I seek to build is broadly ecumenical. I am trying to convince not merely the adherents of some particular moral conception or theory – Lockeans or Rawlsians or libertarians or communitarians for example. Rather, I am trying to convince the adherents of *all* the main views now alive in Western political thought. This ambition makes the task much harder, because I must defend my conclusion on multiple fronts, fielding parallel arguments that address and appeal to diverse and often mutually incompatible moral conceptions and beliefs.

This ecumenical strategy has been confusing to some who complain that I am unclear and inconsistent about the baseline relative to which the global poor are supposedly harmed by existing institutional arrangements.[14] They are right that I do not provide a single consistent such baseline. But they are wrong to see this as a flaw. If I want to convince readers with diverse ideas about morality and justice, then I must support my conclusions with diverse arguments. And these may have to appeal to diverse baselines. A state-of-nature baseline is relevant to a reader with Lockean or Nozickian views. But a Rawlsian will reject such a baseline, insisting that the existing distributional profile should be compared to the profiles achievable under alternative feasible institutional arrangements. To satisfy readers of both kinds, I need to give different arguments to them, each with a different baseline. This is more work, to be sure. But the pay-off is that my case cannot justifiably be dismissed as dependent on some partisan moral premises or theory which readers may feel free to reject.

The ecumenical strategy is broadest and most explicit in the final chapter, which argues for a global resources dividend. My first step there is to show that our world is pervaded by what, following Tom Nagel (Nagel, 1977), I call radical inequality (Pogge, 2002, p. 198):

1. The worse-off are very badly off in absolute terms.
2. They are also very badly off in relative terms – very much worse off than many others.
3. The inequality is impervious: it is difficult or impossible for the worse-off substantially to improve their lot; and most of the better-off never experience life at the bottom for even a few months and have no vivid idea of what it is like to live in that way.
4. The inequality is pervasive: it concerns not merely some aspects of life, such as the climate or access to natural beauty or high culture, but most aspects or all.
5. The inequality is avoidable: the better-off can improve the circumstances of the worse-off without becoming badly off themselves.

I go on to assume that most of my readers demand more than the fact of radical inequality between us and the global poor as proof that we are *harming* them. I also assume that different readers differ on the question of what is missing. To satisfy more readers, I present *in parallel* three second steps of the argument, each of which shows in a different way that the existing radical inequality involves us in harming the global poor. All three strands of the argument lead to the conclusion that today's massive and severe poverty manifests a violation by the affluent of their negative duties: an immense crime in which we affluent citizens of the rich countries (as well as the political and economic "elites" of most poor countries) are implicated.

ENGAGING HISTORICAL CONCEPTIONS OF SOCIAL JUSTICE

In one strand of the argument I invoke the effects of a common and violent history. The present world is characterized not only by radical inequality as defined, but also by the fact that "the social starting positions of the worse-off and the better-off have emerged from a single historical process that was pervaded by massive grievous wrongs" (Pogge, 2002, p. 203). I invoke these historical facts specifically for readers who believe that it matters morally how radical inequality has evolved. Most of the existing international inequality in standards of living was built up in the colonial period when today's affluent countries ruled today's poor regions of the world: trading their people like cattle, destroying their political institutions and cultures, and taking their natural resources. Around 1960, when the colonizers finally left, taking what they could and destroying much else, the inequality in *per capita* income between Europe and Africa had grown to 30:1, and vast inequalities existed also in education, health-care, infrastructure, and legal and political organization. These inequalities greatly disadvantaged Africans in their dealings with governments and corporations of the affluent countries. This disadvantage helps explain why the Europe/Africa inequality in *per capita* income has since risen to 40:1. But even if *per capita* income had, since 1960, increased a full percentage point more each year in Africa than in Europe, this inequality would still be 20:1 today and would be fully erased only early in the twenty-fourth century.

Readers attracted to historical-entitlement conceptions of justice disagree about the conditions an historical process must meet in order for it to justify gross inequalities in life chances. On this point, I can once more afford to be ecumenical. The relevant historical crimes were so horrendous, so diverse, and so consequential that no historical-entitlement conception could credibly support the conclusion that our common history was sufficiently benign to justify even the radical inequalities in starting positions we are witnessing today.

In short, then, upholding a radical inequality counts as harming the worse-off when the historical path on which this inequality arose is pervaded by grievous wrongs. "A morally deeply tarnished history must not be allowed to result in *radical* inequality" (Pogge, 2002, p. 203). This is the moral rationale behind Abraham Lincoln's forty-acres-and-a-mule promise of 1863, which of course was quickly rescinded. And it is the rationale for saying that we are not entitled to the huge advantages we enjoy from birth over the global poor, given how these inequalities have been built up.

Some critics may seem to address this strand of the argument when they point out that the radical inequality between Europe and Africa might have come about even without colonialism.[15] Perhaps Europe could have "taken off" even without slavery and stolen raw materials, and perhaps the resulting inequality would then have been equally great. In the absence of conclusive proof that, without the horrors of European conquest, severe poverty worldwide would be substantially less today, Risse suggests, we are entitled to keep and defend what we possess, even at the cost of millions of deaths each year. (I wonder if he would make the same argument against the forty-acres-and-a-mule proposal.)

As a response to the first strand of the argument, this complaint is irrelevant. The first strand addresses readers who believe that the *actual* history *is* relevant. These readers will say: "Yes, if things had transpired as in Risse's hypothetical, then the citizens of the affluent countries might not, by upholding the radical inequality, be harming the global poor. But this has no bearing on whether such upholding of radical inequality constitutes harm in the *actual* world with its *actual* history."

Still, Risse's complaint resonates with other readers who believe that it is permissible to uphold an economic distribution if merely it *could* have come about on a morally acceptable path. It is such readers that the second strand of my argument addresses. To be sure, *any* distribution, however skewed, *could* have been the outcome of a sequence of voluntary bets or gambles. Appeal to *such* a fictional history would "justify" *anything* and would thus be wholly implausible. Locke does much better, holding that a fictional history can justify the status quo only if the changes in holdings and social rules it involves are ones that all participants could have rationally agreed to. He also holds that in a state of nature persons would be entitled to a proportional share of the world's natural resources. He thus makes the justice of any institutional order depend on whether the worst-off under it are at least as well off as people would be in a Lockean state of nature with a proportional resource share (see Pogge, 2002, pp. 16, 137–39, and 202–03 for a fuller reading of Locke's argument). Locke held, implausibly, that this condition was fulfilled in his time, claiming that "a King of a large fruitful territory [in the Americas] feeds, lodges, and is clad worse than a day Laborer in England" (Locke, 1960, §41, see §37). I argue that this condition is *not* fulfilled for the global poor today who, living below even the day laborers in Locke's England, are coercively denied "enough and as good" (Locke, 1960, §27, §33) of the world's natural resources without having access to an equivalent substitute.

Readers inclined to a Lockean conception disagree about the relevant state-of-nature baseline that determines how bad the worst social starting positions imposed by a just social order may be. On this question I can once more be ecumenical. However one may want to imagine a state of nature among human beings on this planet, one could not realistically conceive it as producing an enduring poverty death toll of 18 million annually. Only a thoroughly organized state of civilization can sustain horrendous suffering on such a massive scale.

Catering to Lockeans, the second strand of my argument invokes the uncompensated exclusion of the worse-off from a proportional share of global resources: the present world is characterized not merely by radical inequality as defined, but also by the fact that "the better-off enjoy significant advantages in the use of a single natural resource base from whose benefits the worse-off are largely, and without compensation, excluded" (Pogge, 2002, p. 202). The better-off – we – are *harming* the worse-off insofar as the radical inequality we uphold excludes the global poor from a proportional share of the world's natural resources and any equivalent substitute.

The point I was making about Locke is quite similar to one Satz puts forth in a tone of criticism. For Locke, she says, "property rights, however acquired, do not prevail in the face of desperate need" because "everyone has an original pre-appropriation claim-right to an adequate subsistence from the resources of the world."[16] This is correct, although the poor can really have a claim only to a proportional resources share, not to adequate subsistence, because there may simply not be enough to go around. But why does Satz speak in this context of a "*positive* 'property right' of the needy in the means of subsistence?"[17] What *are* positive as opposed to negative property rights? Does Satz want to say that we affluent have merely a positive duty toward the needy? This would suggest that our property rights do prevail after all – that our assets are ours though we ought to give away some. But Satz correctly presents Locke as rejecting this picture: we affluent have *no* rights to property, however acquired, in the face of the excluded. Rather, *they* have a right to what we hold. When we prevent them from exercising this right – when we deprive them of what is justly theirs – then we violate this original right of the poor and we harm them. In this way it is a violation of a *negative* duty to deprive others of "enough and as good" – either through unilateral appropriations or through institutional arrangements such as a radically inegalitarian property regime (this is argued at length in Pogge, 2002, ch. 5).

Let me sum up the first two strands of the argument. These strands address readers for whom the justice of the present economic distribution or of present economic arrangements turns on their actual or imaginable history. I conclude that such conceptions of justice cannot justify the status quo. One may try to justify the coercively upheld radical inequality today by appeal to the historical process that *actually* led up to it. But this appeal fails because the actual historical process is massively pervaded by the most grievous wrongs. Alternatively, one may try to justify this coercively upheld radical inequality by appeal to some morally acceptable *fictional* historical process that *might* have led to it. On Locke's permissive version of this account, some small elite may appropriate all, or almost all, of the huge cooperative surplus produced by modern social organization. But such an elite must not enlarge its share even further by reducing the poor below the state-of-nature baseline so that this elite's share of the cooperative surplus is actually more than 100 percent and the share of the poor correspondingly less than zero. As it is, the citizens and governments of the affluent states are violating this negative duty when we, in collaboration with the ruling cliques of many poor countries, coercively exclude the global poor from a proportional resource share and any equivalent substitute.

ENGAGING BROADLY CONSEQUENTIALIST CONCEPTIONS OF SOCIAL JUSTICE

Most contemporary theorists of justice endorse neither of these historical views. Instead, they hold that an economic order and the economic distribution it shapes should be assessed by its foreseeable effects against the background of its feasible alternatives. Thus Rawls considers a domestic economic order to be just if it produces fair equality of opportunity across social classes and no feasible alternative to it would afford better prospects to the least advantaged.

The third strand of my argument addresses such broadly consequentialist conceptions which invoke the effects of shared social institutions. The present world is characterized not only by radical inequality as defined, but also by the facts that: "There is a shared institutional order that is shaped by the better-off and imposed on the worse-off. This institutional order is implicated in the reproduction of radical inequality in that there is a feasible institutional alternative under which so severe and extensive poverty would not persist. The radical inequality cannot be traced to extra-social factors (such as genetic handicaps or natural disasters) which, as such, affect different human beings differentially."[18] When these further facts obtain, so I claim, then the better-off – we – are *harming* the worse-off insofar as we are upholding a shared institutional order that is *unjust* by foreseeably and avoidably (re)producing radical inequality.

Now there are many different such broadly consequentialist conceptions of justice which judge an institutional order by comparing its distributional effects to those its feasible alternatives would have. These conceptions differ along three dimensions. They differ in how they characterize the relevant affected parties (groups, persons, time-slices of persons, etc.). They differ about the metric for assessing relevant effects (social primary goods, capabilities, welfare, etc.). And they differ about how to aggregate relevant effects across affected parties. Once again, my response to such diversity is ecumenical. I am trying to specify very minimal conditions of justice that are widely accepted. Most broadly consequentialist theorists agree that a national economic order is unjust when it leaves social and economic human rights unfulfilled on a massive scale even while there is a feasible alternative order under which these human rights would be much better realized. Most theorists would demand more, of course. But I need no more for my purpose, because our global economic order does not even meet the very weak requirements that form the common core of the various broadly consequentialist theories of economic justice defended today.

As we have seen, the second strand of my argument, operating on Lockean terrain, conceives justice in terms of harm: prevailing economic arrangements and the present economic distribution are shown to be unjust in virtue of the fact that they harm many by forcing them below any credible state-of-nature baseline. It is worth stressing, then, that the third strand of my argument, catering to broadly consequentialist conceptions of social justice, does not, *pace* Satz,[19] conceive justice and injustice in terms of an independently specified notion of harm. Rather, this third strand relates the concepts of *harm* and *justice* in the opposite way, conceiving harm in terms of an independently specified conception of social justice. On my ecumenical response to broadly consequentialist conceptions of social justice, we are *harming* the global poor if and insofar as we collaborate in imposing *unjust* social institutions upon them.

Moreover, *pace* Patten,[20] this third strand of my argument is not addressed to libertarians, who indeed reject any non-historical, broadly consequentialist assessment of social institutions. Libertarians are addressed by the first and, to some extent, by the second strand. To be sure, the third strand, like the two others, is meant to support the conclusion that the immense catastrophe of world poverty manifests not merely the affluents' failure to fulfill their positive duties, but also, and more importantly, their massive violation of their negative duties. But the moral significance of this conclusion can be appreciated far beyond the confines of the libertarian school. Nearly everyone in the affluent countries would agree that our moral duty not to contribute to the imposition of conditions of extreme poverty on people and our moral duty to help protect people from harm in whose production we are implicated in this way are each more stringent than our moral duty to help protect people from harm in whose production we are not materially involved.[21]

As I try to implement the third strand of my argument, specifically for a human right to basic necessities, it involves three main tasks. I seek to show that it is, among broadly consequentialist conceptions, a minimal and widely acceptable demand of justice on all national institutional schemes that these must be designed to avoid life-threatening poverty insofar as this is reasonably possible. I then seek to show that this demand of justice applies not merely to any domestic institutional arrangements, but to the global order as well. And I must then show, thirdly, that there are feasible alternatives to the existing global institutional order under which life-threatening poverty would be wholly or largely avoided.

Task One is easy. There simply is no broadly consequentialist conception of social justice in the field that purports to justify, within one national society, radical inequality of the kind the world at large displays today. To be sure, Paton is right to point out that some libertarians (Nozick) do purport to justify such extreme inequalities. But they do this by appeal to historical conceptions of social justice; and I have sketched my response to such justifications in the preceding section.

Task Two involves a highly complex argument to which I cannot possibly do justice here.[22] So let me here concentrate on Task Three, on which my critics have focused most of their attention.

THE CAUSAL ROLE OF THE GLOBAL INSTITUTIONAL ORDER
IN THE REPRODUCTION OF SEVERE POVERTY

Many critics believe that I see the global institutional order as *the main* cause of world poverty. And they respond that, in light of the incompetence, corruption, and oppression prevalent in so many poor countries, this claim is simply not credible or, at the very least, unsupported by empirical evidence. They are wrong on both counts.

Let us begin with a quick general reflection on causes. In the simplest cases, multiple causes *add up* to produce an effect. Thus the smoke in a bar is the sum of the smoke released by all the smokers. In the case of world poverty, however, the relation among causes is more complex in at least two ways. One complexity is that the different causes of poverty, such as global institutional factors and national policies, influence one another's effects.[23] How harmful corrupt leaders in poor countries are, for example, is strongly influenced by whether the global order recognizes such leaders, on the basis of effective power alone, as entitled to sell us their country's resources, to borrow in its name, and to use the proceeds to buy the means of internal repression.

Given this special complexity, it is not correct to identify my assertion that *most* severe poverty worldwide was and is avoidable through global institutional reform with the claim that the existing global institutional order is *the main* cause of world poverty. My assertion is perfectly compatible with the assertion that most severe poverty worldwide was and is avoidable through better national policies and better social institutions in the poor countries. To put it simplistically, the interaction between the two sets of causal factors is not so much additive as multiplicative. The worse each set of factors is, the more it also aggravates the marginal harmful impact of the other.

But if, as development economists like to stress, most severe poverty worldwide was and is avoidable through better national policies and better social institutions in the poor countries, does this not show that our global institutional order is morally acceptable as it is? Am I not, as Patten put it,[24] demanding too much from ourselves, given that the ruling elites in the poor countries could also eradicate much poverty?

Now it is true that many of these elites are incompetent, corrupt, and oppressive. Failing, as badly as we are and often worse, to honor their negative duties not to harm, they are indeed responsible for most severe poverty worldwide. But this is quite compatible with the advantaged citizens in the rich countries also being responsible for most severe poverty worldwide. For it is equally true that most such poverty was and is avoidable through a better global institutional order. Given this basic symmetry, we cannot accept Paton's judgement that *we* should not be required to stop *our* contribution until *they* are ready to stop *theirs*. If this were right, then it would be permissible for two parties together to bring about as much harm as they like, each of them pointing out that *it* has no obligation to stop so long as the other continues.

The situation is roughly analogous to that of two upstream factories releasing chemicals into a river. The chemicals of each factory would cause little harm by themselves. But the mixture of chemicals from both plants causes huge harm downstream. In this sort of case, we must not hold each factory owner responsible for only the small harm he would be causing if the other did not pollute. This would leave unaccounted-for most of the harm they produce together and would thus be quite implausible. In a case of this kind, provided each factory owner knows about the effluent released by the other and can foresee the harmful effects they together produce, each owner bears responsibility for his marginal contribution, that is, for as much of the harm as would be avoided if he alone were not discharging his chemicals. Each factory owner is then responsible for most of the harm they jointly produce.

Despite this symmetry in my causal account, my critics nonetheless have a point when they accuse me of explanatory globalism[25] (in analogy to the explanatory nationalism of which I am accusing the majority of development economists [see Pogge, 2002, §5.3]). This accusation is accurate in that I *focus* much more on global than on national factors. I do this, because these are the factors that my readers and I are morally responsible for and because, not unrelatedly, these factors are grossly neglected by development economists of all stripes, by the media, and by the citizens of the affluent countries for whom I am writing.

And I have another reason for paying more attention to the causal role of global factors in the reproduction of massive severe poverty. This further reason depends on the second special complexity I mentioned earlier, which is that the causes of world poverty also influence one another. As the global institutional order is *shaped* by the political leaders of the most powerful countries, who in turn are selected and shaped by their domestic institutional arrangements, so the global institutional order powerfully *shapes* the national regimes especially of the weaker countries as well as the composition, incentives, and opportunities of their ruling elites. For example, corrupt rule in poor countries is made much more likely by the fact that our global order accords such rulers, on the basis of effective power alone, the international resource and borrowing privileges just described (see Pogge, 2002, §4.9, 6.3, 6.4). These privileges provide strong incentives to potential predators (military officers, most frequently) to take power by force and compel even the most well-intentioned rulers, if they want to maintain their hold on power, to allow such potential putschists corruptly to divert state revenues. The global order thus exerts a strong influence upon the weaker and poorer countries, which makes them considerably more likely to have corrupt and oppressive national regimes. Not all of them will have such regimes, of course, but many of them will, as is well-illustrated by Nigeria and many other developing countries in which the resource sector accounts for a large fraction of GDP (see Lam and Wantchekon, 1999 and Wantchekon, 1999). This is *another* reason to focus on global factors – especially on those that affect the quality of national regimes in the poorer countries.

Let us now look at the evidence I have for believing that severe poverty is largely avoidable through global institutional reforms. Because the effects of sweeping reforms are harder to assess, I discuss in some detail several small reforms and their likely effects. In the WTO negotiations, the affluent countries insisted on continued and asymmetrical protections of their markets through tariffs, quotas, anti-dumping duties, export credits, and subsidies to domestic producers, greatly impairing the export opportunities of even the very poorest countries. These protections cost developing countries hundreds of billions of dollars in lost export revenues (see Pogge, 2002, §4). Risse believes these protections will be phased out. Let us hope so. Still, these protections certainly account for a sizable fraction of the 270 million poverty deaths since 1989.

MODERATE AND FEASIBLE REFORMS OF THE GLOBAL INSTITUTIONAL ORDER

Are there other feasible reforms of the existing global order through which severe poverty could be largely or wholly avoided? The reform I discuss in most detail involves a small change in international property rights (see Pogge, 2002, ch. 8). In accordance with Locke's inalienable right to a proportional share of the world's resources or some adequate equivalent, this change would set aside a small part of the value of any natural resources used for those who would otherwise be excluded from a proportional share. I show how this *global resources dividend* (GRD) could comfortably raise one percent of the global social product specifically for poverty eradication. And I outline how these funds could be spent so as to provide strong incentives toward better government in the developing countries.

The proposed GRD in the amount of one percent of the global product would currently raise about $320 billion annually, or fifty-six times what all affluent countries combined are now spending on basic social services in the developing world. What sort of impact would this money have? Consider health care. The WHO Commission on

Macroeconomics and Health, chaired by Jeffrey Sachs, has put the cost of providing basic medical care in the developing world at $62 billion annually and has estimated that this initiative alone would prevent about 8 million deaths from poverty-related causes each year.[26] Another $20 billion could go to incentivize research into the so-called neglected diseases which, because they affect mostly the poor, are grossly under-researched thus far: hepatitis, meningitis, dengue fever, leprosy, sleeping sickness, Chagas disease, river blindness, leishmaniasis, Buruli ulcer, lymphatic filariasis, bilharzia, malaria, tuberculosis, and pneumonia. There would be money to give every human being access to clean water and electricity. There would be money for free nutritious meals in schools that children could attend free of charge (thanks to the IMF, many schools in developing countries are now charging attendance fees). There would be money to subsidize micro-lending which has been highly effective in recent decades even while charging interest rates of around 20 percent. And there would be money to relieve the crushing debt burden often accumulated under wholly undemocratic regimes[27] that is weighing down many of the poorest countries.

Critics have worried about domestic cooperation. But how many governments would refuse the offer to spend large amounts of money in their country? Consider India, which has about 30 percent of the world's poor and currently receives about $1.7 billion annually in all kinds of official development assistance from all rich countries combined. Under the reform, some $96 billion of GRD funds could be spent there, greatly benefiting also India's pharmaceutical industry, its agricultural sector, its construction firms, its minimum wage level, its unemployment rate, and its tax intake. India's politicians would be extremely eager to cooperate in securing India's share of the GRD funds.

The GRD, though it re-channels money from the consumers of re-sources to the global poor, is not, *pace* Satz,[28] a form of aid. It does not take away some of what belongs to the affluent. Rather, it modifies conventional property rights so as to give legal effect to an inalienable moral right of the poor. For libertarians, this is the right not to be deprived of a decent start in life through a grievously unjust historical process. For Locke, this is the pre-institutional right not to be excluded, without equivalent substitute, from a proportional share of the world's resources. For broadly consequentialist theorists of justice, this is the right not to have imposed upon one an institutional order that is unjust by virtue of the fact that under this order, foreseeably and avoidably, many human beings cannot meet their most basic needs.

Patten claims that mine is just an exercise in re-labeling. But by assuming that I must really be calling for aid and assistance, he is begging the question I raise. Our moral failure in the face of world poverty is a mere failure to aid only if we really are morally entitled to the huge advantages we enjoy, from birth, under present institutional arrangements. And this is exactly what I am denying – by appeal to how our advantages arose historically, by appeal to Locke's resource-share criterion, and by appeal to the massive life-threatening poverty to which the existing global institutional order foreseeably and avoidably exposes the majority of humankind.

Patten worries that if the rich countries were to implement my proposals, they and their citizens would be unfairly disadvantaged vis-à-vis the elites of many poor countries who would continue to refuse to shoulder their fair share of the cost of eradicating global poverty.[29] The details of the GRD proposal show that no country could avoid the levy on resource uses without incurring even greater surcharges on their exports (and possibly imports as well). Still, Patten is right that some politically privileged people in poor countries (and some economically privileged people in rich countries!) will manage to contribute less than their fair share to the eradication of world poverty. What is baffling is how Patten can deem this unfairness a sufficient reason to release us from our duty to contribute.

I suspect he is once more tacitly assuming here that our relevant duty is a duty to aid and that the literature on fair sharing of the burdens of positive duties is therefore relevant. Perhaps one may indeed refuse to contribute one's fair share to a morally urgent aid project on the ground that others similarly placed successfully avoid contributing theirs. But appealing to this thought again assumes what I dispute: that the status quo involves us in violating only *positive* duties toward the global poor. Once it is accepted that we are violating our negative and intermediate duties toward the poor, Patten's postulated permission seems absurd. One may not refuse to bear the opportunity cost of ceasing to harm others on the ground that others similarly placed continue their harming. Thus, in particular, we are not entitled to go on inflicting harm upon the global poor on the ground that others (predatorial elites in the poor countries) are also continuing. Likewise, we may stop some from harming third parties, and compel some to mitigate harms they have caused, even when we are unable so to stop and to compel all who do harm in a similar way. Thus, in particular, we are no more barred from setting up a GRD by the fact that some of the affluent would unfairly escape its effects than we are barred from setting up a criminal-justice system by the fact that some crimes and criminals are unfairly neither prevented, nor deterred, nor punished. Yes, some will get away with murder or with enriching themselves by starving the poor. But this sad fact neither permits us to join their ranks, nor forbids us to reduce such crimes as far as we can.

NOTES

1 Among 6227 million human beings (in 2002), about 831 million were undernourished, 1197 million lacked access to safe drinking water, and 2747 million lacked access to basic sanitation (UNDP, 2004, pp. 129–30). Some 2000 million lacked access to essential drugs (www.fic.nih.gov/about/summary.html). Some 1000 million had no adequate shelter and 2000 million lacked electricity (UNDP, 1998, p. 49). Some 876 million adults were illiterate (www.uis.unesco.org) and 211 million children (aged 5 to 14) did wage work outside their family, 8.4 million of them in the "unconditionally worst" forms of child labor, "defined as slavery, trafficking, debt bondage and other forms of forced labor, forced recruitment of children for use in armed conflict, prostitution and pornography, and illicit activities" (ILO, 2002, pp. 17–18). Females and people of color are heavily overrepresented in all these horrifying statistics (UNDP, 2003, pp. 310–30).

2 See http://users.erols.com/mwhite28/war/1900.htm for the figures and the relevant literature supporting them.

3 Notably Gerald Gaus: "Radio Interview on Pogge's *World Poverty and Human Rights*" on *Ideas and Issues* (WETS-FM), 19 January 2003, www.etsu.edu/philos/radio/gaus-wphr.htm; and Risse (2003).

4 See www.bls.gov/cpi/home.htm.

5 See www.census.gov/ipc/www/worldhis.html.

6 See http://iresearch.worldbank.org/Povcal/Net/jsp/index.jsp for later figures.

7 To 2,812 million (Chen and Ravallion, 2001, p. 290).

8 The ratio in average income between the fifth of the world's people living in the highest-income countries and the fifth living in the lowest income countries "was 74 to 1 in 1997, up from 60 to 1 in 1990 and 30 to 1 in 1960. [Earlier] the income gap between the top and bottom countries increased from 3 to 1 in 1820 to 7 to 1 in 1870 to 11 to 1 in 1913" (UNDP, 1999, p. 3; see p. 38). The trend picture is no more encouraging when one compares the incomes of households worldwide via purchasing power parities: over a recent five-year period, "world inequality has increased . . . from a Gini of 62.8 in 1988 to 66.0 in 1993. This represents an increase of 0.6 Gini points per year. This is a very fast increase, faster than the increase experienced by the US and UK in the decade of the 1980s . . . The bottom 5 percent of the world grew poorer, as their real incomes decreased between 1988 and 1993 by 25 percent, while the richest quintile grew richer. It gained 12 percent in real terms, that is it grew more than twice as much as mean world income (5.7 percent)" (Milanovic, 2002, p. 88).

9 Gaus: "Radio Interview on Pogge's *World Poverty and Human Rights*"; Alan Patten: "Remarks on Pogge's *World Poverty and Human Rights*" at *Author Meets Critics* session at the Eastern Division Meeting of the American Philosophical Association, 30 December 2003.

10 Gaus: "Radio Interview on Pogge's *World Poverty and Human Rights*"; Debra Satz: "Comments on Pogge's *World Poverty and Human Rights*" at *Author Meets Critics* session at the Eastern Division Meeting of the American Philosophical Association, 30 December 2003.

11 Patten: "Remarks on Pogge's *World Poverty and Human Rights*."

12 Notably Satz: "Comments on Pogge's *World Poverty and Human Rights*."

13 I repeatedly warn against this misunderstanding in formulations such as this: "I hope I have made clear enough that this is not presented as a strict, or lexical, hierarchy: It is generally acknowledged that a higher moral reason can be outweighed by a lower, if more is at stake in the latter" (Pogge, 2002, p. 240, n. 207; see also p. 132 and p. 241, n. 216).

14 Notably Satz: "Comments on Pogge's *World Poverty and Human Rights*," and Patten: "Remarks on Pogge's *World Poverty and Human Rights*."

15 Notably Risse (2003).

16 Satz: "Comments on Pogge's *World Poverty and Human Rights*," p. 16.

17 *Ibid.*

18 *Ibid*, p. 199.

19 Satz: "Comments on Pogge's *World Poverty and Human Rights*."

20 Patten: "Remarks on Pogge's *World Poverty and Human Rights*"

21 These comparisons, once again, hold constant the cost or opportunity cost of the required conduct to the duty bearers as well as the reduction in harm it brings to the beneficiaries.

22 See Pogge (2002), ch. 4, and Pogge (2004).

23 Discussion of the other complexity begins six paragraphs down.

24 Patten: "Remarks on Pogge's *World Poverty and Human Rights*."

25 This accusation is due to Patten: "Remarks on Pogge's *World Poverty and Human Rights*," though he uses the less fitting term "explanatory cosmopolitanism."

26 *The Economist*, 22 December 2001, pp. 82–83.

27 An especially dramatic example of this perverse consequence of the international borrowing privilege is played out in Rwanda: "Perhaps there was no better reflection of the world's shabby treatment of post-genocide Rwanda than the matter of the debt burden incurred by the Habyarimana government. The major source of the unpaid debt was the weapons the regime had purchased for the war against the RPF, which had then been turned against innocent Tutsi during the genocide . . . incredibly enough, the new government was deemed responsible for repaying to those multilateral and national lenders the debt accrued by its predecessors" (International Panel of Eminent Personalities, 2000, §§17.30, 17.33).

28 Satz: "Comments on Pogge's *World Poverty and Human Rights*."

29 Patten: "Remarks on Pogge's *World Poverty and Human Rights*."

CHAPTER 8

In the national interest

Allen Buchanan

THE DOMINANCE OF A DOGMA

Few deny that the national interest should play a major role in foreign policy. But often much stronger assertions about the national interest are made or, more frequently, uncritically assumed to be true. The strongest of these, and the one explicitly endorsed by many state leaders and diplomats, as well as many theorists of international relations, is that

A state's foreign policy always ought to be determined exclusively by the national interest (the Obligatory Exclusivity Thesis).

"Foreign policy" here is understood very broadly, to encompass the state's policies of making war and seeking peace, its posture toward international law, its participation in the global economy through treaties concerning trade and communications infrastructures, international financial and monetary regimes, and the provision of aid to other countries.

Hans Morgenthau, one of the most influential international relations theorists of the twentieth century, unambiguously proclaimed the supremacy of the national interest, asserting that it should be "the one guiding star, one standard thought, one rule of action" in foreign policy (Morgenthau, 1952, p. 242). Taken literally, Morgenthau's assertion presupposes that every foreign policy decision affects the national interest one way or the other. Since this is dubious, and because I am interested in evaluating the more plausible versions of the idea that the national interest should reign supreme in foreign policy, I will understand the Obligatory Exclusivity Thesis as acknowledging that some decisions may not affect the national interest one way or another and as permitting other considerations to guide policy when that is the case.

Let us say, then, that the Obligatory Exclusivity Thesis is that whenever a policy-maker or decision-maker has the opportunity to act in a way that furthers the national interest, she ought to do so, where "furthering" means maximizing – doing what is best, so far as the national interest is concerned. The Obligatory Exclusivity Thesis implies that where the national interest conflicts with other values, the national interest should always take precedence.

A somewhat weaker claim about the supremacy of the national interest is the Permissible Exclusivity Thesis. It is always permissible for a state's foreign policy to be determined exclusively by the national interest. If a state chooses, it may subordinate all other values to the pursuit of the national interest in any case.

To many people who are not diplomats, state leaders, or international relations theorists, even the weaker Permissible Exclusivity Thesis will seem counter-intuitive because it seems to allow the most extreme selfishness, permitting a state to refrain from any action to promote the well-being of foreigners or to protect them against the grossest human rights violations even when this could be done at little cost, whenever such action does not best promote the national interest. It is doubtful, for example, that most citizens of the US believe that their country's humanitarian aid to famine victims in other countries is justified only when it maximizes US national interest. This is not to say that they believe that the US should supply foreign aid to the detriment of its more important interests, but rather that some foreign aid is justified even if alternative uses of the same resources would be more beneficial to the US.

If this is a widely held view, then it is at odds with what has been the dominant view among diplomats and state leaders, and probably among international relations theorists as well. The quote from Morgenthau above shows that he endorsed the Obligatory Exclusivity Thesis, and similar quotes could be produced from other prominent international relations theorists. Given that many thoughtful scholars of international relations tend to accept it, the Obligatory Exclusivity Thesis must be taken seriously, even if it seems obviously false to most of us.

My focus in this essay, however, is on the weaker Permissible Exclusivity Thesis, for two reasons. First, it is less demanding and therefore should be easier to justify than the Obligatory Exclusivity Thesis; second, if I can show that the Permissible Exclusivity Thesis is indefensible, this will count against the Obligatory version as well: if it is not permissible to do something, then it cannot be obligatory to do it.

In this essay I subject the Permissible Exclusivity Thesis to critical examination. I argue that if there are any human rights, then a weighty burden of argument is on those who subscribe to it, not on those who reject it. I then argue that this burden of argument has not been borne – that attempts to justify the Permissible Exclusivity Thesis fail. My conclusion will be that those state leaders, diplomats, and international relations theorists who claim to believe in human rights but endorse the Permissible Exclusivity Thesis are in an untenable position.

ATTEMPTS TO JUSTIFY THE PERMISSIBLE
EXCLUSIVITY THESIS

Before proceeding to a critical examination of arguments to support it, I want to stress that the Permissible Exclusivity Thesis needs to be supported. There is nothing natural or commonsensical about the assertion that foreign policy may be – much less ought to be – guided exclusively by the goal of maximizing the national interest. To the contrary, on its face this thesis is diametrically opposed to the acknowledgement that there are human rights – rights that all persons have regardless of whether they are our fellow citizens. It is also apparently at odds with the commonsense belief that a rich and powerful state such as the US from time to time ought to act charitably toward less fortunate peoples by supplying aid in times of disaster, even if, strictly speaking, justice does not require it. Because the Permissible Exclusivity Thesis itself takes no position on what the national interest is, one cannot assume congruence between pursuit of the national interest and respect for human rights or the promptings of charity.

It is also important to understand that proponents of the Permissible Exclusivity Thesis are wrong if they assume that it only allows the subordination of concerns about the human rights of persons in *other* countries to the pursuit of the national interest. The Permissible Exclusivity Principle asserts that it is permissible, in the domain of foreign policy, to do whatever is necessary to further the national interest, including violating the most basic human rights of anyone whose rights stand in the way of that goal, whether or not he is a fellow citizen. Taken literally, the Permissible Exclusivity Principle is a much more radical doctrine than might first appear.

It is a mistake to assume that the national interest in any area of policy, including foreign policy, is always congruent with the interest of every citizen. Indeed, to the extent that it makes sense to speak of a national interest as something to be pursued in its own right, it must be something distinct from the interests of each of the citizens, and this means that the national interest and the interests of a particular citizen or group of citizens can be in conflict. Although foreign policy decisions are directed toward preserving or altering relationships between the state and institutions or groups beyond its borders, there can be circumstances in which a particular foreign policy that is directed toward the national interest may be very harmful to some citizens. For example, it might be in the national interest to sacrifice a group of citizens who are being unjustly imprisoned by a foreign power.

So the Permissible Exclusivity Thesis does not recognize the sanctity of human rights at home while denying it abroad; it is thoroughly impartial in subordinating all values, including the protection of human rights in any venue, to the national interest, so far as foreign policy is concerned. In addition, the Permissible Exclusivity Thesis would allow wars of aggression against harmless, rights-respecting countries – if, for example, the national interest (not just the national survival or the need to avoid a major set-back to the national interest) required expropriating their oil. Given how abhorrent its apparent implications are, the Permissible Exclusivity Thesis requires a justification.

The Fiduciary Realist Justification for Permissible Exclusivity. This is the first of three attempts to justify the assertion that foreign policy may be exclusively directed toward maximizing the national interest. Fiduciary Realism holds that the overriding moral obligation of state leaders is to act to maximize the national interest, by virtue of her role as fiduciary.

Proponents of this view often assume that the state leaders are entrusted with serving the well-being of the people of the states they lead, and then use the term "the national interest" as if it were synonymous with the well-being of the people. Of course it is easy to criticize this usage by pointing out that on some interpretations the national interest and the interest of the people of the state as a whole are not only distinct but in conflict – for example when the national interest is understood as the interest of the dominant ethnonational group in the state, to the detriment of a minority group. However, regardless of how one interprets "the national interest," the Fiduciary Realist Justification does not justify the Permissible Exclusivity Thesis.[1]

According to the Fiduciary Realist Justification, what is justifiable and even obligatory for state leaders is impermissible for others who do not occupy this role. The proper conduct for state leaders is not to act amorally; they are to serve steadfastly a higher moral principle, subordinating all other values, personal or private, to it. Their fiduciary duty is to conduct foreign policy with an exclusive concern for the national interest. According to this view, exclusive pursuit of the national interest is obligatory and hence trivially it is permissible.

Much more would have to be said to make this view at all credible, for the simple reason that becoming a fiduciary does not wipe the moral slate clean. If I agree to become your guardian or your financial counselor or your doctor, this does not relieve me of all pre-existing moral obligations, and it certainly does not extinguish those obligations that are the correlatives of human rights.

Even a fiduciary role as basic as that of parent does not relieve one of such fundamental moral obligations. There are limits – some of them provided by human rights – as to what a parent may do to save her child. She may not kill someone else's child and take its liver to transplant into her own dying child, for example. So if the Fiduciary Realist argument is to succeed, it must show that this particular fiduciary role – the role of state leader – is profoundly different.

It is at this point that the second term in the phrase "Fiduciary Realism" comes into play. To make the case that state leaders ought to or may subordinate all values to the pursuit of the national interest, it is necessary to embrace a set of empirical beliefs about the world of international relations that is associated with Realism or what might be called Hobbesian Realism. The adjective "Hobbesian" is appropriate because this version of Realism portrays the condition of states in the international system as being like that of individuals in Hobbes's state of nature.

Hobbesian Realism portrays the world of international relations as a massive assurance problem. Even if any one state were willing to curb its pursuit of self-interest, it would be irrational to do so under the conditions that obtain in international relations, that is, in the absence of assurance that its self-restraint will not be taken advantage of by other states.

These conditions are said to be as follows: (a) there is no global sovereign, no supreme arbiter of conflicts capable of enforcing rules of peaceful cooperation, (b) there is (approximate) equality of power, such that no state can permanently dominate all others, (c) the fundamental preference of states is to survive, (d) but (given conditions (a), (b), and (c)) what is rational for each state to do is to strive by all means available to dominate others in order to avoid being dominated. (e) In a situation in which all states strive to dominate, without constraints on the means they employ to do so, moral principles are inapplicable.

Contemporary political scientists sometimes utilize a somewhat different conception of Realism which, though consistent with and grounded in the four assumptions stated above, may warrant being made explicit.

For political realists, international politics . . . is a struggle for power but, unlike domestic politics, a struggle dominated by organized violence. (Keohane, Nye Jr., 2000, p. 20)

On this view relations among states are thoroughly competitive, military competition is the dominant form of international competition, states function as unitary actors whose dominant issue is military security, and whatever cooperation exists among states is derivative on the struggle for military security. In that sense there is only one issue for every state: how to achieve security against hostile force; all other issues matter only so far as they bear on this.

As entrenched as Hobbesian Realism still is in certain quarters, it is untenable. Its sweeping empirical generalizations about international relations are far from being self-evident truisms; they are indeed disconfirmed by a balanced view of the facts. My aim here is not to provide a thorough refutation of Hobbesian Realism but only to sketch the outlines of such a critique in sufficient detail to show that this view of international relations is too flawed to serve in a justification of the Permissible Exclusivity Thesis.

Some of the most interesting work in international relations in the past two decades provides considerable evidence that international relations are not a Hobbesian war of each against all. There are stable patterns of peaceful cooperation, some bilateral, some multistate, some regional, others genuinely global. These include financial and monetary regimes, trade agreements, structures for scientific cooperation, environmental accords, and international support for human rights, economic development, labor standards, and disaster relief.

Furthermore, as critics of Realism point out, it would be dogmatic and inattentive to the facts to say that in all these cases cooperation is derivative on the competition for military dominance. The issues that concern states are not so hierarchically structured (with military security at the apex of the pyramid) as the Hobbesian Realist assumes. Extensive cooperation occurs in a number of areas in which military security is not a concern.

Survival is not an issue, much less the paramount issue, in many contexts of state interactions. (Consider, for example, relations between Britain and the United States over the last 120 years or so, or relations among most Western European states over the last fifty years.) Nor is it true, as the Hobbesian Realist claims, that states are roughly equal in power and hence in vulnerability. Powerful states can afford to take risks in effort to build cooperation and they also face lesser risks of others defecting from cooperative commitments because the costs of betraying their trust may be very high. Furthermore, the information revolution greatly facilitates the communication upon which trust depends.

Perhaps most important, contrary to the Hobbesian Realist, state preferences are neither fixed nor uniform among states. The positive (that is explanatory, as distinct from normative) liberal theory of international relations marshals impressive evidence for the thesis that state preferences (more precisely the preferences expressed by state leaders in foreign policy) vary, depending upon the internal character of the state and its domestic society (Slaughter, 1993; Moravscic, 1997). Of equal significance is the fact that state preferences change over time as a function of the activities of various groups within the state, particularly as these interact with and are empowered by transnational and international governmental and non-governmental organizations and institutions. For all of these reasons, Hobbesian Realism's picture of the world of international relations is sufficiently inaccurate to undercut the argument that state leaders have an absolute fiduciary duty to act only in the national interest.

There is another flaw in the Fiduciary Realist justification for the Permissible Exclusivity Thesis. It lies not in a mistaken understanding of the facts about international relations, but rather in the assumption that the national interest is of such unique moral importance that it makes sense for state leaders to make it the exclusive goal of their endeavors. Consider just how strong the Permissible Exclusivity Thesis is: it entails that pursuing an additional increment of benefit for a nation that is already exceptionally rich and already enjoys excellent protection of human rights *always* should have priority over every other end, including making great improvement in the well-being of the world's worst off people.

The proponent of Permissible Exclusivity might reply that even if maximizing the national interest is not the most fundamental goal morally speaking, it is the only proper goal for state leaders, who are after all fiduciaries for their peoples. To do otherwise would be to violate the terms of the social compact by which state leaders are empowered to serve as leaders.

This reply assumes what is to be justified. What is at issue is how we ought to understand the state leader's fiduciary role and in particular whether her obligation to pursue the national interest (or the interests of the people of her state as a whole) is to be understood as absolute or constrained in some way by concern for the human rights of persons in other states. What the proponent of Permissible Exclusivity needs – but has failed to supply – is a cogent account of why, despite the fact that the goal of maximizing the national interest is not a morally fundamental goal, state leaders, as fiduciaries, ought to treat it as if it were. The answer cannot be that this is what they are expected to do as the executors of foreign policy, because our question is what the goal of foreign policy should be.

Here the advocate of Permissible Exclusivity appeals to a particular conception of the nature of the state that I have criticized elsewhere, according to which the state is nothing more than an association for the mutual benefit of its own citizens (Buchanan, 2000a). On this conception, the role of the state leader, as a fiduciary whose overriding obligation is to further the national interest, follows from the nature of the state. She is to serve exclusively the interest of her fellow citizens in all she does, including the conduct of foreign policy, because of what the state is: an instrument whose sole legitimate function is to benefit its citizens. The state leader is simply the agent the state apparatus employs to further the interests of the citizens in the area of foreign policy.

This move merely pushes the normative question back a stage, for now we must ask: why should we conceive of the state as an association for the exclusive benefit of its citizens? If there are human rights, this is not how we should conceive of the state; instead, the state should be thought of as a resource, not only for furthering the interests of its own citizens, but also for helping to ensure the protection of human rights. This is fully compatible, of course, with the sensible view that citizens have a special claim on the resources of their state, up to the point that it secures for them an adequate or even a generous level of protection of their human rights.

The Hobbesian Realist view of international relations can be seen as an attempt to provide a reason why the state ought to operate, at least in its foreign policy, exclusively as an association for the benefit of its citizens: no other course of action is rational, given the life-or-death anarchic struggle among states. In other words, even if in principle the state's resources should be used to promote the human rights of persons beyond its borders, in practice we never reach the point where it is rational to do so, due to the Hobbesian nature of international relations. So if it is admitted that it is appropriate for the state leader to attend first to securing adequate protection of human rights for her own citizens, then this is all the Hobbesian Realist needs – if we accept her characterization of international relations. In brief, the Hobbesian Realist can concede that *when the national survival is not at stake,* pursuit of the national interest should not take precedence over human rights, but then quickly add that given the nature of international relations, *the national survival is always at stake.*

However, survival is not always at stake; issues of foreign policy do not all hang together, with every other issue being connected to survival. So our earlier conclusion stands: the Fiduciary Realist Justification for the Permissible Exclusivity Thesis fails.

The Hobbesian Realist understands the national interest in a very determinate, narrow way, as physical security through military dominance. In contrast, some hold that the national interest is the interest of the nation, understood as an ethnonational (or, in the case of fascism, racial) group. The idea here is that the national interest is the interest of the nation living its distinctive kind of life, pursuing its special destiny, and so forth. When combined with the premise that the interest of the nation is the highest moral value, this does entail Permissible Exclusivity. But of course the needed premise is repugnant, both because no rational explanation has ever been given of why the interest of the nation is the highest moral value and because of the atrocities committed by those who proclaim that it is.

The Instrumental Justification for Permissible Exclusivity. The second attempt to show that even though there are human rights, it is permissible for foreign policy to be determined exclusively by what best promotes the national interest concedes that although the national interest is not the supreme moral value, conditions in international relations are such that those who conduct foreign policy should act as if it is.

The Instrumental Justification is analogous to arguments that try to show that overall utility is maximized, not by pursuing it directly, but by following rules other than the principle that utility is to be maximized. The Instrumental Justification for Permissible Exclusivity concedes that in principle the pursuit of the national interest ought to be constrained by consideration for the human rights of foreigners, but also holds that under the conditions prevailing in international relations the best outcomes for everyone (or at least for most of humanity) will occur if each state aims exclusively at maximizing the national interest in foreign policy. For the Instrumental Justification for Permissible Exclusivity to work, it must include a convincing explanation of why respect for the human rights of all is best achieved by each state exclusively pursuing its national interest. The needed explanation presumably would be of the invisible hand variety – the world-political analog of the theory of the ideal market.

The theory of the ideal market explains how self-interested individuals can achieve mutually beneficial outcomes – but only when a constellation of robust conditions is present, including secure property rights, access to (perfect) information about goods and services, the absence of monopoly, and zero transaction costs. It is difficult to imagine what the analogous conditions would be in the case of international relations, especially since states are quite different from actors in a market.

The fatal weakness of the Instrumental Justification is that the needed explanation has not been produced and it is doubtful that it could be. There are too many obvious instances in which the exclusive pursuit of the national interest results in disregard of the human rights of persons in other states, without offsetting gains in the protection of human rights of others. The difficulty, then, is that there is neither a theory to show why a global harmony of interests would be achieved through the interactions of exclusively self-interested states under certain ideal conditions, nor any reason to believe that if the theory were produced our world would sufficiently approximate these ideal conditions to make the Instrumental Justification for Permissible Exclusivity credible.

Hans Morgenthau offers an interesting twist to the Instrumentalist Justification, one that has the advantage of not requiring an invisible hand explanation. According to Morgenthau, it will be better for humanity, not just for the people of a particular state, if each state exclusively pursues its own interest, because any attempt to shape foreign policy by moral values will lead to moral imperialism and ultimately to fanatical, highly destructive conflicts among states.

Morgenthau thus provides a different reason than that offered by the Hobbesian Realist for why the state ought to be regarded simply as a resource for pursuing the interests of its own citizens, as an association exclusively for their mutual benefit. He holds that this is how the state should be understood because a more ambitious role for the state will lead to disaster for all (Morgenthau, 1985). Ironically, Morgenthau's defense of the Permissible Exclusivity Thesis is cosmopolitan: it is for the good of humanity that states should exclusively pursue the national interest in their foreign policies.

Morgenthau appears to assume that (1) each society has its own view of morality, that there is little or no commonality of values among societies, and that (2) once a state attempts to guide its foreign policy by morality rather than the national interest, it will eschew tolerance and attempt to enforce its views on other states regardless of costs to others and ultimately to itself.

However, he presents no evidence to show that there is no significant commonality among different societies' moral points of view. He merely observes that the cosmopolitan, aristocratic value system that was previously shared by (Western) diplomats disappeared with the advent of democratization, without considering the possibility that there is growing global culture of basic human rights that represents a minimal moral consensus.

Given that a shared morality performs certain functions that all societies need (they are after all, *human* societies), it would be very surprising if societies had as little in common as Morganthau assumes. Indeed we should expect some congruence of basic moral principles across societies, given the roles that morality plays in human life: in particular, coordinating behavior and providing relatively peaceful means for resolving or avoiding the more common mutually destructive conflicts that can occur wherever human beings go about the basic tasks that all humans must perform.

As Stewart Hampshire has observed, there is a lethal tension in the view that there is a fundamental diversity in *basic* ethical principles, because for something to count as a *basic* ethical principle it must be grounded in and responsive to human interests (rather than in the parochial interests that some humans happen to have) (Hampshire, 1989, p. 90). By the most basic ethical principles Hampshire means those that prohibit behavior resulting in the worst harms to which human beings – all human beings – are vulnerable. But if this is so, then it is hard to see how different societies, so long as they are societies of human beings, could disagree greatly in their most basic ethical principles.

More important, Morgenthau's argument overlooks the fact that there is an apparently broadening global culture of basic human rights, evidenced not only by human rights treaties signed by states, but by the growing power of transnational organizations to exert pressure on states to comply with these treaties (Risse, Ropp, and Sikkink, 1999, p. 199). It is true that there is disagreement about the precise contours of even some of the least controversial human rights and much controversy about whether some rights – especially those recognizing robust economic entitlements – really are human rights. But none of this should blind one to the fact that there is considerable consensus on a minimal, core conception of human rights that include the rights against slavery and involuntary servitude, the rights to physical security of the person, including the right not to be tortured or to be subject to arbitrary arrest, and the right not to be excluded from political participation on the basis of race.

In addition, this growing consensus on basic human rights operates within an international institutional framework that places significant constraints on the moral imperialism that Morgenthau rightly dreads. First, the idea of human rights still functions within a state-centered system that values state sovereignty very highly and an international legal system that prohibits humanitarian intervention without UN Security Council authorization and also prohibits aggressive war. Second, due to the admission of newly liberated colonial peoples in the 1960s and 1970s to the UN, and due to the growing appreciation for cultural diversity in most of the more developed and powerful states, it is more difficult for any state to try to impose on the world its own peculiar conception of morality.

Third, Morgenthau wrongly assumes a sharp distinction between the national interest and a society's moral values. This is to proceed as if the national interest is something exogenously determined, as if a group's interest is in no way shaped by its conception of its relationship to the realization of its moral values. But if the national interest and the society's moral values are not so separable, then the attempt to avoid what Morgenthau takes to be the risks of a morally guided foreign policy by cleaving to the pursuit of national interest is doomed.

Finally, Morgenthau overlooks the possibility that one way to reduce the risk of moral imperialism and hence the destruction it causes is to establish international legal structures that recognize the importance of diversity by helping to secure for all persons the rights to freedom of religion and freedom of conscience as well as a prohibition against aggressive war. Yet for these structures to function effectively, they require support from states, especially powerful ones, and sometimes in circumstances that do not best promote the national interest.[2] Reducing the risk of moral imperialism may in fact be incompatible with the exclusive pursuit of the national interest.

Morgenthau's admonition to states to stick to the pursuit of national interest might be sound advice for a world in which the major threat to human well-being is horrendously destructive competition for world domination among states driven by intolerant, totalizing ideologies, unconstrained by a global culture of human rights, by international institutions prohibiting aggressive war and upholding the sovereignty of states, and by a resolve on the part of the most powerful states to avoid global total war; but this is not to say that it is wise counsel for our world.

The basic flaw in Morgenthau's defense of Permissible Exclusivity is that it wrongly assumes that the only alternatives are (i) the exclusive pursuit of national interest (somehow defined in a morally neutral way) and (ii) unconstrained moral imperialism. So Morgenthau's argument from the risk of pursuing moral values in foreign policy does not justify the Permissible Exclusivity Thesis.

EXPLAINING THE POPULARITY OF THE PERMISSIBLE EXCLUSIVITY THESIS

Given the weakness of the putative justifications for the Permissible Exclusivity Thesis, we need an explanation of its popularity. It is not so hard to explain why state leaders would find Permissible Exclusivity attractive and encourage its acceptance by their fellow-citizens. Because of the elasticity of the notion of national interest, acceptance of Permissible Exclusivity greatly augments the power of state leaders, since it allows them to pursue the national interest without constraint, whenever faced with a decision that will affect the national interest one way or another. And for leaders who seek to base their power on appeals to nationalism, the idea that all that matters is the national interest provides them with a powerful resource for manipulating public opinion and sentiment – and for mobilizing co-nationals against supposed enemies within or outside the state. To explain the appeal of the Permissible Exclusivity Thesis to others, especially to those who are not already motivated by a deeply felt nationalism, may be somewhat more difficult.

The more general appeal of Permissible Exclusivity may be mainly negative: it looks attractive because what is assumed to be the alternative is so unpalatable. There are two different assumptions about what the alternative is that cast Permissible Exclusivity in a comparatively favorable light. But neither assumption, I shall argue, is plausible.

Sometimes those who support Permissible Exclusivity proceed as if the only alternative is a kind of starry-eyed utopianism, an attempt to implement principles of justice right here and now, without regard for the realities of power and the fallibilities of human beings. However, to assume that this is the only alternative to exclusive pursuit of the national interest is either to confuse appeals to morality with "moralizing" or to overlook the distinction between ideal and non-ideal normative theory that those who take human rights seriously can and often do observe.

As a pejorative term, "moralizing" presumably refers to naive attempts to change behavior solely by appeals to moral principles, perhaps combined with a tendency to see issues that are not truly moral issues as being so. Plainly, those who appeal to the importance of human rights and their relevance to foreign policy need not be guilty of these errors. The most effective human rights activists demonstrate by their behavior that appeals to morality alone do not suffice, but must be accompanied by efforts to create additional incentives for moral behavior (for example, by lobbying with the European Union to make better protection of human rights a condition for admission of new states). And a moral view that focuses on the most basic human rights as minimal standards can hardly be accused of injecting morality into all areas of human life. So the charge that appealing to human rights as a constraint on the pursuit of the national interest is "moralizing" is not cogent.[3]

It is also a mistake to assume that those who believe that human rights should play a role in foreign policy naively believe that actions we could undertake now in the name of morality will produce a perfectly just world or that they are unaware that premature or ill-crafted efforts at reform can be counterproductive. Those who take human rights seriously need not neglect the distinction between ideal and non-ideal theory.

Ideal theory specifies the general principles that a just world order would conform to; non-ideal theory proposes second-best principles for our far from ideal world and attempts to show how we should go about the task of moving closer toward the ideal situation. To recognize the distinction between ideal and non-ideal theory is to acknowledge that how we strive for justice must take considerations of feasibility into account.

In fact the ideal/non-ideal distinction is often tacitly invoked by human rights advocates when they are confronted with the question of how to respond to human rights violations. For example, many human rights activists acknowledge that although female genital mutilation (at least when it involves total excision of the clitoris) is a violation of human rights, nothing whatsoever follows from this about the advisability of attempting to force people to stop engaging in the practice. They understand that attempts to force this reform, especially if they originate from outside the cultures in which clitidorectomy is practiced, may well be counterproductive and are also likely to be implemented in ways that show disrespect for people in other cultures that are still suffering the effects of colonialism.

In other words, one can acknowledge that certain practices violate basic human rights, but also recognize that efforts to end them must be informed by considerations of feasibility broadly understood. Believing that human rights should matter in foreign policy need not entail stupidity or callous disregard for history and cultural context.

There are, of course, many mistakes that advocates of reform in the name of justice can make if they fail to take seriously the distinction between ideal and non-ideal theory and along with it the distinction between being justified in condemning a practice and being justified in intervening to change it. But the fact that this is so does nothing to establish that states should only pursue the national interest and never allow moral considerations to shape their foreign policy.

There is a another explanation of the popularity of the Permissible Exclusivity Thesis that does not rest upon the false assumption that the only alternative to exclusive pursuit of the national interest is impractical moralizing. It assumes, instead that we are faced with a choice between exclusive pursuit of the national interest and a thoroughly impartial cosmopolitanism that allows no special priority at all for the national interest. This view assumes that once we concede that the national interest should not be the end all and be all of foreign policy, we have committed ourselves to something that most would find quite unpalatable: the position that our national interest should be fully subordinate to the demands of global justice, that our state should count our interests no more than the interests of foreigners, and that consequently we must be prepared to sacrifice our national interest for the sake of morally improving the world.

Like the claim that anyone who believes that the pursuit of national interest should be constrained by regard for human rights is a naive idealist, this is a caricature of the position it attacks. To deny that the national interest may always take precedence over human rights concerns one need not embrace the equally extreme position that the national interest counts for nothing or should always be subordinate. For one thing, given that the world is divided up into states – given the absence of a world government capable of promoting the interests of humanity – there is good reason for having a division of moral labor in which individual states are held primarily responsible for the welfare of their own citizens.

However, this is not to say that states must be understood as having an unconstrained mandate to maximize the national interest no matter what. When a state has secured an adequate level of human rights protection for all its citizens, it can no longer plausibly plead that the fate of those in other countries is none of its concern. For those who have the good fortune to live in states where human rights are generally well protected to continue to devote all the resources of their state exclusively to maximizing their own well-being when many in other states lack minimal protection for their most basic human rights is not compatible with taking human rights seriously.

The choice, then, is not between the Permissible Exclusivity Thesis and a thorough-going impartial cosmopolitanism that rejects any special place for the national interest. Once this simple point is acknowledged, it is no longer possible to justify Permissible Exclusivity by claiming that the alternative to embracing it is unacceptable.

Notice also, how unpersuasive it would be to argue that once we admit considerations other than the national interest into the foreign policy debate, we will be on a slippery slope toward the excesses of human rights utopianism or thoroughly impartial cosmopolitanism. If history is any indication of what the future will be like, the danger is not that states will neglect the national interest in an ecstasy of self-sacrificial cosmopolitanism. On the contrary, the greater risk is that they will continue in systematically devaluing the claims of persons in other states.

LIBERATING THE DISCOURSE OF FOREIGN POLICY

Once we jettison the dogma that foreign policy should or even may exclusively further the national interest, our orientation to the world beyond our borders undergoes a transformation. This is not to say that foreign policy decisions become easier, only that they can now take into account the full range of relevant values. Instead of asking only "Is humanitarian intervention (or a more permissive immigration policy or a preventive war against terrorists or their allies, or the creation of an international criminal court) in our national interest?" we can now ask: "Would this policy choice promote human rights and can it be pursued in a way that is compatible with according a reasonable priority to our more important legitimate national interests?" In other words, once we are freed from the unwarranted constraint of assuming that only the national interest matters, we can begin to face the difficult but necessary question of how we are to balance a concern for the human rights of others with a proper special regard for our own country's welfare. We can now at least ask whether a genuine commitment to the human rights of all persons is compatible with continuing to guide policy exclusively by the goal of forever improving our own situation in a world in which so many people beyond our borders do not even approximate our standard of human rights protection. Once we dispense with the dogma of the supremacy of the national interest, we can begin to ask the right questions.

NOTES

This essay is a much shortened and modified version of "Beyond the national interest," which appeared in a special issue of *Philosophical Topics* on global inequalities, edited by Martha Nussbaum and Chad Flanders (30, 2 [2002], pp. 97–131).

1 In "Beyond the national interest" I explore alternative understandings of the national interest.

2 This point is due to Martha Nussbaum.

3 Cohen (1985, pp. 6–7) exposes this confusion between morality and moralizing (or moralism).

CHAPTER 9

Cosmopolitan respect and patriotic concern

Richard W. Miller

Even in countries where average income and wealth are much greater than in the world at large, most people take themselves to have a duty to show much more concern for the needs of compatriots than for the needs of foreigners in their political choices concerning tax-financed aid. For example, in the United States, most reflective, generally humane people who take the alleviation of poverty to be an important task of government think they have a duty to support laws that are much more responsive to neediness in the South Bronx than to neediness in the slums of Dacca. This patriotic bias has come to play a central role in the debate over universalist moralities, moralities whose fundamental principles prescribe equal concern or respect for all individuals everywhere and lay down no independent, fundamental duty toward people in a special relation to the agent. Particularists, that is, those who locate an independent principle of group loyalty in the foundations of morality, challenge universalists to justify the pervasive patriotic bias in tax-supported aid that is a deep-seated commitment of most of those who are, in general, attracted to universalism.[1]

So far, universalist justifications of patriotic bias in aid have not risen to the particularist challenge. Granted (as Goodin noted in an important contribution to this debate), if someone has equal concern for all humanity everywhere, she will take certain considerations of efficiency to favor a worldwide system of institutional responsibilities including special responsibilities toward compatriots, as opposed to similarly needy foreigners. People's tendency to be more sensitive to compatriots' deprivation than foreigners' concentrates the collective attention of an effective social group and facilitates the deliberative coordination of giving; on the whole, people have a better understanding of compatriots' needs, and can more easily provide aid to the needy within the nation's borders. However, the grim facts of international inequality override these considerations, when one assesses bias toward compatriots in a per-capita rich country as compared with the poor of the world at large from a perspective of equal concern for all. The neediness of people in countries such as Bangladesh is desperate enough, their local resources meager enough, their numbers great enough, and current transportation, information, and transnational institutions are effective enough, to put responsibility for the needy of per-capita poor foreign countries on a par with responsibility for needy compatriots in per-capita rich ones, when responsibilities are allocated in ways that most efficiently provide for worldwide needs.[2]

The other main universalist strategy for justifying special concern for compatriots has appealed to mutual benefit as the appropriate basis for unchosen terms of cooperation.[3] Tax-financed giving to compatriots is more apt than tax-financed giving to foreigners to be part of an arrangement in which, over the long run, the contribution of each is compensated by proportionate benefits. For example, domestic giving often contributes to an insurance scheme that is in the long-run self-interest of current benefactors, or serves as a means by which the better-off compensate worse-off compatriots for otherwise unrewarded benefits of their participation in shared institutions. However, a rationale for aid that is *solely* based on long-term mutual benefit will hardly satisfy the vast majority of universalists, who think that those who contribute more to social output can have a duty to make sacrifices over the long run to help those who contribute less when the lesser contribution is due to unchosen disadvantages. Yet once the moral relevance of neediness is acknowledged, it is hard to see why it loses force across borders.

The particularist challenge has begun to seem so powerful that it forces a choice between abandoning universalism and abandoning the patriotic bias in tax-financed aid that is a deep commitment of the vast majority of reflective people who are otherwise strongly attracted to universalism. I will describe a way of avoiding this hard choice, a way of basing a special duty expressing this bias on a universalist morality. For reasons I sketched in connection with Goodin's proposal, I do not think this reconciling project can succeed on the basis of a universalist morality of equal concern for all. Instead, I will derive the patriotic bias from a morality of equal respect for all. A plausible comprehensive morality of universal respect produces a strongly biased duty of special concern for compatriots in matters of tax-financed aid, largely because it dictates a special interest in leading a social life based on mutual respect and trust and a special commitment to provide adequate incentives for compatriots to conform to the shared institutions that one helps to impose on them. (The required incentives are not proportionate to contribution.) In a moral discussion, guided by this perspective, between Kevin, a corporate lawyer living in a rich suburb of New York, and Khalid, who collects scrap metal in a slum of Dacca, Kevin could say, "In my political choices, I must give priority to helping my needy compatriots if my most important relations of interdependence are to be based on respect and trust, and if those compatriots are to have an incentive that their self-respect requires if they are to uphold political measures I help to force upon them." Khalid could accept this rationale even though he suffers from the worldwide consequences of Kevin's sort of patriotic bias, because his own moral responsibility leads him to accord a special importance to the kind of social and political relations Kevin seeks, an importance that entails allowing others to treat the pursuit of such relations in their own lives as a basis for choice among rules for giving.

According to this argument, special concern for those in certain unchosen relations to oneself, including relations of specially intense interdependence and mutual subordination, *is* part of the foundations of morality, but it is not an independent part. Such special concern is entailed by a comprehensive universalist morality of equal respect for all.

THE BIAS

The attempt to meet the particularist challenge requires a more detailed description of its terms, that is, the terms of a bias toward compatriots in tax-supported aid that is plausibly ascribed to most reflective people who are otherwise strongly attracted to universalism. In defining this bias, I will construe "compatriot" broadly, as including all long-term, law-abiding fellow-residents of a country. Particularists are in no position to claim that there is a pervasive attachment to a substantial bias of narrower scope: as recent American controversies over denials of benefits to resident aliens imply, there is no broad consensus that mere law-abiding, long-term residents deserve much less concern than those with such further accoutrements as fellow-citizenship or fellow-membership in a cultural or ethnic community that predominates within the country's borders. Still, it is probably common coin that fellow-citizenship strengthens duties of public aid to some degree and that cultural or ethnic ties can justify some special aid (for example, the special support that the Federal Republic of Germany has given ethnically German immigrants from eastern Europe). My arguments for the larger bias will also suggest how these smaller ones might be justified.

In addition, the proper appreciation of the particularist challenge depends on assessing the strength and depth of the pervasive patriotic bias. The broad consensus to which particularists appeal does not just dictate patriotic bias in most countries or in circumstances of approximate international equality. It entails a patriotic bias in tax-supported aid, despite the grim facts of international inequality, in all or virtually all of the most technologically advanced and materially productive countries, the ones that are, per-capita, relatively rich, as well as in all other countries. The "virtually all" is meant to allow for the possibility of a few countries in which deprivation is so rare that the project of government aid to the needy is, properly, concentrated on foreign aid. On a sufficiently rosy view of Liechtenstein, Liechtensteinian concentration on foreign aid would offend no widespread view of patriotic duty.

In addition to this strength, the prevalent bias is deep in the sense of being insensitive to the outcome of certain empirical controversies. In particular, the bias toward compatriots in per-capita rich countries does not depend on pessimism about the efficacy of helping foreigners in poor countries through foreign aid. Even if optimism on the Oxfam model is right, and, dollar for dollar, feasible varieties of foreign aid would be an especially economical means of relieving suffering, the primary concern should be aid to compatriots. (This is not to deny that the pervasive patriotic bias is conditional on other empirical assumptions, which might reasonably be questioned. Rather than seeking to describe these presuppositions at the outset, I will use a morality of equal respect to reveal them, as the factual assumptions in a case for favoring compatriots which rests on this moral foundation.)

Finally, it will be useful to distinguish two kinds of bias that are both prevalent and both fall under the heading "patriotic bias in tax-supported aid." The first is priority of attention to compatriots' needs, that is, a commitment to oppose policies seriously detracting from provision for relevant needs of compatriots. The second is budgetary bias toward compatriots, that is, support for a total aid bill in which tax-supported aid to foreigners is a small proportion of tax-supported aid to compatriots. Both biases are prevalent, but they are not the same. If Americans were to satisfy the first priority, removing all relevant burdens from compatriots, they would live in a world in which many foreigners in per-capita poor countries still struggled with similar burdens. In principle, these needs could generate further moral duties so demanding that they require support for an aid budget mostly devoted to foreigners' needs, violating the second, budgetary bias. ("Charity begins at home" does not exclude the possibility that discharging all duties to give will mostly require giving to strangers in the end.)

Given the facts of international inequality, an argument for budgetary bias in rich countries must be based on a prior case for some form of biased attention to compatriots' needs. Observing this order, I will begin by arguing that full and equal respect for all dictates priority of attention, and then describe the additional considerations sustaining budgetary bias.

Although I have committed myself to defending a strong, deep form of patriotic bias in tax-supported aid, I have said nothing about bias in private, voluntary contributions. And it is a striking fact (which ought to make particularists nervous) that there is no broad, deepseated consensus that cosmopolitanism in individual charity is wrong. Americans who respond to appeals of the Save the Children program can check a box that indicates their desire to help a child who lives in the United States. Those who check the "Where the need is greatest" box instead (or the "Africa" or "Asia" box) are not widely held to have violated a duty. My argument from equal respect to patriotic bias in political choice will not, in fact, support the corresponding private duty. This helps to account for their different roles in the pervasive consensus, and so, helps to confirm the argument itself.

COSMOPOLITAN RESPECT

Any universalist morality worthy of the name will ground moral obligations on some fundamental standpoint in which everyone's life is regarded as equally valuable. Because of the facts of international inequality, it seems impossible to ground duties of patriotic bias in tax-financed aid on a standpoint of equal concern for all. But, on the face of it, according equal value to different people's lives does not entail equal concern for them. I certainly regard the life of the girl who lives across the street as no less valuable than the life of my own daughter. But I am not equally concerned for her. For example, I am not willing to do as much for her. The existence of obstacles to her enjoying the pursuit of her goals is a prima facie reason for me to help remove the obstacles, but my special concern for my own goals, including my wishes for my daughter, can provide a legitimate excuse for neglecting to help, without any of the disrespect involved in treating her life as less valuable than others'.

Three broad, interrelated themes in Kantian moral theory, which are well-connected with moral common sense, define one highly attractive approach to questions of right and wrong in the space that I have just created for universalisms not grounded on equal concern for all. First of all, rather than grounding obligation on equal concern, this approach makes equal respect fundamental. One avoids moral wrongness just in case one conforms to some set of rules for living by which one could express equal respect for all, as distinguished from equal concern for all.

Of course, there are a variety of ways of specifying the demands of equal respect. A second common feature of the universalisms from which I will derive a patriotic bias is something like Kant's view that the rules expressing equal respect for all are the rules that could be the joint, self-imposed, fully autonomous legislation of all. Kant's emphasis on full autonomy is not essential, here. Within this tradition, Scanlon, for example, describes the relevantly unanimous legislation as any total system of shared rules that no one could reasonably reject, while Rawls, in his most Kantian phase, took the principles of justice to be shared premises for political discourse through which each could express her highest-order interests in fair terms of cooperation and the rational revision of final ends. Despite these differences, the various more specific Kantianisms can each be seen as specifying and defending, in its own way, a vaguer, more colloquial standard deploying the ordinary notion of self-respect whose rich moral implications Hill has explored.[4] At least to a first approximation, broadly Kantian universalism affirms that a choice is wrong just in case it violates every set of shared rules of conduct to which everyone could be freely and rationally committed without anyone's violating his or her own self-respect.

As Scanlon has emphasized, some such principle is a natural development of the extremely attractive thought that avoiding moral wrongness is a matter of avoiding actions that are not permitted by rules that are relevantly justifiable, as a shared code of conduct, to those burdened by the action.[5] In this moral context, the irrelevant justifications are those depending on the burdened one's fear or ignorance or her lack of self-respect. It may have been rational for the native peoples of nineteenth-century Rhodesia to accept the rule, "If black, give up your land when whites demand it," since otherwise they would have been subjected to fierce repression, but this hardly shows that Cecil Rhodes and his henchmen did no wrong. Obviously, one does not justify rules in a morally relevant way by getting a victim to accept them out of misinformation or muddle. Finally, justifications that lead to acceptance because of the victim's lack of self-respect (alternatively: her taking her life to be less valuable than others') do not make the permitted conduct all right. If all slaves in the ante-bellum South had shown a lack of self-respect by freely accepting the rules that made them property of whites, support for slavery would still have been wrong.

A final common feature of broadly Kantian moralities is the distinction they draw between negative and positive duties. These universalisms condemn those who lie or initiate the use of force in pursuit of mere personal advantage, but they do not impose a duty to make every sacrifice that would improve the world on balance. It is enough to adopt policies through which one takes on one's fair share of world improvement. One must adopt policies toward giving that impose some lifelong sacrifice. Otherwise, one could not claim to regard the lives of the needy as just as valuable as one's own. But grave self-sacrifice is not required, even if it is productive of great good.

Suppose I see a full-size adult fall, headfirst, out of a tenth story window. No one else is nearby. Because of my deep knowledge of ballistics and anatomy, I know that if I rush to catch him, I will save his life, by cushioning his fall and keeping his head from striking the sidewalk. But if I cushion his fall, I am very likely to break some bones, which will heal, perhaps painfully and incompletely, in the course of several months. Even if there is no question that the cost of helping to me would be much less than the cost of not helping to the man hurtling toward the sidewalk, I can do my fair share in making the world a better place while turning down this chance for world-improvement.

The limits to burdensome giving derive from the fundamental view of moral impartiality. I do not show disrespect for the person falling out the window, do not express the attitude that his life is less valuable than my own, in saving my bones from breakage. Even if specially needy, one shows no lack of self-respect in letting others withhold aid when the cost to them is severe injury. (Thomson's violinist will be quite disturbed if you unplug him, but given the cost of continued connection, he will not take this as an expression of disrespect and will not display a lack of self-respect in accepting a moral code permitting the unplugging.)[6]

No doubt, my brief, relatively colloquial statements of the demands of equal respect have to be elaborated – for example, to cope with special problems of noncompliance posed by those who do not share in the fundamental moral attitude. No doubt, much more has to be said to justify this approach to morality. Still, I hope I have evoked a familiar strand of universalist thinking, which has been developed and defended for decades, indeed centuries. If, as I hope to show, the broadly shared features of this sort of universalism entail the routine patriotic biases, this will, at least, rebut the particularist claim that no currently viable version of universalism has room for the duties of patriotic bias that express a strong conviction of most people who are otherwise attracted to universalism.

PATRIOTIC PRIORITY

The morality of equal respect for everyone that I have described creates a duty to give priority, in providing tax-financed aid, to the serious deprivations of compatriots. In particular, one must give priority to relieving serious burdens due to inferior life-prospects among compatriots, that is, inferior chances of success in pursuing life-goals given equal willingness to make sacrifices. This priority does not totally exclude support for foreign aid in the presence of relevant domestic burdens. Still, until domestic political arrangements have done as much as they can (under the rule of law and while respecting civil and political liberty) to eliminate serious burdens of domestic inequality of life-prospects, there should be no significant sacrifice of this goal in order to help disadvantaged foreigners. Here, significant sacrifice consists of foreseeable costs to a disadvantaged compatriot so severe that she need not willingly accept them, even though she equally values everyone's life and realizes that these costs to her are part of an arrangement helping even more disadvantaged others. For example, poor people in virtually all per-capita rich countries confront low prospects of interesting, valued work, effective political participation, and intellectually liberating education and are at special risk of long-term ill-health, in the absence of extensive aid. These are the sorts of grave burdens that one can be unwilling to take on, as part of an arrangement that relieves even more serious burdens of others, even though one respects them and regards their lives as no less valuable than one's own.

There are two main arguments for this duty of prior attention to compatriots. Both involve special concerns, specially attentive to domestic life-prospects, that are entailed by commitment to the outlook of equal respect that I have described. The first is an argument from excessive costs in lost social trust, the second an argument from the need to provide compatriots with adequate incentives to obey the laws one helps to create.

First of all, consider the cost in disrupted social trust of the failure to provide tax-financed aid sufficient to relieve serious burdens of inferior life-prospects among compatriots, when this shortfall is due to provision for neediness abroad. As a consequence of this shortfall, disadvantaged compatriots would suffer from inferior life-prospects that better-off compatriots do not try to alleviate because their concern for the needy is diffused worldwide. Inevitably, this will reduce the extent to which the disadvantaged can be relied on to cooperate with advantaged compatriots on the basis of their rationally pursuing shared goals, as opposed to their merely acquiescing in the superior coercive power of the state, or deferring out of self-abnegation, or cooperating because they lack awareness of what is going on. For example, if this global evenhandedness is well entrenched, needy compatriots cannot be expected to take part in a trusting and respectful political practice of using principled persuasion to seek common ground. The avoidable burdens of seeking self-advancement under the nation's laws and policies make it psychologically insupportable to engage respectfully in the political process that ultimately enforces these rules. So, in response to a settled commitment to the worldwide diffusion of concern, the domestic disadvantaged will, inevitably, with-draw from politics or treat politics as a means of exerting pressure on others, with no special role for principled persuasion.[7] For similar reasons, the worldwide diffusion of concern would be accompanied by less friend-liness in the routine interactions with non-intimates that determine the overall tone of life. Rather than being based on mutual respect and trust, people's relations of interdependence with compatriots would often be based on resentful fear or servility, the horror from which Huck Finn and Jim made their lonely escape.[8]

Admittedly, someone committed to the morality of equal respect will not be interested in receiving trust that depends on attitudes of disrespect for others. (Huck would have been a much worse person if he had not been reluctant to purchase social trust on this basis from his fellow-whites.) However, the limits to trust on the part of the domestic disadvan-taged do not reflect their lack of full and equal respect for disadvantaged foreigners. For patriotic priority of attention is violated only when they suffer losses sufficiently serious that they do not have to take them on, as part of provision for neediness elsewhere, in order to express full and equal respect for all.

Like the risk to one's bones of cushioning the man hurtling toward the sidewalk, this cost in distrust of foreign aid violating patriotic priority is a legitimate excuse for not helping, an excuse that could be part of the code endorsed by someone who has full and equal respect for all. This assess-ment (which is, I hope, plausible at the outset) gains credibility when one reflects on the role of the interest in basing dependence on trust and respect in rationalizing the morality that I have described. The uncondi-tional commitment to live by some code that all could freely, rationally, and self-respectfully share can require foreswearing indefinitely great advantages, because they depend on exploitation or domination that such codes prohibit. Yet doing the right thing is always one rational option for a normal human being. What normal human interest could rationalize the life-practice of someone who foreswears advantages violating those bases for general agreement, while otherwise pursuing the projects to which she is personally attached?

The answer would seem to be: an interest in having one's relationships of dependence be relationships of mutual respect and trust. All of us have reason to want to be able to rely on others to act in ways that we expect to benefit us, acting in these ways despite tempting opportunities to benefit themselves by noncompliance. The morally responsible people among us, those who seek to avoid wrongdoing, do not want others' dependability to be due to their fear, irrationality, or lack of self-respect, even if these sources of compliance are reliable. Their overriding preference, when they depend on others, is for dependability based on common concerns which each can willingly embrace even if everyone regards her life as no less valuable than anyone else's. Such a person, if a middle-income US citizen, would not really prefer to be Louis XIV, even after the Fronde has been suppressed and putting to one side the inferiority of seventeenth-century medicine. Using coercion and superstition to frustrate peasants' interests in relaxed enjoyment, creative reflection, and meaningful work is, in the end, too disgusting a prospect.

Because this overriding preference that one's relationships of dependence be based on mutual respect and trust is what rationalizes an overriding commitment to self-regulation by rules expressing equal respect for all, one can express this commitment in choices giving special weight to the promotion of those trusting relationships in one's own life. (In much the same way, when a concern for another's well-being is motivated by love, one expresses that concern in choices giving special weight to continued loving interaction with the other. "I wish her well, and I don't care whether I ever see her again" is not an expression of loving parental concern.) So, in a morality based on rules expressing equal respect, the fact that aid to disadvantaged compatriots is specially important for one's engagement in trusting, respectful forms of interdependence provides a legitimate excuse for patriotic bias.

It might seem that the argument from social trust to patriotic bias underrates the bearing of foreign needs on respect and trust, in two different ways. First of all, this argument might seem to ignore the existence of international economic interdependence. But the argument is only meant to justify a bias, and only relies on the fact that interdependence among compatriots is specially intense and specially vulnerable to distrust and disrespect. This special vulnerability is, in part, a consequence of the political vulnerability implicit in the compatriot relation: politically active people support the coercive imposition of laws on their compatriots. (It is largely because of my location in a distinct network of political vulnerabilities that social distrust in Quebec does not taint my social life, even though I live much closer to Quebec than to most of the United States.)

In the second place, the argument so far might seem to ignore the socially disruptive effects of the poverty in poor countries that foreign aid could relieve. The violation of primary attention to compatriots' needs by people like Kevin would reduce social trust on the part of people like Carla, who lives in the South Bronx and makes a meager living cleaning other people's apartments. Nonetheless, the increased foreign aid might lead to strengthened bonds linking Khalid and his compatriots, as Khalid's situation becomes less desperate. Perhaps, because of the special desperation of the worst-off in the poorest countries and the cheapness of the measures that would relieve it, violation of patriotic priority in per-capita rich countries would be part of the most efficient means of promoting social trust worldwide. If so, would not the special interest in social trust that is implicit in equal respect for all exclude, rather than support, patriotic bias, making consequent costs to oneself as irrelevant as costs of forgoing feasible theft or exploitation?

Since I am trying to justify a bias deep enough to be compatible with optimistic views of the efficacy of foreign aid, the supposition about the special effectiveness of foreign aid in the worldwide enhancement of social trust is certainly fair. But taking this efficacy to cancel the excuse for neglecting foreign needs would involve a misunderstanding of a morally responsible person's special valuing of relationships of mutual respect and trust. It would be like the mistake of supposing that someone who specially values the relationship of parental nurturing must be willing to neglect his daughter if this is needed to save two other people's daughters from parental neglect. Granted, if the special valuing of a relationship is a dictate of moral responsibility, then all instances of it, everywhere, are specially valuable. However, as Scheffler has recently emphasized, the special valuing of a relationship entails, not just a high appreciation of the value of its instances, but taking participation in this relationship with another to be a specially demanding reason for appropriate forms of concern for the other.[9] I do not specially value the relationship of parental nurturance if I willingly neglect my child just because this is part of a more effective way to promote nurturance in the world at large. Kevin does not specially value social trust if he jeopardizes his relationship with compatriots such as Carla so that foreigners such as Khalid may enjoy more trust on balance. By the same token, Khalid, as a morally responsible person, will take relations of respect and trust to be specially important and will all the more regret the social strains of Bangladeshi poverty. But, taking such relations to be specially valuable, he will take their maintainence to be a specially powerful reason for action. This is why Khalid, despite his plight, need not condemn Kevin's favoritism toward compatriots, in order to show self-respect.

So far, I have argued that a certain bias is all right, not that it is morally obligatory: the better-off in per-capita rich countries have a legitimate excuse for giving priority to compatriots' needs in their political choices. However, because the topic is the political choice to support laws forcing some to help others and the patriotic bias is based on an interest that all morally responsible people share, this lemma is a short step removed from the theorem asserting a duty of priority in attention to compatriots' needs in tax-financed aid. It shows a lack of respect for another to force her to do more than she must to do her fair share in the task of world-improvement. Because of the cost in social trust, someone would be forced to do more than her fair share if she were taxed according to laws violating patriotic priority. So support for such laws is wrong. On the other hand, such laws as are needed to sustain domestic social trust would be supported by every compatriot committed to equal respect for all: the better-off because of the social interest implicit in that commitment, the worst-off for material reasons, as well. If a political arrangement would be supported by every morally responsible participant, that is, every participant committed to equal respect for all, then each has a moral duty to support it.

Like Rawls's discussions of "excusable envy," this first argument for patriotic bias appeals to a psychologically inevitable limit on trust and respect. Even if the domestic disadvantaged could overcome this limit, engaging in trusting, respectful political activity and avoiding both resentment and servility despite worldwide diffusion of concern, there would be a second basis for patriotic priority of attention, the need to give priority to compatriots' needs in order to avoid unjust domination.

Anyone engaged in political choice is engaged in projects which, if they succeed, will result in laws that all compatriots are forced to obey. Equal respect for all is incompatible with supporting the coercive enforcement of terms of self-advancement under which some are seriously burdened, regardless of their choices, in ways that could be alleviated at relatively little cost to the advantaged. More specifically, suppose that current laws enforce rules of peaceful private self-advancement that guarantee that some compatriots will be seriously burdened by inferior life-prospects unless their advantaged compatriots help to lift these burdens: losers in competition in one generation convey seriously inferior capacities to get ahead to their children. Suppose that there are measures through which suffering from inferior life-prospects could be alleviated without imposing losses on the advantaged, through taxation, that are at all as great as the alleviation. (The taxation used to improve the education of Carla's child will lower the life-prospects of Kevin's child, but the cost to the one is much less than the gain to the other.) In this situation, support for the status quo would show disrespect for the disadvantaged. After all, someone whose life-prospects are burdened by such laws could not willingly uphold a shared social standard allowing these burdens to be imposed in spite of the small costs of change, unless that sufferer lacked self-respect.

From the perspective of equal respect that I have described, the appropriate assessments of benefits and burdens would, surely, rule out support for laissez-faire capitalism in virtually all per-capita rich countries and require aid exceeding current measures, on any hypothesis about the efficacy of domestic aid that coheres with optimism about the efficacy of foreign aid. For, assuming such efficacy, there will be gains to the disadvantaged from wide-ranging policies requiring taxation of the rich that will be much more important than the costs in luxuries and comforts lost through such taxation. Someone rationally committed to forgoing all advantages depending on violation of rules that others could rationally, self-respectfully share must accord special importance to the prerequisites for participation in a social life regulated by rules rationally shared by self-respecting cooperators. Such a willing cooperator will regard it as extremely important to have resources for informed and rational reflection over how to live and what laws to support, to have an influence on a par with the influence of others on laws and, more generally, on one's social environment, to have work that is valuable to oneself, under one's own intelligent control in important ways, and recognized as valuable by others, and to have opportunities for the leisure, affection, and whimsy that are needed for self-expressive living. These are all human requirements for taking part in a social life in which one's self-respect is displayed and supported. Because her commitment to rules sustaining such a social life is unconditional and because she regards everyone's life as equally valuable, a morally responsible person will express her special commitment to these values in comparing gains for some and losses for others. So she will take the burdens on people like Carla to be specially severe and costs for people like Kevin of relieving them to be relatively moderate.

Note that the domestic aid required by the broadly Kantian perspective is more demanding than relief required by considerations of mutual benefit. The standard of mutual benefit would legitimate a situation in which Kevin's and Carla's different life-expectations are proportional to expected differences in contribution, due to advantages of Kevin's that are not traceable to their choices. But Carla would display a lack of self-respect in accepting burdens due to these unchosen differences (such as the difficulties of growing up in a crime-ridden neighborhood, brought up by a single tired, distracted, ill-educated parent and taught by weary, cynical teachers.) She would be like a slave who accepts the distribution of income between slaves and plantation-owners if it reflects the greater economic importance of plantation-owners' coordination of production and exchange, giving no weight to the facts that slaves are denied literacy and large networks of acquaintance and that major economic agents refuse to deal directly with them.

The sticking point in using this argument about unjust subordination to support patriotic bias is the resemblance between Kevin's relationship to Carla and Kevin's relationship to Khalid: the inferiority of Khalid's life-prospects is at least as stark, its burdens at least as severe, and, on optimistic views of the efficacy of foreign aid, it would be even easier to alleviate the burden at little cost to Kevin. However, because of two further differences, Kevin can favor Carla without showing disrespect for Khalid and Khalid can willingly accept such bias without showing a lack of self-respect.

First, Kevin takes part in a political process resulting in the coercive enforcement of laws governing compatriots, not foreigners. Because morally responsible people specially value relationships of mutual respect and trust, they regard it as specially important not to take part in the coercive imposition of arrangements that participants could not rationally, self-respectfully uphold. After all, in specially valuing a relationship, one both regards participation in it as providing a special reason for appropriate forms of concern *and* regards its opposites as relationships one has special reason to avoid – the more powerful the opposition, the stronger the reason. If I specially value friendship, I must be specially concerned not to tyrannize others – even more concerned than I must be to avoid benefiting from others' tyrannizing. Similarly, if I specially value relationships of mutual respect and trust, I must be specially concerned to avoid coercively dominating others in ways that they could not self-respectfully uphold, and this concern should take priority over my interest in alleviating inferior life-prospects due to rules for self-advancement in whose creation and coercive enforcement I do not participate. Kevin, then, expresses his commitment to equal respect for all, not his disrespect for Khalid, in Kevin's special concern for life-prospects determined by rules he helps to impose. And Khalid, for his part, shows no lack of self-respect in accepting a moral code requiring such special concern of the likes of Kevin. The endorsement of rules reflecting an attitude that makes it rational to have equal respect for all can entail no loss of self-respect.

In the second place, the different baselines appropriate to assessing the impact on life-prospects of domestic and of international interactions make the moral pressure to supplement transnational interactions with foreign aid much less than the pressure to add policies of aid to domestic economic arrangements. We can attribute domestic inequalities in life-prospects on the scale of those separating Kevin and Carla to their domestic institutions because, in the absence of enduring, effectively enforced domestic institutions, everyone's life-prospects would be virtually nil, as compared with their actual life-prospects. International inequalities in life-prospects are not attributable to transnational institutions to the same extent, since rich and poor economies would differ quite substantially in prosperity in the absence of interaction between them. Indeed, the miserable record of per-capita poor countries that have pursued autarky suggests that the benefit of current interaction to those affected in poor countries is an improvement in life-prospects on the scale of corresponding improvements in rich countries. In some cases, there is, no doubt, an exploitive inequality. Still, the difference in the relevant baselines makes it much easier for Khalid than for Carla to accept advantages of Kevin's without loss of self-respect.

Even though these arguments for patriotic bias have turned on the need to avoid certain negative phenomena of resentment and unjust domination, the underlying perspective of equal respect makes adequate provision for needy compatriots a legitimate source of pride. One should be all the prouder of improving the world because one has avoided insensitivity to morally relevant differences, in the process of world-improvement. In addition, a morality of equal respect for all has room for a positive appreciation of someone's supporting aid advancing patriotic goals because of her loyalty to her compatriots. A well-integrated person who is committed to the morality of equal respect will have a non-instrumental desire to play an active role in a community in which people care for one another and contribute to the flourishing of common projects whose success is important to the success in life of each. After all, it would not be rational to be so concerned to live by rules that others willingly share, if one were perfectly content to be a harmless isolate or to interact with others on the basis of utterly self-centered goals. This general aspiration to community can certainly be satisfied by international cooperation. Some of us have life-projects and resources permitting us to cooperate in cosmopolitan communities of university intellectuals, social democrats, music lovers, or whatever. However, for most people, the broadest form of communal interaction corresponding to their desires and resources is participation in a national community in which the enhancement of compatriots' well-being and the flourishing of a shared way of life are a source of collective pride. So proud engagement in a national community is a centrally important way of realizing an aspiration of anyone fully committed to the universalist morality of equal respect.

BUDGETARY BIAS

Suppose that a broadly Kantian morality of equal respect for all does require priority of attention to compatriots' needs. The remaining task is to compare the domestic aid and foreign aid columns in the ideal budgets of virtually all per-capita rich countries, to see whether the respective sums express the budgetary bias, according to which the total aid bill that morally responsible citizens must support is very largely devoted to compatriots.

In these ideal ledgers, two general considerations magnify the domestic sum or discount the foreign sum. The magnification is due to the special expensiveness of helping a poor person in a per-capita rich country successfully pursue interests that a morally responsible person will regard as centrally important. For example, in a per-capita rich country, making a valued contribution through interesting work in which one is not bossed around requires a relatively expensive education. Interactions in which one expresses one's personality in ways that are recognized and appreciated require relatively expensive housing and clothing. In a morality of equal *concern* for all, this higher cost of living decently would tend to reduce the amount of provision for the worst-off of per-capita rich countries, since provision for the poor in per-capita poor countries more efficiently satisfies needs. But the same cause has an opposite effect if priority must be given to sustaining social trust and providing incentives for supporting domestic institutions among poor compatriots.

The other general consideration, which systematically reduces the sum in the foreign column, is the sharing of responsibilities for worldwide needs. The arguments so far combine with Goodin's considerations of efficiency to sustain a conclusion that is, in any case, more or less obvious: the better-off people in per-capita rich countries have the only major responsibility to pay taxes to aid their needy compatriots. On the other hand, if there is no difference in benefit from international exploitation and no difference in the proportion of relevantly deprived compatriots, there will be no difference in the extent to which people in different per-capita rich countries have a duty to make sacrifices to help the poor in poor countries. This responsibility is shared among people in rich countries, while their domestic responsibilities are not.

In addition, the perspective of full and equal respect for all ascribes a substantial responsibility for poor compatriots to people in per-capita poor countries, a responsibility quite out of proportion to local resources, based on the moral importance of local autonomy. A self-respecting person will seek participation in control over her government, the coercive apparatus that dominates her life, and (if she would protect the self-respect of others) she will want this control to reflect the ongoing achievement of agreement based on appeals to shared principles. This preference for shared deliberation is served by substantial local responsibility for the poor of poor countries. Dependence on the benevolent will of others who are not bound by shared political deliberations is not to be avoided at all cost, even the cost of starving to death, but it is a form of dependence that a self-respecting person will seek to avoid at serious cost.

Against the background of these general factors magnifying the aid budget for domestic needs and reducing the budget for foreign needs, we must now assess the specific reasons why tax-financed aid to the poor in poor countries might be part of the fair share of world-improvement of people in a rich country. First, the international economic regime might give rise to inequalities in life-prospects that are burdensome to people in poor countries, burdensome in ways that beneficiaries in rich countries could alleviate at much less cost than the alleviation produced. This would be similar enough to the domestic situations dictating tax-financed aid to the disadvantaged to provide a reason for international aid if it entails no significant sacrifice of the domestic projects. However, because of the previously noted differences in baselines of non-interaction, the impact of the international economic regime does not seem dramatically unequal in its effects on life-prospects.

Because the distribution of natural resources is so clearly morally arbitrary and the imposition of barriers to access to natural resources is so obviously in need of justification, those who call for increased foreign aid (a proposal that I am *not* opposing) often emphasize the need to compensate for inequalities in the international division of control over natural resources.[10] However, this specific inequality seems to add little to a case for foreign aid based on unequal benefit from international economic interactions as a whole. Materially based wellbeing in the world at large is almost entirely the consequence of what is done to work up raw materials, which are otherwise usually as valueless as a cup of crude oil in a kitchen. So a case for transfer based on inequality should largely depend on unequal net benefits of whole systems of production and exchange, the argument from exploitive interaction that I have been mitigating. Through this de-emphasis on inequalities in natural resources as such, one avoids the embarrassment of rating the pressure to give on resource-poor Japan as less than the pressure on resource-rich Canada, and one puts no pressure at all on the resource-rich Republic of the Congo.[11]

Another consideration, especially salient from a perspective of equal respect, is the impact of closed borders. Poor foreigners who want to take advantage of the better opportunities for honest self-advancement in rich countries are usually kept out. This creates a duty of concern for consequent increased burdens.[12] But the concern should be shared among rich countries restricting immigration. Moreover, it does not attend to the poor whose local ties and lesser resources make emigration an unattractive option. And it must be balanced against both losses to the home country due to emigration and losses the poor who currently live in per-capita rich countries can suffer when poor immigrants become their compatriots, subjects of patriotic priority.

These are the main reasons for aid to the foreign poor that might be based on specific kinds of interactions with them. With domestic magnification and foreign discounting on the bases previously described, would they create a total aid budget in which foreign aid was more than a small proportion of domestic aid, in any remotely typical per-capita rich country? I have offered reasons to suppose that the answer is "no." There are factual presuppositions in this case for budgetary bias – above all, in the assessment of exploitive international benefits – which cannot be justified quickly, perhaps cannot be justified in the final analysis. But note that a conclusive empirical argument for these presuppositions is not needed to meet the particularist challenge. Many thoughtful people committed to substantial domestic aid have a patriotic budgetary bias that is, itself, conditional on these factual assumptions. For example, *if* they were to conclude that an *un*biased budget could provide the domestic basis for social trust and the adequate political incentive that I have described *and* that such a budget would be needed to return their nation's proportionate share of benefits of interaction with people in poor countries that are exploitive in the sense that I described, then they would not take support for such a budget to violate a moral duty. Their patriotic convictions do not conflict with a universalist morality that makes budgetary bias conditional on their plausible view that the actual extent of international exploitation is not that enormous.

In addition to duties to help the foreign poor that depend on the nature of relationships and interactions with them, there is certainly a prima facie duty to help others just because they are suffering. But the net impact on an ideal budget of this prima facie duty to relieve world suffering is severely constrained, in any remotely typical per-capita rich country, by the combination of the domestic burdens of disadvantage and the limits of the sacrifice that moral responsibility requires as a means to aid the needy to whom one is not bound by morally significant relationships and interactions.

Given the patriotic priority of attention established in previous sections, provision for foreign poverty must not involve a significant departure from the project of relieving serious burdens of domestic inequality. With the possible exception of a few small and specially favored societies, all advanced industrial societies seem to require market-based economic arrangements generating burdensome inequalities, on pain of inefficiency that would make life even worse for the worst-off. On views of the efficacy of domestic aid that cohere with reasonably optimistic views of the efficacy of foreign aid, the totality of laws and policies that could relieve such burdens are diverse, extensive, and financially demanding.

Suppose that all that could be done to help the domestic disadvantaged was done. At that point, in virtually all per-capita rich countries, the burdens of domestic aid would have pushed many of the better-off to a margin at which further transfer on the same scale involves losses not required by equal respect for all (hence, losses that should not be coercively imposed). No doubt, the consequent marginal costs in fatigue, detachment, and nonfulfillment on the part of the better-off would, still, be less important than the associated gains for poor foreigners, on the scale of values of a morally responsible person. Giving up interesting vacations, teaching another class each semester, and moving to a smaller house on a noisy street would be a loss on my part smaller than the gain for someone in Mali benefiting from improved sanitation my sacrifices finance. Still, such a loss, willingly endured just to help the needy, is serious enough to exceed the demands of equal respect for all. Neither the refusal to cushion the falling man at the cost of a broken arm which takes three months to heal nor the refusal to invite a very charming waif to join one's household for a year when he will otherwise starve is an expression of the view that the needy one's life is less valuable than one's own. These are expressions of self-concern falling well short of contempt for others. The losses imposed on the better-off when the project of worldwide aid is pursued well beyond relief of the burdens of domestic disadvantage are as substantial. For example, a rational, responsible, self-respecting professor could choose to endure discomfort as great as suffering from a broken arm that takes three months to heal, or choose to take in a boarder for a year, in exchange for avoiding the losses I have described, losses of a sort that seem inevitable if the overall project of aid is pushed so far beyond its patriotic stage that there is no patriotic budgetary bias, overall.

I do not claim that it is certain that domestic needs are as hard to relieve as these arguments for budgetary priority suppose. But, again, this is not necessary to justify the patriotic bias that most humane people otherwise attracted to universalism actually share. If it were to turn out that the elimination of burdensome domestic life-prospects in per-capita rich countries would leave the better-off free to make a similar, additional sacrifice for the sake of foreign needs while still doing no more than equal respect for all demands, many of those now committed to budgetary bias would abandon this bias, with great joy. The pervasive bias is conditional on a plausible hypothesis about the daunting requirements of domestic aid.

Still, because of her special interest in social trust and in adequate incentives for political cooperation, someone who respects everyone, worldwide, will adopt this plausible pessimism as her working hypothesis. She will insist on budgetary bias until helping her poor compatriots proves to be easier than she fears.

NOTES

Earlier versions of this paper were presented to the New York Society for Philosophy and Public Affairs in 1997 and to the Philosophy Program at the City University of New York Graduate Center in 1998. I am indebted to the subsequent discussions, in which comments by Virginia Held, John Kleinig, William Ruddick, Sybil Schwarzenbach, and others advanced my thinking on these topics. I have also benefited from Henry Shue's incisive criticisms of an earlier draft, comments on related work by Greg Demirchyan, Thad Metz, David Phillips, and Robert Wallace, and suggestions by the editors of *Philosophy and Public Affairs*.

1 David Miller develops a detailed and powerful version of this particularist challenge in (1995), chapter 3. Other recent versions have been presented in criticisms of Nussbaum's cosmopolitan ethic (see especially Fletcher (1994) and Bok (1996)) and in defense of communitarianism (see, for example, Sandel (1996), especially p. 17).

2 See Goodin (1988). He acknowledges that international inequalities can override patriotic restrictions on responsibility, on pp. 684–86.

3 Dagger's appeal to reciprocity (1985) has been especially influential.

4 See especially Hill (1973).

5 See Scanlon (1982), especially pp. 110–17.

6 See Thomson (1971), pp. 48f.

7 For a powerful and detailed portrayal of the trusting and respectful political practice in which participants seek common ground through principled persuasion, see Cohen (1989).

8 The milieu that is jeopardized includes the "friendly civic relations" whose nature and value Schwarzenbach describes (1996), with illuminating reference to Aristotle's account of *politike philia*.

9 See Scheffler (1997), especially pp. 196, 206. However, in using a comprehensive morality of equal respect to balance special obligations to compatriots against obligations to the poor of the world, I am resisting Scheffler's pessimism about the availability of a single moral outlook which gives adequate scope both to special responsibilities and relationship-independent duties to help the disadvantaged (see pp. 207f). I agree that no single moral outlook can integrate the proper valuing of special relationships with the pursuit of overall distributive fairness if the latter must express equal or impartial concern for all. But here, as elsewhere, the identification of moral equality with equal respect is a basis for cautious optimism about the capacities of universalist moral theory.

10 Thus, in (1994b), Pogge's central proposal to reduce international inequality is a global resources tax, because this is "an institutional proposal that virtually any plausible egalitarian conception of global justice would judge to be at least a step in the right direction" (p. 199). Beitz begins his pioneering argument for a global original position by noting that the unequal distribution of natural resources would create a Rawlsian reason to reduce international inequality regardless of the status of international interactions (1975, pp. 288–95).

11 Neither Pogge nor Beitz, I should add, regards the unequal distribution of natural resources as the centrally important aspect of international inequality in the final analysis, given the actual nature of worldwide economic activity.

12 As I argued in (Miller, 1992), pp. 299f.

CHAPTER 10

Persons' interests, states' duties, and global governance

Darrel Moellendorf

I

The central claim of cosmopolitanism is that we owe duties of justice to all the persons of the world. If this claim is true, it would seem to have profound implications for the arrangement and powers of institutions of governance. Agreement about the truth of the central claim of cosmopolitanism is consistent with significant disagreement about its requirements. One source of this disagreement has to do with the content of justice. I shall not focus much on this matter here. Another source has to do with which duties of justice are global. Disagreements arise about whether certain duties of justice are owed to compatriots or to non-compatriots. Varieties of cosmopolitanism may be different responses to the fact that global governance is currently for the most part delegated to states.

In this essay I shall argue that the best account of duties of justice is as associative duties. I then discuss whether a global association exists; although the evidence is not unambiguous, it seems to support the view that there is an economic association. I go on to argue that taking duties of global justice seriously is consistent with ignoring or discounting certain interests of non-compatriots within a system of global governance that includes states. But just global governance requires at least global institutions that would ensure that duties of distributive justice are fulfilled and global or regional institutions to protect other interests of persons in cases of state failure.

Most of what I say about the content of justice is insufficient. I assert little more than I need in order to discuss the role of the state and global institutions in securing global justice. Nor do I discuss other pressing matters of global justice, such as the distribution of costs associated with global climate change and combating infectious diseases and the global institutions and regulatory regimes required by the existence of national militaries, currencies, and trade rivalries. Clearly, a full account of global governance requires much more than I can offer here.

II

The best defense of the central claim of cosmopolitanism must be based in part upon contingent facts about the world in which we live, facts of the association of persons in particular (Moellendorf, 2002, pp. 31–39). Suppose that facts about the world are unimportant to the central claim of cosmopolitanism, and that the claim follows from the demands of personhood alone (O'Neill, 2000, p. 194). This view seems implausible in light of the heavy burdens of duties of justice. Two features of the duties of justice make them particularly burdensome. The first is that in very many cases they require action, not merely non-interference. For example, a proper response to the violation of important liberties requires restraining and perhaps even prosecuting and punishing the violator. The second feature can also be seen from the preceding example. Duties of justice often require institutional construction and maintenance.

An application of the account of the burdens of justice to a thought experiment indicates a problem with claiming that duties of justice are owed to all persons regardless of association. Imagine persons in two societies, A and B, separated by some great distance (which is of course technologically relative), which have no on-going interaction, but are aware of the existence of each other and have a general understanding of their respective circumstances. Perhaps they have sent emissaries on one or two occasions or they receive annual news from each other. I assume that basic moral duties exist between persons across this divide. The claim that in addition duties of justice exist, entails that if persons in A are aware that persons in B do not enjoy, say, freedom of conscience, then the persons in A have a prima facie duty to intervene in the affairs of B to protect the liberties of persons there, even to the extent of constructing and maintaining institutions to protect these liberties. This conclusion is not absurd, but it seems highly implausible.

Given the demands of justice, it is more plausible to limit the persons to whom it extends. The limit I believe to be most sensible is the border of associations. This is not completely satisfactory since the category of association is somewhat vague. An association is an interaction of a special type. An association is strong to the extent that it is enduring, comprehensively governed by institutional norms, and regularly affecting the highest order moral interests of the persons associated. Weak associations blur into mere interactions. And so the limit between where an association ends and interaction begins is not always clear. Nonetheless certain applications are. The modern state is an association. A group of friends in discussion is not. Determining where an association exists often requires careful attention to facts.

The vagueness that results from limiting the duties of justice to the borders of associations could be avoided if they were limited instead to relationships in which persons interact directly with the possibility of causing harm. For example A has a duty of justice to B if and only if A has harmed B or A could harm B.[1] This, however, would limit the persons obligated beyond what is plausible. For according to this account a person's duty of justice to the vast majority of her compatriots is negligible since her causal relation to them is weak.

Another possibility would be to limit claims of justice to societies in which people actually cooperate for mutual advantage (Barry, 1982). This would eliminate considerable vagueness. A duty of justice would exist between two people only if their interaction produced mutual benefits. But this suffers from the same problem as the account that would limit duties of justice to persons who interact directly. It would rule out too many cases in which intuitively duties of justice exist. For example, if A were sufficiently oppressed by B, justice would not govern then the relationship between A and B.

The most plausible view holds that duties of justice are associative duties. They are special duties that we have to other persons due, in part, to the kind of association that we have with them. But it is implausible to claim that associations bring moral duties into existence where none existed before. If A and B have no moral duties at all to one another, why would they have any when they became associates? The more plausible view is that duties of justice develop out of pre-existing moral duties. Pre-existing moral duties become fruitful and multiply themselves in the richness of an association.

There is nothing unusual about claiming that relationships change the character of general moral duties. For example, suppose that we have a duty of equal respect to all persons, but that I make a promise to my colleague to help her move her belongings. In this case, respect may require that I treat my colleague differently than everyone else, namely that I help her move her belongings. Something analogous is true of associations. If a group of people find themselves taking shelter together during a hurricane, equal respect requires that they establish a manner of distributing the emergency provisions that is fair to all.

Not all associations generate duties of justice, however. Clubs are associations that generate moral duties. But the duties generated are not duties of justice. The reason for this has to do with both the scope of the effects of membership in structuring public life and the nature of one's membership. One's fraternal relationships do not structure the background of one's public relationships, although they may occasionally be a source of significant advantage. Moreover, membership in clubs is largely voluntary and typically may be renounced with comparatively few opportunity costs. Duties of justice arise among persons when their on-going association is largely non-voluntary and constitutes a significant part of the background for the various relationships of their public lives. And duties of egalitarian justice, in particular, arise in this situation if all persons are owed a morally basic duty of equal respect.

Another source of vagueness in this account of duties of justice is evident. Whether an association is sufficiently extensive in its reach or effects to constitute a significant part of the background of the public lives of persons will at times be difficult to assess and may be relative to societal institutions and norms. For example, whether families create duties of justice between family members will depend upon the extent of the effects of family life. Although we might wish to purge vagueness from our account of justice on grounds of ease of application, the indeterminacy, as expressed in the family example, seems appropriate.

Two noteworthy consequences follow. First, different kinds of associations might have principles of justice that differ in content. The principles of justice that govern the association might protect only those moral interests that the association affects. For example, suppose that all persons have fundamental security rights. From the fact that A and B are engaged in an association that affects their access to resources, it *might* not follow that A has a duty to construct and maintain institutions to ensure that B enjoys her security rights. Second, associations might generate duties of justice when they provide part of the background for the various public relationships of persons. The modern world is complex and persons are members of multiple associations that generate duties of justice, such as provinces, states, and the global economy.

III

The sort of contingent facts that would justify the central claim of cosmopolitanism then would be facts that justify the view that a global association exists, that it is largely non-voluntary, and that it is a significant part of the context of one's various public relationships. The principles of justice that would follow from this sort of global association would depend upon the moral interests that this association affects. Some political philosophers are skeptical that duties of distributive justice can be derived from a global economic association alone, even if there is one (Miller, 2004). The general idea is that only political associations generate duties of justice because political ideals make concerns about social inequality particularly pressing. I think it would be hard to deny the premise but I doubt that it entails the conclusion. The claim that we are rightfully concerned to limit inequalities if we are committed to political equality does not entail that there are no other grounds for limiting inequality.

An economic association can have profound effects on its members' public lives. It can determine their opportunities for advancement, leisure, and longevity as well as their access to education and health care, opportunities for political participation, and the pursuit of worthwhile personal goals. Moreover, such an association may be non-voluntary. Respect for persons requires that we consider the fairness of the association's distribution of the benefits and burdens, in other words its distributive justice. Consider John Rawls's intuitive approach:

The intuitive notion here is that this structure contains various social positions and that men born into different positions have different expectations of life determined, in part, by the political system as well as by social circumstances. In this way the institutions of society favor certain starting places over others. These are especially deep inequalities. (Rawls, 1999b, p. 7)

We should be concerned about fairness domestically because the basic structure assigns people to very unequal positions regarding what they can expect over the course of their lives. If we take equal respect seriously, such inequality must be a concern since it may be very hard indeed to justify such unequal life expectations to those who are underprivileged. But the same considerations would apply to a global economic association as well.

Consider some of the evidence of increasing global economic association noted by the United Nations Development Programme (UNDP, 1999, p. 25):

World exports averaged 21 percent of a state's GDP in the late 1990s compared to an average of 17 percent in the 1970s.
Foreign direct investment (FDI) reached $400 billion in 1997, seven times the levels in real terms of the 1970s.

The daily turnover in foreign exchange markets increased from $10–20 billion in the 1970s to $1.5 trillion in 1998.

International bank lending grew from $265 billion in 1975 to $4.2 trillion in 1994.

An increase in world exports from 17 to 21 percent is impressive. Moreover the poorest countries are the most deeply integrated into world trade. For example, sub-Saharan Africa had an export to GDP ratio of 29 percent as compared to 15 percent for Latin America (UNDP, 1999, p. 31). Nonetheless these figures are hardly resounding evidence of a global economic association. The skeptic could argue that the vast majority of economic activity still occurs within state borders and not across them. Additionally, the growth in FDI does not clinch the cosmopolitan case since many countries, indeed the poorest, have hardly been recipients of this at all. Of the $400 billion of FDI noted above, 58 percent went to developed countries and only 37 percent to developing countries, and of the latter 80 percent went to just twenty countries, China in particular (UNDP, 1999, p. 31). The last and second to last countries on the UNDP's human development index in 1999, Sierra Leone and Niger, had net investment inflows of only $4 million and $1million respectively (UNDP, 1999, p. 56).

One response is to argue that a threshold of economic integration is not required. Charles Beitz claims the following:

The justification of international principles does not depend on the extent of existing patterns of international interaction or the details of the institutions that organize them. On the other hand, if there were no international basic structure – if for example, there were no appreciable international capital flows, little trade, no international economic institutions, and only rudimentary forms of international law – then we would not find principles of international distributive justice of any practical interest. (Beitz, 1999, p. 539)

Suppose that the existence of even minimal global integration suffices for claiming that justice applies since justice would apply to those activities and institutions that are producing integration. This is consistent with the associational nature of duties of justice, but given the facts about FDI in the poorest countries and their level of exports, it is not clear that this view would support a *global* principle of distributive justice that binds persons in the wealthy states to those in the poorer ones. Additionally, suppose that the argument for other non-distributive duties of global justice rests on the existence of an economic association (as I shall argue), it would then seem that not much at all follows about *global* justice from this argument. If the world is insufficiently integrated economically, it is all the more doubtful that it is sufficiently integrated politically. For the political integration of the world is decidedly less advanced than the economic integration.

A great deal would seem to hang on the existence of a global economic association. There are several reasons to think that there is a stronger global economic association than the figures noted above might suggest. First, even if trade does not constitute the majority of any state's GDP, it does have a profound impact on the economies of very many countries. The Asian economic crisis of the late 1990s had huge ripple effects. States with economies heavily dependent upon exporting basic resources such as petroleum and precious metals expected dramatic declines in their GDP as a result of the Asian crisis, 14 to 18 percent in Angola and Kuwait and 9 percent in Zambia (UNDP, 1999, p. 41).

In trying to make sense of the interconnected nature of the global economy Robert Keohane and Joseph Nye, Jr. have employed the terms "network effects" and "network interconnections" to refer to complicated and not well-understood causal connections that make the prediction of global economic and political phenomena difficult.

Unexpectedly, what appeared first as an isolated banking and currency crisis in a small "emerging market" country, had severe global effects. It generated financial panic elsewhere in Asia . . . prompted emergency meetings at the highest level of world finance and huge "bail-out" packages . . . and led to widespread loss of confidence in emerging markets and the efficacy of international financial institutions. Before that contagious loss of confidence was stemmed, Russia had defaulted on its debt (August 1998), and a huge US-based hedge fund, Long Term Capital Management, had to be rescued . . . Even after the recovery had begun, Brazil required a huge IMF loan, coupled with devaluation, to avoid financial collapse in January 1999. (Keohane and Nye Jr., 2000a, pp. 199, 200)

Trade figures alone would not have predicted these effects. And their existence is reason to believe that there is more to the global economic association than trade figures suggest.

Additionally, the FDI figures noted above may minimize the actual importance of foreign investment in global capital formation. Victor F. S. Sit argues that FDI in 1997 was 64 percent of the world's gross fixed capital formation (Sit, 2001, p. 12). Moreover the FDI figures may fail to note the full effect of foreign investment in domestic economies by a substantial amount since foreign investment is often a condition of domestic financing and financing from third-party countries. According to Sit, total FDI related investment after adjusting for these other sources is about four times that normally measured in official statistics (Sit, 2001, p. 13). Additionally, as the UNDP and many others have observed, competition to attract foreign investment leads countries to make significant changes in their regulatory regimes. "The pressures of global competition have led countries and employers to adopt more flexible labour policies, and work arrangements with no long-term commitment between employer and employee are on the rise" (UNDP, 1999, p. 37).

Finally, the role of international financial institutions in the global economic association is noteworthy. In his survey of International Monetary Fund (IMF) and World Bank lending between 1980 and 1998, William Easterly put together a database of 126 loans (Easterly, 2000). Between 1987 and 1991 loans to the low-income, debt-distressed countries in Africa (most of these have relatively little FDI), amounted to 15.4 percent of the countries' real GDP and 75 percent of real imports (World Bank, 1994). The conditionality associated with IMF and World Bank loans from the 1980s onward gave these financial institutions considerable voice in the policies of poor countries that were in many other ways not greatly integrated into the global economy.

Economic integration resulting from trade, FDI, and the activity of international financial institutions seems to support the belief that a global economic association exists. Moreover, the case for a global economic association is likely to grow stronger with time as the tendency seems to be toward increasing integration. One barrier to further integration is the protectionism of the developed world. The United Nations Conference on Trade and Development (UNCTAD) estimates that low technology countries are together losing out on $700 billion per year in export earnings due to protectionism in the developed world. This amounts to more than four times the annual capital inflow into the developing world due to FDI (UNCTAD, 1999). These tariffs have come under scrutiny and criticism in part as a result of the establishment of the World Trade Organization, which many developing countries had hoped would bring greater access to developed world markets. Such criticism may serve eventually to be a unifying point for developing countries, and thereby enhance their bargaining position vis-à-vis the developed world, ultimately effecting greater integration.

IV

Accepting that people owe duties of justice to all the persons of the world does not decide the matter of which duties are owed and whether different duties may be owed to different persons on the basis of their citizenship. So, the central claim of cosmopolitanism does not entail that persons owe all other persons of the world, regardless of citizenship, the same duties. Furthermore, if we assume that states mediate duties between persons, the central claim of cosmopolitanism does not entail that, in the normal course of things, states owe non-citizens the same treatment as they owe their citizens and residents (Shue, 1988). Indeed this latter view is probably inconsistent with a working international system of states since it would require state expenditures for everything from education, infrastructure, policing, and defense to be allotted so as to provide equal treatment by each state for all persons of the world. Even if a system of interstate transfers could be devised to achieve this end, states, as we know them, would have little point. If states have any moral justification, then a plausible cosmopolitan view will have to be somewhere between the view that states may completely neglect the claims of non-citizens, barring exceptional circumstances, and the view that states owe all the persons of the world equal treatment.

Consider the following claims about the relative importance of non-citizens' interests in state policy:

(A) States may discount some of the interests (that justice protects) of non-citizens to some degree short of complete neglect all of the time.
(B) States may discount some of the interests (that justice protects) of non-citizens to some degree only under appropriate circumstances.
(C) States may ignore some of the interests (that justice protects) of non-citizens all of the time.
(D) States may ignore some of the interests (that justice protects) of non-citizens only under appropriate circumstances.

Recall that my claim above was a conditional one. If states have any moral justification, then a plausible cosmopolitan view will have to be somewhere between the view that states may completely neglect the claims of non-citizens, barring exceptional circumstances, and the view that states owe all the persons of the world equal treatment. The antecedent of the conditional, that states have some moral justification, is slightly controversial among cosmopolitans.[2] In section VI, I offer reasons for accepting the antecedent.

In each of the above four formulations one could substitute "some of the interests" with "all of the interests" to get four additional formulations. But the resulting claims would be inconsistent with cosmopolitanism, as I understand it. Given the facts of globalization and the moral requirement of equal respect, there are certain interests of non-citizens that can neither be discounted nor ignored, for example their interest in a fair scheme of distribution of the benefits and burdens of the global economic association.

One might contend that duties directed toward these interests can be fulfilled by the state of which a person is a citizen or resident. This is false. The requirement of fairness ranges over all of the benefits and burdens of the global association. In the absence of global institutions of distributive justice, the resources of, say, Malawi cannot be distributed to Malawi citizens in any way that would allow a citizen of France to meet her duties of justice to the citizen of Malawi. So, to fulfill the duties of distributive justice among non-compatriots, states must respond through a distribution scheme that treats equally the interests of all persons in the global association.

v

What are the merits of the four claims listed above? It is not possible to evaluate claims that it is consistent with justice to discount or ignore some interests of non-citizens without some discussion of which interests generally are the proper concern of justice. For example, if the ground of global justice is an economic association, perhaps the proper concern of global justice includes only economic interests. The argument of this section will be somewhat circuitous, for it will amount to a defense of claims (b), (c), and (d), but the defense will require offering reasons to believe that the global economic association provides grounds for defending liberal and democratic rights and liberties.

Let's turn first to claims (c) and (d), that there are interests of non-citizens that states may sometimes ignore. Suppose that global justice requires that all persons' basic liberties be secured. An individual state may do this very well. A global system of states, each of which preserves basic liberties for its citizens and residents, may relieve the individuals of the world from having to secure these liberties for all others (Goodin, 1988). In such a system states could ignore some of the interests of non-citizens. The example's limitation to states that preserve basic liberties entails that (d) is true, namely that states may ignore some of the interests (the interests associated with enjoying basic liberties) of non-citizens only under appropriate circumstances and that (c) is false with respect to those interests. For if the justification for ignoring basic liberties of citizens of other states is simply that they are secured by their states, then the interests may not be ignored when not secured by those states.

The argument of the previous paragraph, however, rests on a supposition, namely that global justice requires that persons' basic liberties be secured. This might not follow from the global *economic* association. There are two reasons, however, to believe that it does. First, realizing the goods of economic association requires basic liberties, among others freedom of contract, movement, and unionization. And, freedom of conscience and thought are required in order to exercise one's own judgements about how to evaluate the fruits of the economic association. Second, although the association may be economic, the interests that it affects are not only economic. Rather, other fundamental moral interests are also affected, such as the ability of a person to live a life that is in significant ways chosen. Economic associations threaten such interests routinely. Hence, the existence of an economic association engenders other duties of justice in addition to duties of distributive justice.

The foregoing argument expands the list of interests of non-citizens that states must sometimes protect from economic ones to other basic liberties. Must states also act sometimes to secure the *democratic* rights of non-citizens? Suppose that states are justified because they fulfill the duties of protecting basic liberties that all persons have to one another. If democratic states ensure such liberties better than non-democratic ones, then there is a derivative duty to help construct and maintain democratic state structures. This instrumentalist consideration is, of course, not the only defense of democracy. Institutions required by global justice, on whatever grounds, should function according to principles that are consistent with the basic values that generate duties of global justice in the first place. The operation of public institutions according to principles of majority rule and non-exclusion may be required by respect for persons. Additionally, democratic deliberation may be the best means for reaching an understanding of the content of economic needs.[3]

Are there any reasons in support of (c), that states may ignore some of the interests (that justice protects) of non-citizens all of the time? I have argued that due to the global economic association non-compatriots have duties either to protect the basic liberties of all or to establish and maintain states, which protect these liberties for their citizens. But states are associations that generate duties of justice; and these duties would seem to be candidates for duties that exist only between compatriots. Perhaps then there is a duty among non-compatriots to establish and to help sustain states that protect the basic liberties of citizens and a duty only among compatriots to ensure fairness within the political process. The moral ground of the first duty follows from an economic association, while the moral ground for the second might follow only from the political association that (in the best case) fulfills the first duty. This would not be altogether surprising. For in other cases institutions that ensure that certain moral duties are fulfilled between persons can be the grounds for additional moral duties with a narrower scope. For example, citizens have a duty to protect one another that is fulfilled in part by a judicial system; and within that judicial system lawyers have special duties of zealous representation only to clients.

Perhaps, historically, states have come into existence where there was some pre-existing social or political association. But the erection of a legal edifice creates additional duties, such as for example equal treatment under the law. One candidate for a duty between compatriots only is the duty to ensure equal protection under municipal law. Another is the duty between compatriots to ensure that social inequalities do not undermine the democratic ideal of equal opportunity to participate in the governance of the state. Is it plausible that non-compatriots may have duties to one another to construct and support states that protect basic liberties and democratic rights, but that they do not have duties to ensure that the citizens of these states maintain these other requirements of justice within the state?

Here we seem to be pulled in opposite directions. On the one hand, the idea of democracy presupposes that a populace be able to determine its political fate. Duties to non-citizens to support fairness within states would narrow the scope of democratic self-determination considerably. On the other hand, we are supposing that states have duties to non-citizens to construct and support states that secure basic liberties and democratic rights, and equal participation under the law and equal opportunity to participate in governance would seem to be covered by these liberties and rights. This last claim is a strong reason to take equal protection and equal participation as objects of global duties. Moreover, doing so may still be consistent with respecting a measure of democratic self-determination. If the interests in equal protection under the law and equal opportunity to participate in governance are to be treated along with the interests in basic liberty and democratic rights, then principle (D) would apply to them, which is to say that states may ignore them for non-citizens if and only if they are being satisfied by their states. However, some room remains for the politics of self-government. This room is defined by the scope of the basic structure of domestic society.[4] States may, indeed must, ignore the interests of non-citizens that are not interests normally secured by the basic structure. This provides a defense of (c), that states may ignore some of the interests that justice protects (namely those that the basic structure does not protect) of non-citizens all of the time.

Turning now to claims (A) and (B), are there interests of non-citizens that states may discount, rather than ignore, some or all of the time? Here is a reason to believe so: the force of duties of justice is proportional to the degree of association. This claim is plausible if duties of justice are by nature associative duties. Hence, the interests of persons with whom we are only weakly associated generate weaker duties. And therefore states as mediators of duties between persons may discount the interests of those with whom the state's citizens are only weakly associated. This is, then, a defense of (B), that states may discount some of the interests of non-citizens to some degree only under appropriate circumstances.

This argument does not, however, support (A) that there are interests of non-citizens that states may discount all of the time since the permission to discount interests is contingent on a weak association. Indeed, it is hard to imagine interests of non-citizens that states could in all situations discount, if this means that these interests are recognized as making demands, but demands that in all circumstances are weaker than those of citizens. This would not follow from the existence of sub-associations since the ignorable claims of (c) make no demands on non-compatriots (not weaker ones). So, it is hard to see how it would follow at all.

The practical force of the argument in support of (B) would be that in making trade-offs between the interests of citizens and those of non-citizens, with whom citizens are only weakly associated, under conditions of resource scarcity, states would have a reason to prefer citizens. This is not to say that there may not be other reasons to prefer non-citizens. The severity of need of non-citizens may be much greater, for example. Hence, moral casuistry in this regard might be complicated.

The argument for discounting the interests of non-citizens where the association is weak has several practical limitations. In a system of global governance that preserves some role for states, states would mediate certain of the duties between persons. So, if the citizens of state X have more to do with persons in one particular region of state Y than with persons in other regions, then the fact that the duties of the citizens of state X with respect to the citizens of state Y are mediated by the interactions of the two state structures will often require that the citizens of state X treat all citizens of Y equally. For the citizens of state Y must be ensured equal protection under the law by their state structure. Moreover, there is probably no accurate way to grade associations for the strength of duties that they generate. All distinctions will be rough, imperfect, and somewhat intuitive. Treating various non-citizens differently on the basis of their citizenship, where citizenship is taken as an indicator of strength of association, may engender resentment that is unhelpful for other forms of global cooperation. This is especially the case if the second practical limitation is true, since justified different treatment may be hard to distinguish from invidious discrimination.

The upshot of this section is that states are permitted to ignore all of the time those interests of non-citizens that typically are not protected by the basic structure of states, other interests if and only if they are protected by suitable state or global structures, and that states are permitted to discount all of those duties that its citizens have to those non-citizens with whom they are only weakly associated, although in practice such discounting may be very hard to achieve without prohibitively high moral costs.

VI

What institutions does this account entail? Would a just global order contain states? Would it require global institutions as well? The argument of sections IV and V assumed the existence of states and considered what the implications of the existence of states would be for the assignment of the duties of global justice. There are good reasons for thinking that a just global order would contain states. It is quite likely that the best way to secure many basic liberties and democratic participation would be through a system of global governance that includes states with limited sovereignty with respect to certain functions in a territory. This is, of course, a speculative conclusion and not an empirical generalization since the majority of existing states are not particularly good at securing basic liberties. According to the UNDP, 106 countries still restrict important liberal and democratic freedoms (UNDP, 2002a). But presumably states could do a better job with appropriate changes. In addition, limited jurisdiction over a piece of territory smaller in size than the whole globe does not place nearly as much power in the hands of political leaders as would jurisdiction over the whole globe. Limited jurisdiction allows for greater ability to resist oppression from the inside and the possibility of resisting it from the outside as well. Additionally, institutions of governance at the state level, as opposed to the global level, would more easily accord with the democratic ideal of providing persons with an equal opportunity to participate since the sheer scale of global institutions requires greater political distance between those who run them and those who are affected by them.

Suppose that a state fails to ensure basic liberal and democratic liberties and rights. The duty to do so then reverts to persons of the world and their agents. I have been assuming in the previous sections that their agents would be the states of which they are citizens. If so, then the various states of the world would have duties to address the injustice where possible and where the moral costs of doing so are not disproportionate. This may not be the best system of governance to address the problems of state failure. Instead, international or regional actors may be more disinterested, may have greater legitimacy, and have greater material capacity than individual states. Moreover, international and regional deliberative bodies may be better able impartially to weigh the reasons for and against intervening on behalf of justice.

According to the version of cosmopolitanism that I am defending, an abiding concern of global justice is meeting the duties of distributive justice. The present global economic association contains massive inequalities. In Rawls's words, these inequalities are "especially deep." For example, the total income of the world's richest 1 percent of people is equal to that of the poorest 57 percent (UNDP, 2002b, p. 19). For a great many people extreme poverty is a problem: 1.3 billion people live on less than a $1 Purchasing Power Parity a day; the same number lack access to clean water; and 840 million children are malnourished (UNDP, 1999, p. 28). The United Nation's International Children's Emergency Fund (UNICEF) reports that 30,500 children under five die every day of mainly preventable causes (UNICEF, 2000).

It is inconceivable that an account of justice that is based upon equal respect for persons could tolerate this poverty. There is no plausible defense of the claim that these destitute children deserve their condition. Nor have they freely contracted with others only to find that their investment of work or capital did not realize expected gains. It would be disrespectful to claim that their plight is a permissible outcome of their parents' mistakes. Discounting their misery against the greater good enjoyed by others (even if it were optimal), fails to take their claims seriously.

If distributive justice requires addressing global inequality, redistribution within states alone is inadequate. For state-level institutions can only fulfill whatever duties of distributive justice exist between compatriots. Just global governance will require global institutions at least to insure that duties of distributive justice are fulfilled. These institutions will have to gather revenue globally and monitor resource provision within various states.

With regard solely to the core content of justice – the duties to protect liberal and democratic liberties and rights and the claims of distributive justice – a minimally adequate system of global governance requires an international system of reasonably just states, global or regional bodies to handle situations of state failure, and global institutions to address social inequality. Although my limited focus has not allowed me to discuss matters of global climate change and infectious disease, I assume that some sort of egalitarian sharing of the costs associated with these follows from a defense of egalitarian distributive justice. Additionally, regimes of global governance will require institutions for reasons that do not flow directly from justice. The reasoning will often indirectly rely on justice but more directly upon the lessons of history. History has demonstrated that the international state system requires a forum for states to engage in conflict resolution and cooperation, that international trade requires management, and that states may have problems meeting their financial obligations and stabilizing their currencies and therefore require international lending institutions. Nothing that I have argued here is meant to deny such arguments from history.

NOTES

My thanks to those in the audience at Bennington College who offered comments on an earlier version of this paper and to Patrick Hayden and Paul Voice for criticisms. I am grateful to the James Hervey Johnson Charitable Educational Trust for a grant that helped me to complete the paper.
1 Thomas Pogge holds that one has a duty not to allow the institutions that one cooperates in to harm others. (Cf. Pogge, 2002, p. 171.)
2 For defenses of a global state see Nielsen (1988), Singer (2002, p. 199) and Cabrera (2004).
3 This point runs through much of Sen (1999). See pp. 78–79, 80, 110, 147–48, 153–54.
4 Cf. Rawls (1999b, pp. 6–7) for the general account of the basic structure.

CHAPTER II

The demands of justice and national allegiances

Kok-Chor Tan

Basic to the idea of nationality is the belief that individuals have special ties and loyalties to their fellow nationals, and that these ties and loyalties can generate certain special obligations among co-nationals. This claim of national allegiances presents an obvious challenge for global distributive justice. The challenge is most acute when global justice is conceived in cosmopolitan terms. On the cosmopolitan view, individuals are entitled to equal consideration regardless of nationality (e.g., Beitz, 1979, 1983; Nussbaum, 1996, 2000; Pogge, 1989, 1998b). A cosmopolitan conception of justice is thus impartial with respect to people's particular national membership. With respect to *distributive* justice, which is my focus here, this view suggests that what counts as a just global distribution of resources and goods is to be determined independently of the actual national allegiances that people have. Yet this understanding of distributive justice seems to be radically at odds with the widely and deeply held commonsense moral belief that individuals may, or are even required to, show special concern for their co-nationals. The requirements of cosmopolitan justice and the fact of national allegiances thus seem to impose conflicting claims on individuals.

If the cosmopolitan idea of justice is to have any appeal for human beings, it must acknowledge the local attachments and commitments people have that are characteristic of most meaningful and rewarding human lives. Among the special ties and commitments that people share are those of nationality. The challenge for cosmopolitans, therefore, is to show how they can accommodate and account for national allegiances *without* compromising their motivating and fundamental commitment to global equality. A theory of global justice that does not accommodate and properly account for the special ties and obligations of shared nationality would not be a theory of justice suited for humanity.

It is worth noting here that the problem of national allegiances does not *only* present a challenge for global egalitarians. It also poses a challenge for liberal theory *itself.* On the one hand, liberalism is believed by many to be cosmopolitan in its aspiration; on the other, it is an increasingly popular view that liberals are also liberal *nationalists.*[1] Indeed Yael Tamir calls nationalism "a hidden agenda" of liberalism, and she writes that "most liberals are also liberal nationalists" (Tamir, 1993, p. 139). If liberal nationalism is an acceptable doctrine, and if national allegiances and cosmopolitan justice do in fact impose conflicting demands on individuals, there is then a serious tension within liberal theory itself – between its cosmopolitan vision, on the one side, and its (hidden) nationalist agenda, on the other.

One way the demands of cosmopolitan justice and the fact of national allegiances may be reconciled is to treat cosmopolitan justice as an "institutional ideal" that is primarily concerned with the global "basic structure" (to borrow Rawls's term) (Rawls, 1971).[2] Cosmopolitans would require that global institutions be informed by principles that treat individuals as equals regardless of their particular national membership. Cosmopolitan principles are to be impartial with respect to nationality in this sense. But within the parameters of a just global structure (i.e. a global structure informed by cosmopolitan principles), individuals may pursue their particular commitments, even nationally derived or based ones, so long as the rules of the global basic structure permit. Cosmopolitan principles, then, are principles *for* the background global institutions within which people (individually or socially, through their national communities, for instance) interact; but it does not directly regulate the choices that people may make within the rules of institutions. Thus, in a just global context, when the resources that a nation actually holds, do *as a matter of justice* belong to it, members of this nation may do with these resources as they wish, including using them to promote specially the interests of their co-nationals, so long as the overall rules of the global basic structure are preserved.[3]

So, while cosmopolitan justice need not reject the exercise of national partiality as such, it requires that the exercise of such partial consideration be confined within the rules of institutional justice *that* are not themselves shaped or influenced by national allegiances. To put the point in a different way, cosmopolitans demand *national impartiality* at the level of the global basic structure, but allow for co-national *partiality* within the rules of a just global structure.[4]

To illustrate this point, let us assume that an impartial consideration of the needs of individuals in the world would require, among other things, a global resource taxation program of the sort envisioned by Thomas

Pogge. The taxation scheme serves to meet the requirements of cosmopolitan justice that takes nationality to be irrelevant from the moral point
of view. That is, it is a part of an institutional scheme that treats individuals equally regardless of their nationality. But within the rules of
this scheme, people may use their post-tax resources and wealth to
further their particular national ends, or any other local commitments
for that matter, so long as the rules of the just scheme permit (Rawls,
2001, pp. 50, 54).

So cosmopolitan justice sets limits on what kinds of national allegiances
individuals may claim. There are limits on what members of a nation can
demand of their compatriots in the name of patriotism; and similarly
there are limits to what members of a nation can do to members of other
nations. One of the central aims of a liberal theory of nationalism is to
establish the limits for acceptable kinds of national commitments. Those
who take cosmopolitan distributive equality seriously will insist that
individuals may favor the interests of their fellow nationals only if the
background global context has satisfied certain cosmopolitan requirements. Within the framework of a global institutional setting that regards
the needs of all individuals equally regardless of nationality, national
allegiances may be given expression. What cosmopolitans deny, contrary
to the claims of some nationalists, is that the baseline entitlements of
individuals may be influenced by the national allegiances that people
have.

But some nationalists may take exception to this way of reconciling
cosmopolitan justice and national allegiances. I will consider two possible
objections. The first is that the subordination of nationality to cosmopolitan justice fails sufficiently to *accommodate* people's national allegiances.
The principles of global justice, on this objection, should be determined
in light of the existing national commitments people have. National
membership is one of the basic factors to be taken into account when
determining what counts as a just global distributive arrangement. To
allow for the expression of national allegiances *only within* the rules of
impartial global justice is to unduly restrict the proper scope of nationality, and the special ties and commitments that a shared nationality
generates. Call this the *accommodation-objection.*

The second objection says that even if this subordination of nationality
to cosmopolitan justice amply allows for the practical expression of the
ties of nationality, it nonetheless fails properly to *account* for the moral
significance of nationality. The subordination of nationality to cosmopolitanism undervalues or under-appreciates the moral significance of

nationality, the objection alleges, because it treats national membership to be *only* instrumental for servicing cosmopolitan ends or principles. Yet national membership can itself be an independent source of moral commitments that are not reducible to some (more) general principles. Cosmopolitanism, in short, cannot provide a proper theory or account of national allegiances. It, on this objection, misconceives the basis of national allegiances. Call this the *conceptual-objection*.

One might say that both objections take cosmopolitan justice to be too demanding in different senses. The accommodation-objection says that it is too demanding in a practical sense – cosmopolitan justice would unreasonably restrict the expression of shared nationality among members of a nation against the demands of cosmopolitan equality. The conceptual-objection says cosmopolitanism is too demanding in a conceptual sense – it is at odds with ordinary people's *conception* of their national allegiances; giving priority to cosmopolitan justice would require people to radically reconceptualize their understanding of their national ties and commitments. At any rate, the instrumentalist view of national allegiance is at odds with how most nationalists understand the ethical basis of nationality. I will further explain, and evaluate, these objections in turn.

ACCOMMODATING ALLEGIANCES

Consider, first, the objection that cosmopolitanism cannot fully accommodate national allegiances. Nationalists who reject the subordination of nationality to cosmopolitan justice do not necessarily reject the idea of global justice per se (see e.g., Miller, 2000, p. 174). What they reject is the cosmopolitan egalitarian ideal that the terms of *distributive* justice ought to be defined independently of people's national commitments.[5] They argue that to confine national allegiances within the rules of cosmopolitan justice is to unduly restrict the realization of such commitments. A proper accommodation of national allegiances must allow people's national affiliations and commitments to shape and limit the kinds of *global* obligations that they may have. To limit people's pursuit of their national commitments against the demands of cosmopolitan justice is to fail to give due regard to the practical requirements of these commitments. National allegiances must be allowed to shape the terms of global justice, and not the other way around as cosmopolitans hold.

This argument can be expressed as an argument in terms of national self-determination. The exercise of national self-determination is one way national allegiances can take expression. The pursuit of national projects and goals free from the interference of others is one way the special ties and loyalties of nationality are reflected and realized. Claims of national self-determination, therefore, ought to limit what global justice can demand of national communities, not the other way around. Or at the very least, the right of national self-determination is one factor to be taken into account when determining what global justice demands. That is, what justice can reasonably demand of people is shaped in part by the national allegiances that people have. As one nationalist theorist puts it, "global justice is not a requirement that sets absolute limits to self-determination, but rather a factor that needs to be balanced against it" (Miller, 2000, p. 178).

To be sure, nationalists can concede that the obligations to "respect basic human rights world-wide" and "to refrain from exploiting vulnerable communities and individuals," do clearly set limits on national self-determination (Miller, 2000, p. 177). But, as the influential nationalist David Miller writes, the obligations of global justice does not extend to showing equal concern in matters of distributive justice to *all* individuals. The "special moral responsibility that compatriots have to one another" is an expression of national allegiance that may limit what global distributive justice can require of individuals (Miller, 2000, pp. 177–78).

The accommodation-objection can thus be summed up in the following question: why should the terms of distributive justice be determined *independently* of people's nationality? That is, should existing national allegiances not be one of the factors that we ought to take into account when determining what individuals owe to each other?

The response to this question, I believe, turns on our general understanding of the concept and role of justice. If we accept that the role of justice is to adjudicate between competing standpoints or claims, then the terms of adjudication by which these claims are to be assessed must be as neutral, or as impartial, as is possible between these competing claims. The terms of adjudication can hardly be described as fair, or even useful, if they are *directly* shaped (and hence distorted) by the views under contention. The ideal of impartiality is thus central to the very concept of justice, and any plausible conception of justice must express this ideal in some appropriate way. As Will Kymlicka neatly puts it, to reject the ideal of justice as impartiality is not to propose an alternative account of justice, but to propose an alternative to justice (Kymlicka, 1990, p. 103). In short, it is basic to the concept of justice that justice takes an impartial perspective with respect to the competing claims that is its purpose to evaluate.

Extending this common understanding of justice to the global context, it follows that the terms of global justice ought to be as impartial as is possible with respect to national standpoints. One central purpose of *global* justice, after all, is to adjudicate and evaluate competing *national* claims and interests; and in order for this adjudicative procedure to be fair, the principles of global justice cannot be shaped or influenced by people's actual national allegiances. They could not be appropriately called principles of global *justice* otherwise. The insistence of nationalists, that existing national commitments may limit and influence the requirements of global justice, therefore, subverts our common understanding of justice. The priority of (nationally) impartial justice over national allegiances derives necessarily from the purpose and concept of justice. To reject an account of global justice that is impartial with respect to nationality (that is, to reject cosmopolitan justice) is not to propose an alternative conception of global justice, but to deny the very idea of global justice.

Global justice properly understood, then, has to be cosmopolitan in the specific sense that it has to be conceived independently of the particular allegiances that individuals have. One cannot reject (this basic aspect of) cosmopolitanism without also rejecting any sensible notion of global justice. To say that global justice must begin from the standpoint of people's national commitments, as some nationalists insist, is to confuse the promotion of national-interests for justice.[6]

It might be said that to restrict national self-determination within the terms of cosmopolitan justice is too demanding because it severely limits what compatriots can in fact distribute to each other. Indeed, some cosmopolitans take this to be a point against liberal nationalism. There is the implication in Gillian Brock's arguments, for example, that some nationalists will find cosmopolitan justice too demanding vis-à-vis their understanding of their national commitments. She points out that liberal nationalists do not "typically request" that one worries about promoting global justice and then worry furthermore about the needs of co-nationals (Brock, 2002, p. 322). The point here, it seems, is that to subordinate nationalist pursuits to the demands of cosmopolitan justice will be seen as overly demanding by nationalists.[7]

However, I am not sure though if taking cosmopolitan equality seriously would radically limit the projects that well-off nations may undertake in the name of national self-determination. Recent studies on globalization have shown, if anything, that even though overall global wealth and production are increasing, inequalities between well-off countries and the worst-off are also increasing. Thus rich countries may do their share in promoting greater global equality without having to compromise significantly on their nationalist commitments. I do not mean here that rich countries are in fact doing their share in promoting global justice; my point is that they can do their share and still have ample resources left over for their particular national projects and goals given both increasing total global wealth and inequalities between the rich and poor.

But, more fundamentally, even if we assume that the requirements of cosmopolitan justice would require a significant restriction on the things that may be done in the name of national allegiance, why should this be thought to be *overly* demanding? Justice, to be sure, imposes demands, but the demands of justice are *reasonable* demands in light of the claims people rightly have. As Rawls has written, to take responsibility for one's ends, one has to exercise one's capacity to revise and reform one's conception of the good in light of one's legitimate entitlements (Rawls, 1999b, p. 371). If cosmopolitan justice does in fact require citizens of well-off countries to limit quite significantly the kinds of things they may do in the name of national allegiance, then this restriction is not only reasonable but required. If we accept as reasonable for the domestic case that justice can impose limitations on people's personal pursuits, there is no reason off hand to reject as unreasonable the global analogue that people ought to limit their national pursuits in light of the requirements of global justice.

David Miller in *Citizenship and National Identity* rejects the above analogy between domestic and global justice (Miller, 2000, ch. 10). Miller does not deny that justice has priority over other goods. He allows that when justice and personal pursuits come into conflict in domestic society (i.e., within a nation-state), considerations of justice override. But this is because, according to Miller, "justice features only on one side of the balance" (Miller, 2000, p. 167) in cases of such conflicts in domestic society. The problem with extrapolating this reasoning to the global context, Miller argues, is that national claims are not analogous to personal claims. Unlike individuals, nations are engaged in the pursuit of social justice "*among their own* members" (Miller, 2000, p. 167, italics mine), and so national allegiances, unlike personal pursuits (or conceptions of the good) in the domestic context, are themselves expressions of social justice. Accordingly, when national commitments and global justice come into conflict, "justice features on both sides" of the balance, and it "ceases to be clear that global justice must take priority" (Miller, 2000, p. 167). In other words, global demands and national commitments present conflicting claims of justice, and to give priority to *global* justice over *national* justice is arbitrary. The priority of justice gives justice dominance over other goods; but it does not give one *claim* of justice dominance over *another* claim of justice.

But Miller's alleged disanalogy between the domestic and global spheres can be questioned. It does not seem to me that there is only a single claim of justice in domestic society, and that therefore "justice [necessarily] features on only one side of the balance" in cases of domestic conflict. There are distinct realms of human activities within domestic society, and these can generate their own distinctive claims of justice (or commitments). Jon Elster, for example, refers to these association-specific claims as claims of "local justice" in contrast to "domestic justice." Local justice applies *within* particular associations *in* a society (e.g., we can talk of justice in a workplace, justice in the family, justice in a cooperative, and so on); domestic justice, on the other hand, applies to the society at large, that is, to the basic structure of the society (Elster; cited in Rawls, 2001, p. 11). And claims of local justice can come into conflict with claims of domestic justice, just as claims of national justice can come into conflict with claims of global justice.

So contra Miller, justice can feature on both sides of the balance in the domestic sphere when different claims come into conflict. Yet we are prepared to give domestic justice priority over local justice. The reason for this is that the pursuit of justice *within* any sphere of human interaction must not violate any *external* principles of justice that also apply to it. For instance, a cooperative *within* a society could have a mutually agreed-on distributive principle that said, for example, "to the greater contributor goes the greater benefit." So this cooperative would distribute its goods among its members along this principle. But this does not mean that this cooperative need not respect the principles of justice applicable to the larger society of which it is also a part. It must, in particular, honor those principles of domestic justice that regulate its dealings with other associations and non-members. For one, this association may not misappropriate the resources of other associations, and then distribute these unjustly acquired resources among its members along its local distributive principle (of "greater contribution").

Domestic justice has priority over any claim of local justice because what members of an association owe to each other cannot be determined without first determining what rightly belongs to that association. This means that claims of local justice are to be subordinated to the claims of domestic justice. Domestic justice dominates over local justice *because* local justice is realizable only in the context of domestic justice.[8] While the principles of local justice may be unique to a particular association, the amount and kinds of goods that its distinctive principles (of local justice) may actually distribute (among its members) cannot be ascertained without addressing the prior matter of domestic justice.

Thus the association-specific principles of local justice are constrained in their application by external principles of domestic justice that also bind the association. A distinct sphere of human activity is not sheltered from principles governing its relationship with other societies just because it is able to generate its own internal principles of justice. To reject this point is akin to saying that a criminal organization need not respect any external claims of justice against it, just because it has its own internal distributive criteria applicable only to its gang members.

So, although Miller is right that national commitments are themselves expressions of justice that may conflict with the demands of global justice, it does not follow that both claims of justice are on a par such that no one claim can take precedence over the other. National justice is attainable only in the context of global justice. Nations have their own domestic distributive principles, and members may have special allegiances and commitments to each other but not to non-members. But national justice does not present a claim of justice that can be realized independently of the claims of global justice. National justice must presuppose justice at the global level, and hence has to be subordinated to its demands. A nation may distribute resources *justly* among its own members only if these resources in fact rightly belong to the nation in the first place, and thus national-level distribution can be just only in a background of global justice (Shue, 1980, ch. 6; 1983). The fundamental question that remains basic to any implementation of national justice is whether the resources or goods that a nation is seeking to distribute among its own members are resources or goods that it is rightly entitled to. The question of global justice is thus unavoidable. For this reason, global justice considerations have a prior place with regard to considerations of national justice. That "justice features on both sides of the balance" in the global context when the demands of global justice and national commitments collide, does not disprove the priority of global justice.

Domestic justice has precedence over local justice because one of the central functions of domestic justice is to adjudicate the competing claims of different associations within society. Likewise, global justice has precedence over national claims of justice given that the function of global justice is to adjudicate competing national claims. The fact of the presence of competing claims of justice does not alone tell against the priority of some claims of justice over others. Some claims of justice are of a higher order because they serve to evaluate other competing claims of justice.

What the above argument shows, moreover, is that even if we accept Miller's premise that the domestic context is disanalogous to the global one because justice features on only one side of the balance in the former but on both sides in the latter, the priority of global justice over national justice is preserved.

The above argument does not deny that nations can have their own distinctive distributive principles; most certainly it does not deny the importance and significance of these local distributive principles. The point is that these distinctive principles, in order to be legitimately fulfilled, must operate in a background context of global justice. And the cosmopolitan's general position, that what rightly belongs to individuals in the world as a whole must be determined independently of their actual national allegiances, remains unrefuted.

Miller's denial that global distributive justice need not have necessary priority over national justice is ultimately premised on this fundamental point, namely, that distributive justice becomes difficult to make sense of once we take the idea outside the national context. Miller writes that outside the boundaries of the nation, there ceases to be any common agreement on the sorts of goods to distribute, agreement on the principles for distributing these goods, and the institutional means for enforcing the distributive requirements. In short, distributive equality is necessarily a nation-bound concept, and so global justice cannot include a distributive component.

But this nationalist line of argument that is so commonly made is, I think, too hasty, and is far from conclusive. Theorists such as Charles Beitz and Thomas Pogge have shown, to the contrary, that there can be global agreement on the goods that ought to be distributed.[9] Moreover, cosmopolitans have suggested that there are methods (developed for the domestic context) that can be adopted for determining what a global distributive principle should look like. For example, some cosmopolitans like Pogge and Beitz have developed Rawls's original position method of justification for the global context. And with respect to the point of institutional enforcement, it is important not to make the crucial mistake of taking justice to be tied to existing institutional arrangements when the goal of justice is to assess institutional arrangements and to require the

establishment of new ones when the ends of justice would be furthered
by this. So more needs to be said why distributive equality fails to have
meaning outside the context of the nation-state. Until then, this skepticism about the coherence of global distributive equality cannot on its own
conclusively refute the priority of global distributive justice.

CONCEPTUALIZING NATIONAL ALLEGIANCES

I have tried to argue that the subordination of national allegiances to
cosmopolitan demands does not unreasonably limit the practical expression of national allegiances. To hold national pursuits to be permissible
only within the bounds of cosmopolitan justice is consistent with how we
understand the relationship between personal pursuits and justice in more
familiar (e.g., domestic) contexts.

But some may argue that even if this subordination of nationality to
cosmopolitan justice provides sufficient space for the practice of national
self-determination, subordinating nationality to cosmopolitan justice
nonetheless offends against most people's understanding of the moral
significance of nationality. National membership is not only instrumentally valuable – to be valued, say, only as a means to some (more) basic
ends. For many individuals, at least according to (many) nationalist
theorists, nationality can also have non-instrumental value because it is
constitutive of a person's well-being or conception of the good human
life. Thus nationality is a good that is valued for itself, for what *it* means
to individuals, and not merely instrumentally for furthering some impersonal goals.[10] To treat nationality as though it has *only* instrumental value
is to empty it of much of its meaning and force.

To treat a relationship as non-instrumental in this sense is to accept
that the relationship *itself* can be the source of its special obligations and
commitments. As Samuel Scheffler writes, "to attach non-instrumental
value to my relationship with a particular person just is, in part, to see that
person as a source of special claims in virtue of the relationship between
us" (2001, p. 100).[11] Thus the moral basis of national allegiances is not
entirely reducible to some general (e.g., cosmopolitan) principle or goal;
rather a person's special relationship with her fellow nationals can *itself* be
the source of her special commitments to them. National allegiances can
be said thus to have a certain "normative independence" – national
affiliation can provide its own groundings for special obligations or
concern without reference to some higher or more general principle.
According to nationalists like Miller, I have an obligation to a fellow

national simply because she is my fellow national. No further justification or explanation is necessary or available. The special relationship between fellow nationals itself supplies the *non-reducible* source of reasons for action (Miller, 1995, ch. 3; also Scheffler, 2001, p. 121).

The conceptual-objection, then, is that in subordinating national commitments to the demands of cosmopolitan justice, cosmopolitans fail to recognize the normative independence of national allegiances. Cosmopolitans regard the worth of national allegiances as reducible ultimately to cosmopolitan principles, the objection charges, and this does not properly appreciate and account for the moral significance of nationality. Accordingly, cosmopolitans are unable to take special relationships and commitments seriously. The objection calls to mind Rousseau's caricature of the cosmopolitan as one who "boasts of loving all the world, in order to enjoy the privilege of loving no one" (Schlereth, 1977, p. 91).

As an illustration, this objection is somewhat analogous to the objection that utilitarians cannot properly account for friendship, because utilitarians, so it is alleged, can accommodate the practice of friendship *only* by showing how the special commitments between friends do in fact produce the greatest amount of happiness for the greatest number of individuals. Yet this way of accommodating the practice of friendship, the objection continues, fails to appreciate adequately the moral significance of friendship. Friends have special claims on each other not just because such special claims serve as a good strategy for maximizing social utility (from the point of view of all persons); rather the relationship itself provides friends with distinct principles for action that are not entirely reducible to more general (external) principles (e.g., Friedman, 1985). The special commitments between friends need not be good-maximizing in the utilitarian sense.[12]

It is true that nationality and friendship are two very different kinds of associations, and nationalists who insist on the non-reducibility of national commitments need further arguments to show how and why, in a non-intimate and impersonal relationship, such shared nationality can provide individuals with an independent source of reasons for action. I will leave this important socio-psychological point aside.[13] For the purpose of examining the accountability-objection in its strongest possible form, I will grant that national commitments are not reducible for the same general reasons that other important *associative* commitments (such as those of friendship) are not.[14] The question before us is thus: does the subordination of nationality to cosmopolitan justice deny the normative independence of national allegiance?

It is not clear to me that it must. The objection seems to me to assume that just because national commitments must be limited by cosmopolitan principles, national commitments must, therefore, be reducible to cosmopolitan principles. But this does not follow. What cosmopolitan justice does is to provide the *limiting conditions* for national allegiances; but this is distinct from providing the *justificatory bases* of such allegiances. And setting the limits of a practice need not entail setting also the moral basis for that practice. It may be left to individuals themselves to understand the source of the moral significance of their national commitments – a person may indeed want to claim that she has a special commitment to another simply because she is her co-national, just as I have a special commitment to, say, my brother *just* "because he is my brother" (cf. Miller, 1995). But this normatively independent justification of special commitments should not trouble the cosmopolitan. Cosmopolitanism need not force on persons any particular understanding of how their associational ties are to be conceived and understood, and thus what the sources of these associative obligations are. What it demands is that the exercise of such ties stays within the limits defined by cosmopolitan justice. And there is nothing reductionist about this requirement. The normative independence of national allegiances is thus respected even as its exercise is limited against other moral considerations.

The analogous case of friendship or kinship is instructive. We do not need to adopt a reductionist account of the worth of friendship or kinship to claim that cronyism or nepotism is wrong. We can accept that the ties of friendship can be internally justified (by reference to the relationship itself – because "she is *my* friend"), while insisting that the exercise of friendship needs to respect certain boundaries of justice. It is one thing to claim that the value of friendship is reducible to principles of justice for society, it is another to say that how one expresses one's friendship must be constrained by these principles. I may care for someone simply because she is a friend; but how I can express that special concern ought to be limited by the other considerations (of justice).[15]

Indeed, while a conception of friendship that reduces the source of friendship commitments to some general criteria external to the relationship of friendship would be a distortion of what friends are for, a conception of friendship that does not acknowledge any boundaries on the commitments of friendship would be just as distorting of the idea of friendship. A reductivist account of friendship undervalues the ideal of friendship; but an account of friendship that observes no constraints on what friends may do for each other grossly inflates it.[16] My point here, to be clear, is just that commonsensical notions of friendship recognize limits on the ties of friendship – what is open to dispute is what these limits are.

Constrainability and reducibility are two distinct features, and the former need not entail the latter. Because cosmopolitan justice can set principled constraints on national allegiances without denying their normative independence, cosmopolitan equality does not come at the cost of undervaluing or under-appreciating the ties of nationality (as the conceptual-objection alleges). Cosmopolitans do not insist on the reducibility of national allegiances to cosmopolitan principles even as they hold that the practice of such allegiances is to respect cosmopolitan boundaries.

Cosmopolitanism, then, need not be seen necessarily as a thesis about individual identity, that is, a theory about how individuals are to see their own place in the world, and how they are to account for their personal projects and social attachments and commitments. As a doctrine about individual identity, cosmopolitanism may rightly be criticized for failing to take into account the allegiances people have if the truly free individual on the cosmopolitan view is one who is culturally detached, and one who must be able to provide impersonal and general justifications for the social ties and commitments that she has. But understood primarily as a doctrine about justice, cosmopolitanism can be agnostic about how individuals are to understand their own conceptions of the good and their special allegiances. It does not demand that individuals provide a particular *form* of justification for their social attachments and commitments before these can be taken seriously. As a doctrine about justice, cosmopolitanism need not deny the normative independence of social attachments; all that it demands is that these attachments and commitments be compatible with the requirements of justice impartially conceived. Thus once we distinguish cosmopolitan demands of global justice from the more encompassing cosmopolitan doctrine about individual identity, the worry that cosmopolitan justice fails to account for the moral significance of nationality, is unfounded.

Indeed, the cosmopolitan view that national allegiances while non-reducible are to be constrained by external considerations provides a more balanced idea of such allegiances. A reductivist notion of allegiances would be at odds with how most people conceive of their national ties; however, a view of national allegiances that treats these allegiances to be beyond the constraints of justice would be just as offensive to our common understandings of national allegiances. Where there is disagreement concerns the limits of these constraints. But I have tried to argue in the previous section that these constraints are to be defined independently of people's national commitments.

CONCLUSION

I began by suggesting that cosmopolitan justice and national allegiances may be reconciled by subordinating the claims of nationality to the claims of cosmopolitan justice. I then tried to show that the concern that this would be too demanding on people's national commitments was unfounded. Against the objection that giving preference to cosmopolitan justice does not fully accommodate the exercise of national allegiances, I argued that it is basic to the concept of justice that partial pursuits be confined within the rules of justice that are impartially defined with respect to these pursuits. Against the objection that cosmopolitanism cannot properly account for the significance of national allegiances because it treats allegiances to be reducible to cosmopolitan principles, I argued that this objection is based on the mistaken assumption that to hold a practice constrainable to a set of principles is to treat it as fully reducible to (or justified by) these principles. The normative independence of national allegiances can be respected by cosmopolitans without compromising on the basic cosmopolitan commitment to equality.

NOTES

This paper was presented at a Symposium on "Globalization and Democracy" at the American Philosophical Association Eastern Division Meeting (2002), and at a conference on "Globalization and Citizenship" at the National University of Singapore (January 2003). I am grateful for the feedback and comments I received at these meetings, and I especially am thankful to Will Kymlicka, C.L. Ten, Daniel A. Bell, Henry Shue, Steven Lukes, and Sor-hoon Tan.

1 For the cosmopolitan liberal position, see Beitz (1979, 1983), Nussbaum (1996), Pogge (1989, 1998b), and Shue (1980, 1983); for the liberal nationalist view, see Kymlicka, 2001; Miller, 1995 and 2000; and Tamir (1993).

2 Rawls himself, on one interpretation, rejects the idea of a global basic structure (Rawls, 1999b). For discussions on this specific point, see Beitz (1979, part III) and Buchanan (2000b). For more on justice as an institutional ideal see Barry (1995), Freeman (2005), and Tan (2004b).

3 This is consistent with Rawls's basic point that "within the framework of background justice set up by the basic structure, individuals and associations may do as they wish insofar as the rules of institutions permit" (Rawls, 2001, p. 50). For one famous account on how Rawls's basic ideas should be globalized, see Pogge (1989, part III).

4 See Beitz (1979), Kymlicka (2002, pp. 268ff), McMahan (1997), Nussbaum (1996, pp. 135–37), Pogge (1998b), Shue (1980, ch. 6).

5 It is important to note that not all liberal nationalists reject the cosmopolitan idea of justice. For one notable example, see Kymlicka (2001 and 2002, pp. 268ff). I try to show the compatibility between liberal nationalism and cosmopolitan justice in "Liberal Nationalism and Cosmopolitan Justice," 2002) and at greater length in *Justice Without Borders* (Tan, 2004c).

6 Again, this is not to say that partial national commitments cannot be pursued; it only says that national goals/projects are to be limited by the principles of global justice that have been impartially arrived at.

7 It seems, then, that given her belief that cosmopolitanism and nationalism are therefore fundamentally at odds, Brock thinks that cosmopolitans should be more skeptical of co-national partiality.

8 To take a specific example, if the difference principle is one of the principles of domestic justice, then an association in this society must comply with this requirement with respect to the rest of society, claims of local justice notwithstanding. The association need not apply this principle in its internal (local) distribution. But the amount of goods it has (relative to other associations) that it may distribute internally (in accordance with its local principle) must be constrained by the difference principle, among other things.

9 The Human Development Indices utilized by the UNDP in its quality of life assessment seems to me to provide a universally accepted and workable cross-national metric for measuring individual well-being.

10 As Scheffler writes, "it is pathological to attach nothing but instrumental value to any of one's personal relationships" (2001, p. 121).

11 See also Miller (1995, ch. 3).

12 The reference to utilitarianism is only illustrative. Similar objections can be raised against Kantians; there is no intention here to tie cosmopolitanism to utilitarianism.

13 For some additional arguments on why nationality can generate "associative obligations" that are normatively independent, see MacIntyre (1984), and Miller (1995).

14 Associative obligations are thus a subset of special obligations in that associative obligations are non-reducible special obligations (whereas other classes of special obligations are reducible – e.g., special obligations between business partners). See Scheffler (2001); also Dworkin (1986).

15 For more on personal pursuits and the impartial requirements of morality, see Kelly (2000).

16 That is, a morally non-reductive yet constrainable account of friendship is most consistent with our ordinary perception of the morality of friendship.

CHAPTER 12

Cosmopolitanism and the compatriot priority principle

Jocelyne Couture and Kai Nielsen

INTRODUCTION

To think about morality seriously is among other things to hope that it can plausibly be made to have some reasonable form of objectivity. What form it can take (if any), and still make sense, is a deeply contested matter (Mackie, 1977). In this essay, we shall argue (1) that an objective morality should take the form of intersubjectivity best captured by the method of general and wide reflective equilibrium; (2) that such a method itself yields a conception of morality that is both (a) universalistic and cosmopolitan and (b) particularistic and contextual. We will further argue that any reasonable morality must be both (a) and (b); (3) that moving on to the domain of normative politics, a justified political morality must be a cosmopolitan morality. Moreover (or so we shall argue), a cosmopolitan morality should, where a nation's sovereignty is threatened or not accepted, yield a liberal nationalism if it is to be a justified political stance. This raises the compatriot priority question and with it, the issue of the consistency of a liberal nationalist cosmopolitanism. We shall consider that in some detail.

I

Let us begin with a brief methodological note on what John Rawls calls wide and general reflective equilibrium. What reflective equilibrium seeks to do is to *discover* patterns of coherence among our considered judgements or, where coherence is not to be found, to *forge* them into such patterns of coherence in good constructivist fashion (Rawls, 1999b, pp. 303–58). Wide reflective equilibrium takes into consideration all matters relevant to justifying our considered moral judgements, while narrow reflective equilibrium takes only our moral considered judgements, middle-level moral rules, and more fundamental moral principles (all of which at all levels may be considered judgements) (Rawls, 1999b, pp. 286–302).

Wide reflective equilibrium then, seeks to discover patterns of coherence not only with our moral beliefs but with the things we know or reasonably believe about society, ourselves and our world: with the best-established factual beliefs, well-established scientific theories (including crucially social scientific theories), history, moral, and political theories, accounts of the functions of morality (where all of these are reasonable), and the like. We get general as well as wide reflective equilibrium when the beliefs and convictions of not just those of a single moral agent so reflecting and investigating are taken into consideration but those of most of the moral agents so concerned and so reflecting and investigating (Nielsen, 1996, pp. 12–19).

We start with particular considered judgements (convictions): usually the ones we hold most firmly. Wide and general reflective equilibrium, far from being a purely coherentist method, takes these considered judgements (taken individually) to have an *initial* credibility. But that does not turn it into foundationalism. For while these considered judgements are taken to have some initial credibility, they gain that credibility (1) by the way they hang together and (2) by the fact that they are the subject of reflective endorsements. Being put in wide reflective equilibrium means that various matters have been reflected on. The considered convictions are neither beliefs expressed by something like atomic or protocol sentences standing quite independently of each other, nor are they just received opinions or self-evident truths. They are rather deeply embedded considered convictions that have our reflective endorsement.

They also are not ethnocentric convictions or cultural prejudices; we may start with some that are, but these considered convictions are winnowed out as we apply wide and general reflective equilibrium. In failing to fit with our other beliefs, including beliefs found in cross-cultural studies, informed accounts of what our world is like, with our other considered convictions and with other people's considered convictions in our societies and in other societies, we will have, with all those convictions before us, *reasons* for criticizing, modifying, and perhaps even abandoning those considered convictions that do not fit together. We will have very good *reasons* for suspecting they are ethnocentric beliefs or cultural prejudices by the very fact that they do not fit with the rest, even after careful attempts to so read them. If they are considered convictions that, after all that rationalizing, still do not fit, then they should either be modified until they do fit or be abandoned. So instead of just having a jumble of sometimes conflicting considered convictions, we will have instead considered convictions resulting from the use of this critical method.

The method of general and wide reflective equilibrium does not yield a final and complete equilibrium. We have no idea of what it would be like to get an unconditional or timeless warrant where inquiry once and for all could come to an end. Any equilibrium, no matter how wide and general and how carefully constructed, can be expected to be replaced by another reflective equilibrium at a later time. We can hope, if we are whiggish, that later equilibria will be more adequate than the earlier ones: that they will take in more considerations, be the result of improved theorizing and that a more perspicuous patterning will obtain. But we do not have any very clear criteria for "the most adequate" here any more than we have for convergence in the sciences. It is not unreasonable to expect some progress here but we will never get any final resting point. Truth may be time independent but justification surely is not.

II

We next want to argue that a careful application of the method of wide and general reflective equilibrium (hereafter called just the method of reflective equilibrium) where modernity is firmly in place will yield a morality that is (a) both universalistic and cosmopolitan and (b) particularistic and contextual and that (a) and (b) can harmoniously fit together. Though, as we shall see, that idea is not without its problems.

To see how a reasonable conception of morality – a conception of morality resulting from the use of reflective equilibrium – will be contextualist/particularist *and* universalistic we will work with examples that will hopefully make this compatibility clear. How people should comport themselves sexually has changed with the advent of AIDS, how a just war (assuming there could be one) could be pursued has changed with the advent of nuclear weapons, how and the extent to which fishing should be pursued has changed with the depletion of fish stocks. Things are plainly in good measure contextual and particular here. In one context a certain particular thing should be done and in other contexts, a different thing should be done. But this is generally determined by the *objective features of the situation* and the accompanying moral judgement is universal: whenever and wherever the objective situation is such that the fish stocks are being extensively depleted then, *ceteris paribus*, fishing should be halted or drastically cut back.

What should be done changes with time, place, and situation principally and importantly because the objective situation is different. As the above examples show, it is the changed objective situation, which often both *causes* and *justifies* the changed moral views. There is nothing that is subjective or relativistic going on here though there is something which is determinately *contextual.*

It is not infrequently the case that for any context S, A should be done. When context S shifts to context Q, then B should be done instead. And when the objective features of S and Q are relevantly different, we should say that for *any* group or persons at time t and in context Q, that B should be done. Or, so as to indicate that things are not quite that straightforward, that in context Q, for any statistically normal person in that context, B should be done. These claims are perfectly universalizable (generalizable) and not infrequently universal (though not always so because of a possible dispute over "relevant differences"). Contextualism and universalism happily cohabit here. In fact they require each other. Many of our beliefs and convictions change because the world changes in certain ways including the people in it.

III

We will now consider a third claim, namely that an adequately justified morality must be, at least for we moderns, a cosmopolitan morality, though one that acknowledges the importance for people of their local and particular ways of doing things. This is again reiterable for all people. Following on that, and moving to the domain of normative politics, we will further argue that in certain circumstances a cosmopolitan will also, and quite consistently so, be a liberal nationalist (Couture and Nielsen, 1998, pp. 579–662, and Kymlicka, 2001, pp. 203–21).

A cosmopolitan is a world citizen, but "world citizenship" should not be taken literally for it is basically the expression of a moral ideal. We, as the Stoics thought, should give our first allegiance to the moral community made up of the humanity of all human beings. We should always behave so as to treat with respect every human being, no matter where that person was born, no matter what the person's class, rank, gender, or status may be. At the core of the cosmopolitan ideal is the idea that the life of everyone matters, and matters equally. This, in broad strokes, is the cosmopolitan moral ideal.

To be committed to such an ideal involves understanding that we are part of and committed to the universal community of humanity whether there is anything actually answering to the idea of there being such a community or not. If we are at all tough-minded, we will realize there is no world community and that the actual world is more like a *swinerai* (pigsty). But this is neither to affirm nor to deny that there could and should be a world community. Whether it obtains or not, we should act to make it obtain or to approximate its obtaining in whatever way we can.

It is also vital that local affiliations do not stand in the way of cosmopolitan commitments to humanity as a whole. We need to keep firmly before our minds, and at the core of our commitments, the cosmopolitan ideal that the life of everyone matters, and matters equally. This very cosmopolitan and egalitarian moral point of view involves as a crucial task of cosmopolitan moral agents to work, as Martha Nussbaum well puts it, "to make all human beings part of our community of dialogue and concern, showing respect [and, we would add understanding] for the human wherever it occurs and allowing that respect to constrain our national or local politics" (Nussbaum, 1997a, pp. 60–61).

Some think that cosmopolitanism wrecks itself on the shoals of the compatriot priority principle, namely the principle that, in certain determinate circumstances, where compatriots' needs and interests clash with those of foreigners, the needs and interests of compatriots should *ceteris paribus* take priority over those of foreigners. It is not infrequently thought that a consistent cosmopolitan *cannot* accept that principle, while any kind of nationalist, including even a thoroughly liberal nationalist, *must* accept it, so right there we can see, it might be said, that cosmopolitanism and liberal nationalism are incompatible. Some, Brian Barry for example, just bite that bullet, reject nationalism *tout court* and opt for cosmopolitanism (Barry, 2001). Others just jettison cosmopolitanism and opt for nationalism, hopefully a form of liberal nationalism. Still others, like Kok-Chor Tan, while sticking with a strong version of the compatriot priority principle, seeks to show that cosmopolitanism and liberal nationalism are compatible and both desirable (Tan, 2002, 2004a, 2004b, and 2005).

Agreeing with Tan that they are compatible and both desirable, we will take a more lax position vis-à-vis the compatriot priority principle. Admitting in some circumstances it has force, we will also argue that in most circumstances the compatriot priority principle is subordinate to cosmopolitan considerations and can *standardly* be benignly neglected. However, as we argue in the last part of this essay, this is not always so. In (for example) situations where open borders become an issue, particularly for small wealthy countries (e.g.: Iceland, Luxembourg, New Zealand), there can *sometimes* be a conflict between a cosmopolitan commitment and a commitment to the compatriot priority principle. This poses a problem for both our form of liberal nationalism and for Tan's form. We are not terribly confident that either of us has the resources to answer it. We tentatively and conjecturally propose a way of resolving that conflict right at the end of our essay.

We shall endeavor in what follows first briefly to state what liberal nationalism is and how it contrasts with ethnic nationalism and other illiberal forms of nationalism and, second, try to clarify the issues described above and hopefully thereby make our take on them compelling.

IV

There are, it is crucial to understand, nationalisms and nationalisms. Some types (ethnic nationalism, for example) are to be despised and resisted and sometimes even to be fought (Couture and Nielsen, 1998). However, of whatever stripe, a nationalist is someone who cares about the nation of which she is a member and seeing, or at least believing, its independence threatened or seeing that it has not yet been achieved, seeks securely to sustain or achieve, as the case may be, some form of sovereignty, or at least some form of self-governance, for her nation. In speaking of a nation, we are speaking of a *people* who constitute a political community; a nation, that is, is a group of people with (a) a distinctive history, traditions, and customs, and, typically but not always (e.g. the Scots), with a distinctive language; in short, what Kymlicka calls a distinctive encompassing (societal) culture and (b) a sense that they are a people sustaining or seeking some form of self-governance (Seymour, 1998).

There are forms of nationalism that are barbaric and vicious while others (*pace* Barry) are liberal and tolerant (Couture and Nielsen, 1998). In their most extreme forms, non-liberal nationalisms engage, when the opportunity is at hand, in genocide and ethnic cleansing. Even in less virulent forms, they are xenophobic, exclusivist, typically racist, tracing national origin to ethnic origin and sometimes even to race. For such nationalists, national identity is in the blood or is an inherited encompassing societal culture or both. Where membership in a nation is marked by descent, we have ethnic nationalism and this is incompatible with universalism or cosmopolitanism or indeed, as Engels put it, with just plain human decency (Nielsen, 1996–1997).

Liberal nationalisms, on the other hand, are thoroughly compatible with universalism and arguably compatible with cosmopolitism. All liberal nationalists are liberal in the sense that Isaiah Berlin, John Rawls, and Donald Dworkin are liberals. They are committed to pluralism and tolerance. Liberal nationalists, like Johann Herder and David Miller, see and stress the vital importance to people of their local identities and attachments which include, in conditions of modernity, national identities, and attachments. Access to national membership is not, on such an account, through descent but through a will to live together and to cooperate and reciprocate. Liberal national membership, on that account, also comes with the cultural attunement from living in a liberal society, accepting the constitutional essentials of that society and a mutual recognition of those similarly attuned. Liberal nationalisms are compatible with universalism and arguably, but controversially, with cosmopolitanism in the ways in which we have shown particularism/contextualism is compatible with universalism. If our argument goes through, the ways in which liberal nationalism support having local identities is compatible with cosmopolitanism.

Brian Barry thinks that liberal nationalism has zero exemplification in our actual world. They are just ideas in some theoreticians' heads (Barry, 2001). But that is plainly false. The independence struggles of Norway and Iceland from Sweden and Denmark respectively were struggles by liberal nationalists, and both the seceding nations and the nations seceded from were liberal societies and all of these societies later became social democratic liberal societies. The struggle between them at the time of their secession, though bitter, was carried out within the framework and parameters of liberal democracies. In our times the powerful and protracted nationalisms in Flanders, Catalonia, Quebec, Puerto Rico, Scotland, and Wales are all liberal nationalisms and the states opposing them are liberal states. Propaganda goes on on all sides; still, the peoples and the nation-states of such nations resulting from secession would remain liberal.

Why can a Catalonian nationalist or a Quebec nationalist not also be a cosmopolitan? Indeed some of them – perhaps even most of them – are. Certainly, at least many of them think of themselves as such. But can they *consistently* be both liberal nationalists and cosmopolitans? We have argued they can, but Kok-Chor Tan has argued that consistency can only be obtained, on our account, by having an impoverished conception of the compatriot priority principle (Tan, 2004a). Yet that principle is so central, or so Tan claims, to liberal nationalism that it needs to be in a stronger form than we sanction. It is liberal nationalism with a strong compatriot priority principle, he claims, that must be shown to be compatible with cosmopolitanism. Tan argues reasonably that, given an adequate conception of the compatriot priority principle, it can. Others have thought that no cosmopolitan can consistently accept the compatriot priority principle. Still others think that there is an irresolvable conflict between cosmopolitanism and liberal nationalism over some key applications of the compatriot priority principle (e.g. over the problem of open borders). It is to these crucial issues, generated by their at least putatively conflicting views, to which we turn.

v

Tan's treatment of the compatriot priority principle is crucial to what is at issue here. We maintain that Tan has in effect, though not explicitly, confined himself to ideal theory here, and that this, in discussing the relations between cosmopolitanism and liberal nationalism, is a defect. What we see when we are doing ideal theory in such contexts is the thesis that individuals or even states may favor in certain circumstances their compatriots and that this is not *in itself* objectionable. This is problematic for a cosmopolitan. We heartily agree with Tan when he says

. . . if the formation and sustaining of special and local attachments are constitutive of any meaningful and well-lived human life, any theory of justice that fails to take seriously these attachments can be renounced as a *reductio ad absurdum*. The aim of justice is not to undermine the good for individuals but to fairly facilitate their pursuit of the good, and it is the good that gives meaning and worth to people's lives. (Tan, 2004a)

Tan further argues that "nationalists have to accept the priority for compatriots as one of the local commitments that individuals do and must develop to live rewarding and rich lives" (Tan, 2004a). This is not something that is *optional* for a nationalist. Thus, given our nationalist commitments, we must "accept the priority thesis as part of common sense morality, and consequently a theory of justice that rejects the priority thesis [as part of ideal theory, we add] is not a theory of justice that is made for humanity" (Tan, 2004a).

Tan argues that for a nationalist, it is not sufficient to say that particular attachments and the compatriot priority principle have instrumental value only. "For serious nationalists, national membership and attachments are not only instrumentally valuable – to be valued only as a means to some more important ends – they are also to be valued for themselves" (Tan, 2004a). Indeed, for most ordinary people, their shared nationality has non-instrumental value because it is constitutive of their well-being or conception of a good human life. Membership in a national community is a good that is valued for itself, for what it means to individuals, and is not merely valued instrumentally because it furthers some impersonal goals. Part of what gives meaning and worth to a shared national membership is the special concern members have for each other's needs. "To regard nationality as having *only* instrumental value is to empty it of much of its meaning and force" (Tan, 2004a).

However, it is important to remember that things can (and usually do) have, both instrumental value and non-instrumental value. Some value walking as an end in itself *and* as a means for keeping healthy. Group membership, including a shared national membership and attachments and (which is something else again) compatriot partiality, could be valued as an end (for the very reasons that Tan gives) and as well be valued instrumentally. To say that that compatriot priority has instrumental value is not to say that it has *only* instrumental value. We need (instrumentally need) local attachments for a society to flourish even if we refuse to acknowledge that anything like that can have a value in itself or even that such notions make sense. We can leave the debate over whether group attachments have value in themselves for the philosopher's closet without disclaiming the *central* role that group membership plays in justice and human flourishing. For practical political argumentation, a sound argument that shows the instrumental value of compatriot priority and the instrumental value of local attachments is sufficient. This could be as true for a serious nationalist concerned with the achievement of the national self-determination of the nation of which he is a member as for anyone else.

In arguing as we just have, we are not committed to a *reductive* program. We are not saying there is "nothing morally significant about national attachments as such," or that the "priority thesis is reducible to cosmopolitan principles." Indeed we think *that* is a mistake and perhaps even an incoherency. What we are saying is that the compatriot priority principle and national attachments have, whatever other value they may or may not have, instrumental value and that this justification is available even for someone, including a serious nationalist, who cannot see anything morally significant about national attachments as such.

We do not want to reject the compatriot priority thesis. However, we want to reject the idea that serious nationalists have to grant this principle an inherent or intrinsic value. Serious and consistent nationalists can, and often do, recognize that national attachments are important precisely because these attachments play a central (instrumental) role in achieving democracy and local as well as global justice. We also want to deny that considerations about the status – instrumental, inherent or intrinsic – of the compatriot priority principle cuts much moral-*political* ice. These are considerations which, when we are thinking concretely and practically about how the world can and should be ordered, we can benignly neglect. That notwithstanding, we can agree with Tan that, *as far as ideal theory goes*, the real challenge for a cosmopolitan nationalist is to show how the cosmopolitan commitment to global egalitarianism can be reconciled with the nationalist principle that compatriots do take priority.

Let us pull some things together. Tan *may* well have a strong case for saying that we should say, that the "compatriot priority thesis is exercisable only against the background global order that is just" (Tan, 2004a). That is why we now, though rather uneasily, treat the compatriot priority principle as exclusively a part of ideal theory, never a part of non-ideal theory, for it is unfortunately only in ideal theory that we can find a global order that is just. The real world does not yield such a picture. We also think that there is some force in saying, as Tan does, that

priority for compatriots must be useful for global justice before it is to have [much] moral significance. For the purposes of cosmopolitan justice, so long as the priority for compatriots is *compatible* with the requirements of justice [we would say global justice], the nationalist need offer no further explanation for his preferences. (Tan, 2004a)

Indeed, here Tan gives a clear instrumental justification to compatriot priority. Our point is that we need no more than that for *political* justification. But we agree that "within the bounds of justice, there is nothing offensive about the compatriot priority claim in itself, and any theory of justice must recognize the fact that forming and pursuing local attachments is part of what it means to live a meaningful human life" (Tan, 2004a). That last statement can be and has been challenged, but we think it can be sustained.

Without retracting any of the criticisms we have so far made of his account, we think this characterization by Tan goes some distance towards meeting what he calls the real challenge for anyone wanting to defend a cosmopolitan position while taking nationalism seriously. To meet that challenge "is to show how the irreducible moral significance of national attachments can be acknowledged and endorsed without surrendering the cosmopolitan commitment to equal respect and concern for all persons" (Tan, 2004a). Compatibility between cosmopolitanism and liberal nationalism all the way along from the most general contexts to concrete ones is maintained and the independent significance of the compatriot priority principle is also maintained while (a) stressing that priority for compatriots can only be allowed where global justice obtains and (b) where it is useful for social justice. We are not sure that we must appeal to (b) as well as (a) but either way we have a meeting of that central challenge to a liberal nationalist who would also be a cosmopolitan *though within the limits of ideal theory alone.* We *generally* (but not in all particular instances) have compatibility between cosmopolitanism and liberal nationalism.

VI

We now want to bring out something of our rationale for saying why we attach, while remaining serious liberal nationalists, less importance to the compatriot priority principle than does Tan and indeed many others. We will set forth two sorts of considerations.

First, and here it is hard to know whether we are talking about ideal theory or not, Tan argues in effect that the compatriot priority principle comes into play within the limits of *global* justice alone. A rich country cannot rightly appeal to the compatriot priority principle in deciding how things are to be distributed between countries. This will later be questioned with respect to open borders. We are inclined to think *au contraire* that the compatriot priority principle only gains much significance when we have to make such choices, that is, when, in such situations, we are concerned with a *non-ideal* theory of global justice.

Consider a case. Suppose a family, say a family of academics, wishes to send their very talented, earnest, and eager daughter to Yale to study art history, something which she has a considerable talent for and is committed to. She very much wants to study at Yale, which is, let us assume, the best place in the world to study art history. But Yale is very expensive. Further, suppose they live in Belgium and that she could study there and get a decent education, including the study of art history at much less expense, but education-wise, Yale is still the perfect place for her given her interests and talents. Further suppose the Belgium government is social democratic and has once again raised taxes in part to direct more money to foreign aid. The Belgium government, let us say, among other things, supports plans for building wells to yield clean water in an impoverished country, say, Sierra Leone. It would like also to provide adequate aid to partially support students like the one described, but cannot afford to do both. It must set some priorities. With our way of looking at things – indeed, we think, with any cosmopolitan and egalitarian way of looking at things – the money should go on the wells. But some conscientious people with a strong conception of the compatriot priority principle would resist that. Is it so obvious what justice mandates here? This is where the compatriot priority has a rationale and some bite even in a world that is anything but just. Even some, like ourselves, who would go for the wells, still feel its force. Should not the compatriot priority principle be overridden in such situations? Here we have something that is up for debate and not just in ideal theory. Our considered judgement is that we should not here give much weight to the compatriot priority principle. But can we get this into wide reflective equilibrium? What should be said here is not evident.

Let us turn to our second importantly different case. Here what we shall say is particularly conjectural and we end up at risk of unsaying what we started by saying. Giving determinate content to our earlier gnomic remarks, we contend that once one leaves the protections of ideal theory, the compatriot priority principle becomes less important though, paradoxically, that is the only place where it could do any non-truistic work.

The best way we can think of bringing this out is by translating this into the concrete and telling a story. The story we give is about Quebec but it could apply to any nation trying to gain sovereignty. We use Quebec only because we are more familiar with it. The first part of this story is realistic; the second is pure fantasy, but with no damage to its force. Now, for the story. It has been widely thought in the last few years that the issue of Quebec sovereignty has finally been laid to rest. With the election in Quebec about a year ago of the provincial Liberals (actually a very conservative party headed by a former Tory federal MP recycled as a provincial Liberal), we have a government that has extensively dismantled many of the social programs (such as, health provisions, day-care provisions, educational provisions, and environmental protection laws) that it took years of struggle to attain. This, along with the heavy-handedness of the federal government, has rekindled the embers of the quest for sovereignty in Quebec. Quite contrary to their intent, the provincial Liberals and the federal Liberals put the issue of sovereignty on the agenda again. It is not unreasonable to expect that the next provincial election will sweep the major sovereigntist party (the *Parti Québécois*) into power and that will be followed by a new referendum and that the vote this time will be *Oui*. It might not happen, but it realistically could.

Now comes the pure fantasy, but still useful part of the story. Suppose that happened and suppose we, as elected MPs, are in the cabinet and are among those responsible for policy formation in the new state. We would centrally recommend five things: first, the restoration and extension, though perhaps in somewhat different forms, of the abolished as well as other social welfare provisions. Second, the securing and extension of the French language as the official language of Quebec and its protection particularly in Montreal where it is demographically threatened. There would also be enhanced provision for English instruction as a *second* language. Quebec, mainly a French-speaking nation of 7 million, is surrounded by 280 million English speakers. For all kinds of practical reasons *Québécois* need to learn English and learn it well, but as *a second language*. But the lingua franca of Quebec should be firmly French. Third, the protection of the culture, traditions, and institutions that go with Quebec's culture. They, of course, would change where people (the citizens of the new country) want them to change, as they surely will, but these changes would not be forced on them from the outside but should be collectively and democratically decided by the Quebec citizens. There would also remain in place at least the traditional protections for the First Nations and the English-speaking national minority. Fourth, the protection of the multicultural nature of the vibrant urban center that is Montreal. Montreal, like many large urban centers around the world, is a culturally rich center where many cultures meet, culturally borrow from each other, and where people of those different cultures frequently intermingle and intermarry. Around our universities, for example, you can, besides French and English, hear on the streets, and often, Chinese, Italian, Arabic, Hebrew, and Hindi. Sometimes these cultures clash usually due to exogenous factors but for the most part they get along, become part of the broader culture – encompassing (societal) culture – and constantly intermingle at work, in school and in university classrooms, and at play. Here we, as does Jeremy Waldron following Salman Rushdie, celebrate our mongrelized, bastardized selves (Waldron, 1992). We gain from hybrid-vigor and our society is enriched from it. Any liberal nationalist should recognize that and seek to preserve and further it in the nation to which she or he is attached in a way such that these minority cultures are accepted and enhanced, and that they neither come into conflict with each other, nor are any of them excluded from access to the long engrained, though ever-changing traditional culture – the (encompassing) societal culture – of the nation. Finally, fifth, we would recommend, consistently with our liberal, nationalist, and cosmopolitan commitments, for the new state of Quebec to have progressive policies of foreign aid, to support international institutions for global justice and peace, to favor cultural exchanges with other countries and cultures, and to adopt external policies that support democratic struggles for national emancipation and national independence wherever they occur in the world.

It is such things that would be the concern of the serious liberal nationalist. Compatriot priority does not come to the fore, at least not in any major way, here. To this it may be responded: but it does, though, not in the way that it is usually thought. To see this, consider the vexing problem of *open borders*. As we have seen, any nationalist (liberal or otherwise) is concerned to protect the cultural integrity of her nation: its language and societal (encompassing) culture. But the liberal nationalist is also a cosmopolitan, an internationalist, and an egalitarian. She has, as Tan puts it, "a cosmopolitan view of global justice, the fundamental premise of which is that individuals are entitled to equal respect and concern regardless of citizenship or nationality, and that global institutions should be arranged such that each person's interests are given equal due" (Tan, 2004a). But the liberal nationalist, if she lives in a rich nation, will have many people clamoring for entry. Many of them will not be political refugees but simply *economic* ones. A country, particularly a small country, could not have a policy of fully open borders without coming to lose any cultural distinctiveness that it may have. Think of Iceland or New Zealand here. Hybrid-vigor is one thing; complete loss of identity along with becoming a tower of Babel and an economic slum is another. Does justice or a commitment to humanity require that?

We are inclined to think that the answer to that question is: no. And that answer does not appeal to the compatriot priority principle or, for that matter, to any *principle*, but instead to factual matters. First, cosmopolitans respect cultural diversity and what they deny is that national attachments should have a priority over our commitments toward the whole of humanity; but in doing so they need not deny that national attachments have a moral value. What they might recommend, in the case we are considering, might be a careful balance between a reasonable opening of their borders and strong measures to protect the culture of their country. Where it does so it also must fully respect the rights of the immigrants. Second, cosmopolitans value equality and this includes economic equality, but economic equality need not be for them an intrinsic and absolute value so that opening the borders will be a good thing even when it reduces the general population in a country to dire poverty. What should be known in order to arrive at a sound decision about opening the borders are, among other things, facts concerning what has been called the "carrying capacity" of a country (Nielsen, 2003, pp. 226–31).

Nationalists could also argue against opening the borders of their country without appealing to the compatriot priority principle. In non-ideal situations where generally rich and powerful countries still keep their borders closed, the liberal nationalist might argue that his country is not morally required to assume *alone* the burdens of global justice. Cosmo-politans can agree with nationalists on that and both can work at changing the world so as to have a better distribution of the burdens of global justice. We tend to agree with Tan when he implies that the appeal to the compatriot priority principle (to oppose the opening of borders, for instance) is not justified in non-ideal cases, but we also want to point out that it is not what ideal theory tells us about a compatriot priority principle that could help us to see what to do – to open the borders or not – when the demands of justice are not met.

On that point, questions can be raised about whether opening the borders is the best strategy to be advocated by cosmopolitans and liberal nationalists when global justice is concerned. Are there any other feasible devices that could yield a worldwide democratic and economic equality (or at least something approximating it) and that both cosmopolitan and liberal nationalists could agree on? Thomas Pogge, in his practical-concrete fashion, has suggested some that would satisfy, as far as we can see, the stringent moral requirements of both liberal nationalism and cosmopolitanism (Pogge, 2002). Here, we have good reasons to think that liberal nationalism and cosmopolitanism are consistent with each other and could be put in *wide and general* reflective equilibrium.

CONCLUSION

We are not trying to solve the morally important and intellectually demanding problem of open borders here. We rather use it to probe the problem of the compatibility of liberal nationalism and cosmopolitanism. Must not cosmopolitans, trying to get their views into wide reflective equilibrium with those of liberal nationalists, be committed, perhaps their gut reactions to the contrary notwithstanding, to some form of com-patriot priority principle? In closing, but with no very considerable confidence, we will attempt to sketch a solution.

Once we get to the hurly-burly world and must deal with an actual problem, such as that of open borders, it gives us a new form of the challenge that both Tan and we try in our distinct ways to meet. It would *seem* that a consistent cosmopolitan *in that context* (i.e. the open-borders context), and perhaps in other *such contexts* as well, would reject the compatriot priority principle and that in *that context* (such contexts) a consistent liberal nationalist would do the same. So it would seem at least that one can be a consistent liberal nationalist cosmopolitan.

However, note the qualifier "in that context" and "in such contexts." That leads us to understand that there are some contexts in which cosmopolitanism and liberal nationalism may conflict but that says nothing about "most contexts" or "many contexts" or even "nearly all contexts." That there are a few *extreme contexts* (if there are) where they cannot consistently go together says nothing about whether they could not massively go together. And that, we think, is what is important. There will always be, as things go, some particular moral and moral-political conflicts and incompatibilities. They will often be very important in the situation to which they apply, but they are not the whole of the matter and they do not gainsay what we have just said. Moral principles and moral-political doctrines like cosmopolitanism or liberal nationalism should not be taken as *unexceptionally* universal in such moral-political discourses. In spite of their often universal form, they will have exceptions. We should not look at moral and political principles as if they were axioms in axiomatic systems and always expect them to yield determinate and non-context-dependent claims. *Normally* cosmopolitanism and liberal nationalism can consistently and peacefully co-exist. There may be *some* cases where they conflict, and where this conflict is not clearly resolvable, if resolvable at all. This is to be expected. It is like both Rawls and Habermas on the liberties of the ancients and the liberties of the moderns; they both take them to be co-original and compatible without it being the case that there will not be *particular* instances where they will conflict. We should not think there is a principle of sufficient reason in moral and normative political discourse. That would be rationalism and non-contextualism raising their ugly heads.

CHAPTER 13

Beyond the social contract: capabilities and global justice

Martha Nussbaum

> But among the traits characteristic of the human being is an impelling desire for fellowship, that is for common life, not of just any kind, but a peaceful life, and organized according to the measure of his intelligence, with those who are of his kind . . . Stated as a universal truth, therefore, the assertion that every animal is impelled by nature to seek only its own good cannot be conceded.
>
> Hugo-Grotius, *On the Law of War and Peace*

> Global inequalities in income increased in the 20th century by orders of magnitude out of proportion to anything experienced before. The distance between the incomes of the richest and poorest country was about 3 to 1 in 1820, 35 to 1 in 1950, 44 to 1 in 1973 and 72 to 1 in 1992.
>
> *Human Development Report 2000*, United Nations Development Programme

A WORLD OF INEQUALITIES

A child born in Sweden today has a life expectancy at birth of 79.7 years. A child born in Sierra Leone has a life expectancy at birth of 38.9 years.[1] In the US, GDP per capita is $34,142 dollars, in Sierra Leone, GDP per capita is $490. Adult literacy rates in the top twenty nations are around 99 percent. In Sierra Leone, the literacy rate is 36 percent. In twenty-six nations, the adult literacy rate is under 50 percent.

The world contains inequalities that are morally alarming, and the gap between richer and poorer nations is widening. The chance of being born in one nation rather than another pervasively determines the life chances of every child who is born. Any theory of justice that proposes political principles defining basic human entitlements ought to be able to confront these inequalities and the challenge they pose, in a world in which the power of the global market and of multinational corporations has considerably eroded the power and autonomy of nations.

The dominant theory of justice in the Western tradition of political philosophy is the social contract theory, which sees principles of justice as the outcome of a contract people make, for mutual advantage, to leave the state of nature and govern themselves by law. Such theories have recently been influential in thinking about global justice, thanks especially to the influential work of John Rawls. In this essay I shall examine that tradition, focusing on Rawls, its greatest modern exponent; I shall find it wanting. Despite their great strengths in thinking about justice, contractarian theories have some structural defects that make them yield very imperfect results when we apply them to the world stage. I shall argue that much more promising results are given by a version of what Amartya Sen and I have called the capabilities approach – an approach that, in my version (rather different here from Sen's) suggests a set of basic human entitlements, similar to human rights, as a minimum of what justice requires for all.

I shall ultimately be arguing that something like my version of the capabilities approach provides us with a promising way of thinking about the goals of development in this increasingly interdependent and interconnected world. Before we reach the positive proposal, however, we must first confront the best attempts made by contractarians to confront the issue of global justice. I shall first describe the two different strategies used by contractarians to address the problems of justice between nations: the strategy of what I shall call the *two-stage bargain*, and the strategy of what I shall call the *global bargain*. Taking John Rawls's *The Law of Peoples* as a best case of the former strategy, I shall argue that this approach cannot provide an adequate account of global justice. The strategy of the *global bargain* looks more promising; but it cannot defend redistribution from richer to poorer nations without departing in major ways from the social contract approach.

Although my arguments in this essay are directed against social contract approaches to global justice, I choose these approaches because they are stronger than some others we have – stronger, in particular, than models of global development based on contemporary economic Utilitarianism. The "human development approach" that I favor can make alliance with contractarians, up to a point, against that crude approach. It is this subtle debate between two worthy opponents that concerns me here. And my main contention will be that we cannot solve the problem of global justice by envisaging international cooperation as a contract for mutual advantage among parties similarly placed in a State of Nature. We can solve them only by thinking of what all human beings require to live a richly human life – a set of basic entitlements for all people – and by developing a conception of the purpose of social cooperation that focuses on fellowship as well as self-interest. Contractarian ways of thinking, especially the idea that we ought to expect to profit from cooperation with others, have untold influence on public debate. My aim is to supply something both new and old, resurrecting the richer ideas of human fellowship that we find in Grotius and other exponents of the natural law tradition.

Before we begin, we need to have before us very clearly three salient features of social contract conceptions on which John Rawls, the most influential modern exponent of that tradition, continues to rely throughout his work – despite the fact that his hybrid theory mixes Kantian moral elements with the idea of a social contract. First, Rawls explicitly endorses the idea that the social contract is made between parties who are roughly equal in power and resources, so that no one can dominate the others. Tracing this idea to Hume's account of the "Circumstances of Justice," as well as to classical social contract doctrine, he insists that this rough equality of the parties is an essential element in his theory, and is his own analogue to the idea of the State of Nature in classical social contract doctrine. Second, and closely connected, the contract is imagined as one made for mutual advantage, where advantage is defined in familiar economic terms, and income and wealth play a central role in indexing relative social positions. Although the Veil of Ignorance introduces moral constraints on the ways in which the parties achieve their own interest, the parties are still imagined as exiting from the State of Nature in the first place because it is in their interest to do so. Thus, while the Veil sharply limits the role played by interest once they enter the Original Position, interest continues to play a large part in determining who is in and who is out at the initial stage: namely, they bargain with rough equals in power and resources, because a contract for mutual advantage makes sense only between rough equals, none of whom can dominate the others. Despite his Kantianism, Rawls remains a contractarian in these two crucial respects. Finally, contract theories take the nation state as their basic unit, conceiving of their contracting parties as choosing principles for such a state. This focus is dictated by their starting point: they imagine people choosing to depart from the State of Nature only when they have found principles by which to live a cooperative life together. This starting point is a grave limitation, as we shall see.

A THEORY OF JUSTICE: THE TWO-STAGE BARGAIN INTRODUCED

The pre-contractarian "natural law" tradition held that relations between states, like the rest of the world of human affairs, are regulated by "natural law," that is, binding moral laws that supply normative constraints on states, whether or not these dictates are incorporated into any system of positive law. The social contract tradition, by contrast, understood the situation that exists between states as a State of Nature, and imagined principles of justice being contracted as if between virtual persons. The clearest example of this two-stage approach, and the most significant for Rawls, is Kant, who writes in *The Metaphysics of Morals* that a state is like a household situated alongside others. Under the Law of Nations, he continues, a state is "a moral Person living with and in opposition to another state in a condition of natural freedom, which itself is a condition of continual war." States ought to "abandon the state of nature and enter, with all others, a juridical state of affairs, that is, a state of distributive legal justice" (Kant, 1970, p. 307). The social contract, then, is applied in the first instance to persons, enjoining that they leave the State of Nature and enter a state. It is then applied a second time over to states,[2] enjoining that they enter some kind of juridical state of affairs.[3]

In *A Theory of Justice*, Rawls continues this Kantian approach. He assumes that the principles of justice applying to each society have already been fixed: each has a "basic structure" whose form is determined by those principles (Rawls, 1971, p. 377). The "basic structure" of a society is defined as "the way in which the major social institutions distribute fundamental rights and duties and determine the division of advantages from social cooperation" (Rawls, 1971, p. 7). It is said to be equivalent to those structures that have effects that are "profound and present from the start," affecting "men's initial chances in life" (Rawls, 1971, p. 7).

We now imagine a second-stage original position, whose parties are "representatives of different nations who must choose together the fundamental principles to adjudicate conflicting claims among states" (Rawls, 1971, p. 378). They know that they represent nations "each living under the normal circumstances of human life," but they know nothing about the particular circumstances of their own nation, its "power and strength in comparison with other nations." They are allowed "only enough knowledge to make a rational choice to protect their interests but not so much that the more fortunate among them can take advantage of their special situation." This second-stage contract is designed to "nullif[y] the contingencies and biases of historical fate."

Rawls says little about the principles that would be chosen in this situation, but he indicates that they would include most of the familiar principles of the current law of nations: treaties must be kept; each nation has a right of self-determination and non-intervention; nations have a right to self-defense and to defensive alliances; just war is limited to war in self-defense; conduct in war is governed by the traditional norms of the law of war; the aim of war must always be a just and lasting peace (Rawls, 1971, pp. 378–79).

Let us now consider the analogy between states and "moral persons." One of its problems is that many nations of the world do not have governments that represent the interests of the people taken as a whole. Even when a nation has a government that is not a mere tyranny, large segments of the population may be completely excluded from governance. Thus Rawls's device of representation is indeterminate. In such cases, if the representative represents the state and its basic structure, as Rawls strongly implies, he is likely by this very fact *not* to represent the interests of most of the people.

A second problem concerns the fixity of the domestic basic structure. Rawls seems to accord legitimacy to the status quo, even when it is not fully accountable to people. One of the things people themselves might actually want out of international relations is help overthrowing an unjust regime, or winning full inclusion in one that excludes them. There is no place for this in Rawls's early scheme.

But the gravest problem with the analogy is its assumption of the self-sufficiency of states. In designing principles at the first stage, the society is assumed to be "a closed system isolated from other societies" (Rawls, 1971, p. 8). (Thus it is no surprise that the relations between states are envisaged as occupying a very thin terrain, that of the traditional law of war and peace.) This is so far from being true of the world in which we live that it seems most unhelpful. Rawls's structure has no room even for a supra-national political/economic structure such as that of the European Union, far less for the complex interdependencies that characterize the world as a whole.

The assumption of the fixity and finality of states makes the second-stage bargain assume a very thin and restricted form, precluding any serious consideration of economic redistribution from richer to poorer nations. Indeed, Rawls waves that problem away from the start by his contractarian assumption of a rough equality between the parties: no one is supposed to be able to dominate the others. Of course, in our world, these conditions are not fulfilled: one probably can dominate all the others. At any rate, the G8 do effectively dominate all the others. To assume a rough equality between parties is to assume something so grossly false of the world as to make the resulting theory unable to address the world's most urgent problems.

Notice, too, that starting from the assumption of the existence and finality of states, we do not get any interesting answer to the question why states might be thought to matter, why it might be important to make sure that national sovereignty does not get fatally eroded by the power of economic globalization. Let us now see whether *The Law of Peoples* solves these problems. I believe that it makes a little progress on some, but none on others; and it introduces new problems of its own.

THE LAW OF PEOPLES: THE TWO-STAGE BARGAIN REAFFIRMED AND MODIFIED

The Law of Peoples "is an extension of a liberal conception of justice for a domestic regime to a Society of Peoples" (Rawls, 1999a, p. 9). As in *Theory of Justice*, Rawls takes the domestic principles and policies of liberal societies as fixed, including their economic policies, and simply inquires into their foreign policies. At the same time, however, Rawls devotes some attention to real-world problems, if only to reassure the reader that these problems can be solved through a structure that fixes the domestic basic structure first, and then addresses, at a second stage, problems between nations. Thus he mentions immigration, only to reassure us that the need for immigration would "disappear" (Rawls, 1999a, p. 9) if all nations had an internally decent political structure. Among the causes of immigration he mentions religious and ethnic persecution, political oppression, famine (which he holds to be prevent-able by domestic policies alone), and population pressure (which, again, he holds to be controllable by changes in domestic policy). In "the Society of liberal and decent Peoples" these causes would not exist. Absent from his list, however, is one of the greatest causes of immigration, economic inequality — along with malnutrition, ill health, and lack of education, which so often accompany poverty.

Similarly, discussing the "burdened peoples," who on account of their poverty will not be part of the Society of Peoples, he justifies not discussing economic inequality between nations by insisting that extreme poverty can be eradicated by reasonable domestic policies: the main causes of wealth are, he says, the political culture of a people, their religious and ethical traditions, and their talents and "industriousness." Such an analysis ignores the fact that the international economic system creates severe, disproportionate burdens for poorer nations, who cannot solve their problems by wise internal policies alone. Clearly in the domestic case Rawls would not consider it sufficient to point out that poor families can get by on thrift and virtue. Even to the extent that this may be true, it does not dispose of the question of justice.

Let us now investigate Rawls's central argument. As in *Theory of Justice*, the device of the Original Position is applied in two stages: first domestically within each liberal society, and then between those societies. However, a major new feature of the book is that Rawls also holds that a decent Society of Peoples includes as members in good standing certain non-liberal peoples, who have " decent hierarchical societies." But of course these societies, being non-liberal, do not apply the Original Position domestically. They have other ways of establishing their political principles (Rawls, 1999a, p. 70). So, there are three applications of the Original Position device: domestically by liberal peoples, then internationally by liberal peoples, then, in a further step, internationally by the non-liberal peoples who decide to sign on to the Society of Peoples.

As in *Theory of Justice*, the traditional concerns of foreign policy are the focus of both second-stage bargains, and a stable peace is at the core of their aspiration. Thus, among the eight principles of the Law of Peoples, six deal with familiar topics of international law, such as independence and self-determination, non-aggression, the binding force of treaties, non-intervention, the right of self-defense, and restrictions on the conduct of war. But Rawls expands his account to include agreement on some essential human rights and a duty to assist other peoples living under unfavorable conditions.

As in *Theory of Justice*, Rawls treats the domestic principles of justice as fixed and not up for grabs in the second-stage bargain. For none of these states, then, will the second-stage bargain call into question anything about their assignment of liberties and opportunities, or, importantly, about their domestic economic arrangements.

On some vexing issues left over from *Theory of Justice*, however, the new work makes progress. Recall that the analogy between states and persons suggested that states somehow represent the interests of the people within them; this, however, we said, is not true of many nations in the world. Rawls now officially recognizes this fact and gives it structural importance. The second-stage Original Position includes only states that respect human rights and have either a liberal-democratic constitution or a "decent hierarchical" arrangement that includes a "common good conception of justice" and a "decent consultation hierarchy." On the outside of the Society of Peoples are "outlaw states," which do not respect human rights, and "burdened societies," which are defined as not only poor but also politically badly organized. Rawls holds that one important task of the Society of Peoples is to restrain the outlaw states. In this way, the argument has at least some bearing on the opportunities of people who are oppressed by these societies. All members, moreover, have duties to assist the burdened societies, which primarily means, for Rawls, helping them to develop stable democratic institutions, which he takes to be the main ingredient of their eventual prosperity. As I have already said, this is a limited understanding of what we owe other nations, but at least it is something.

The most important development beyond the approach of *Theory of Justice* lies in Rawls's recognition of the transnational force of human rights. Membership in the Society of Peoples requires respect for a list of such rights, which constrain national sovereignty. The list is understood to be only a subgroup of those rights that liberal societies typically protect internally, "a special class of urgent rights, such as freedom from slavery and serfdom, liberty (but not equal liberty) of conscience, and security of ethnic groups from mass murder and genocide" (Rawls, 1999a, p. 79). Although this is a clear progress beyond *Theory of Justice*, it is important to notice how thin the list of rights is: it explicitly omits more than half the rights enumerated in the Universal Declaration. Moreover, the fixity of the basic structure entails that no international agreement in the area of human rights going beyond this thin menu will have the power to alter domestic institutions.

So: Rawls makes only a little progress toward a richer conception of international society. Insofar as he does make progress, we can now observe, this progress is made possible not by the contractual approach itself, but by some very dramatic departures from it, in the direction of an approach more like the one I shall favor, which defines a minimal conception of social justice in terms of the realization of certain positive outcomes, what people are actually able to do and to be. The criteria used to judge who is part of the bargain and who is not are ethical outcomes-oriented criteria: respect for human rights. Moreover, it appears that Rawls has jettisoned the traditional Humean criterion of rough equality, in the sense of similar economic circumstances. For clearly enough, nations that uphold human rights are not rough equals at all. Rawls seems to imagine the bargain as taking place between the United States and the nations of Europe and Australasia, which might at least be claimed to be rough equals. But where do we place nations such as India, Bangladesh, and South Africa, liberal-rights-respecting democracies that are grossly unequal to Australia and the others in basic economic advantage? The GDP per capita of the United States is $34,142, that of Bangladesh $1,602, that of India $2,358, that of South Africa $9,401. So these nations are extremely far from being rough equals of the nations of the US, Europe, and Australasia, and also far from being rough equals of one another.

The upshot is as follows. Either Rawls will have to admit that the principles and circumstances that bring societies together to form the second-stage bargain are very different from the Humean "circumstances of justice," with their focus on rough equality and mutual advantage, or he will stand firm on those conditions. If he departs from Hume, relaxing the condition of rough equality and the associated understanding of the motivation of the parties (they can all expect to gain from cooperation), then he can include all the nations I have mentioned, with their staggering inequalities. But then he will have to offer a new account of why they cooperate together, since the bargain can no longer be seen as one for mutual advantage. Peace, of course, is in the interests of all human beings, but, as with the "outlaw states," peace can be promoted externally, so to speak, and need not be promoted by including the poor democracies in the bargain itself. So we must have a richer account of the purposes they pursue together. If, on the other hand, Rawls stands firm with Hume, then he ought to say that India, Bangladesh, and South Africa do not belong in the second-stage bargain, much though his other criteria tell in favor of their inclusion. They are just too poor for the richer nations to gain anything from treating them as rough equals. Rawls has not thought this through; his unclarity at this point makes *Law of Peoples* an unsatisfactory work.

One more aspect of its inadequacy remains to be noted. As we have said, Rawls's Society of Peoples admits "decent hierarchical societies," justifying this move by appeal to a principle of toleration that makes a highly questionable use of the state-person analogy. Rawls argues as follows:

Surely tyrannical and dictatorial regimes cannot be accepted as members in good standing of a reasonable society of peoples. But equally not all regimes can reasonably be required to be liberal, otherwise the law of peoples itself would not express liberalism's own principle of toleration for other reasonable ways of ordering society nor further its attempt to find a shared basis of agreement among reasonable peoples. Just as a citizen in a liberal society must respect other persons' comprehensive religious, philosophical, and moral doctrines provided they are pursued in accordance with a reasonable political conception of justice, so a liberal society must respect other societies organized by comprehensive doctrines, provided their political and social institutions meet certain conditions that lead the society to adhere to a reasonable law of peoples. (Rawls, 1999a, pp. 42–43)

In other words: just as Americans are required to respect the comprehensive doctrines of believing Roman Catholics, and Buddhists, and Muslims, provided they respect the reasonable political conception of justice defended in *Political Liberalism* (Rawls, 1993b), so too a liberal society is required to show respect both for other liberal societies and for decent hierarchical societies, provided that these societies adhere to the constraints and standards spelled out in the Law of Peoples. Toleration is said to require not only refraining from exercising military, economic, or diplomatic sanctions against a people, but also recognizing the nonliberal societies as equal members of the Society of Peoples.

Let us now examine this analogy. In fact, there are both analogy and disanalogy. Inside a liberal society, there are many hierarchical conceptions of the good. These conceptions will be respected as reasonable, provided that their adherents accept, as a constituent part within their comprehensive doctrine, the principles of justice that shape the basic structure of their society.[4] In other words, the religious conceptions must include Rawls's principles of justice, even if originally they did not do so. Comprehensive doctrines that promulgate teachings conflicting with those will not find their speech suppressed, except in the exceptional conditions Rawls specifies in his doctrine of free political speech. Nonetheless, they will not be respected, in the sense of being regarded as members of society's constitutional structure; nor will their proposals be allowed to come forward for straightforward majority vote, since contradictory ideas will be entrenched in the nation's constitution.

In the transnational case, things are very different. The religious or traditional doctrine is tolerated, in the sense of being recognized as belonging to the community of peoples, whenever certain far weaker conditions obtain. There must still be respect for a small list of human rights. But it is clear that a people may win respect in the community of peoples even if property rights, voting rights, and religious freedom are unequally assigned to different actors within the society – men and women, for instance.[5] The requirements of political democracy, equal liberty, and universal suffrage[6] are replaced by the weaker requirement of a "reasonable consultation hierarchy." Even free speech need not be accorded to all persons, so long as certain "associations and corporate bodies" allow them to express dissent in some way, and take their views seriously.

In the domestic case, Rawls's principle of toleration is a person-centered principle: it involves respecting persons and their conceptions of the good. In the transnational case, although Rawls depicts himself as applying the same principle, the principle is fundamentally different: it respects groups rather than persons, and shows deficient respect for persons, allowing their entitlements to be dictated by the dominant group in their vicinity, whether they like that group or not. Rawls still focuses on persons to the extent of insisting on a small list of urgent human rights. But he allows groups to have a power in the national case that they do not have in the domestic theory.

Furthermore, in the domestic case, any concessions that are made to the group are made against the background of exit options: persons are free to depart from one religion and to join another, or to have no religion at all. Rawls knows well that the basic structure of a nation offers no, or few,[7] exit options; this is why he thinks it is so important that the institutions that form part of the basic structure should be just. The basic structure shapes people's life chances pervasively and from the start. And yet in the transnational case, Rawls has lost sight of this insight, allowing a local tradition to shape people's life chances pervasively, in ways that depart from principles of justice, even though there are no exit options for those who do not endorse that doctrine.

I conclude that Rawls's analogy is deeply flawed. So far as his argument goes, at least, there seems to be no moral obstacle to justifying a single far more expansive set of human rights, or human capabilities, as fundamental norms for all persons.

Rawls clearly thinks that if we conclude that another nation has defective norms we will intervene, whether militarily or through economic and political sanctions. But that need not be the case. For we may, and I believe must, separate the question of justification from the question of implementation. We may justify a set of benchmarks of justice for all the world's societies, in public debate, and yet hold that we are not entitled to use military force, or even, perhaps, economic sanctions to impose these standards on a state, except in very exceptional circumstances, so long as that state meets some minimal conditions of legitimacy. The rationale for this deference to the nation is both prudential and moral. Its moral part, well expressed by Grotius, is the idea that national sovereignty is a key expression of human autonomy.

When people join together to give laws to themselves, this is a human act that ought to be respected, even if the decision that is reached is one that is not fully justified from the moral point of view.

THE GLOBAL BARGAIN: BEITZ AND POGGE

A far more appealing use of a contractarian approach is made by Charles Beitz and Thomas Pogge (Beitz, 1979; Pogge, 1989). For both of them, the right way to use Rawlsian insights in crafting a theory of global justice is to think of the Original Position as applied directly to the world as a whole. The insight guiding this strategy is that national origin is rather like class background, parental wealth, race, and sex: namely, a contingent fact about a person that should not be permitted to deform a person's life (Pogge, 1989, p. 247). Pogge and Beitz argue convincingly that the only way to be sufficiently respectful of the individual as subject of justice, within a Rawlsian framework, is to imagine that the whole global system is up for grabs, and that the parties are bargaining as individuals for a just global structure. Both argue, in different ways, that the resulting structure will be one that optimizes the position of the least well off. Pogge's view (which he calls "only illustrative speculation" [Pogge, 1989, p. 273]) envisages an initial global agreement on a list of human rights, which, over time, becomes more robust, including a system of global economic constraints. The list of human rights is considerably thicker than that defended by Rawls: it includes the entirety of the Universal Declaration, plus an effective right to emigrate (Pogge, 1989, p. 272). Natural resources are also subject to redistribution.

The Pogge–Beitz proposal is a big improvement over the two-stage bargain. The global Veil of Ignorance is an insightful way of capturing the idea that a just global order will not be based on existing hierarchies of power, but will be fair to all human beings. One significant difficulty with these proposals is their vague and speculative nature. We are not told in detail exactly how the global bargain will work, what information the parties will and will not have. The world we live in exhibits changing configurations of power at the level of the basic structure itself; even one hundred years ago it would have been difficult to predict what those structures would be. The new structures (multinational corporations, for example) govern people's life chances pervasively and from the start. If the parties do not know their own area and its economic structures, they can hardly choose well. A related area of unfortunate vagueness concerns the role of the nation-state. Pogge and Beitz set out to question the finality and closed character of domestic state structures. But they do not tell us how far they really want to go. Are we standing back so far from current events that the very concept of the state will have to be reinvented, and considered against other options for arranging people's lives? But it is hard to arrange human lives in a complete vacuum. How can we say whether the state is or is not a good structure, without first assessing its relation to other aspects of life, such as trade, the flow of information, the presence of international agencies and agreements? Finally, we need to know more about what primary goods the parties are imagined as pursuing. Pogge depicts himself as following Rawls closely, and yet he also thinks that his parties will agree on a long list of human rights, and will recognize a material basis for liberty. How far does he really intend to depart from Rawls's idea?

These are all questions that might be answered, although an adequate response will probably require departures from the Rawlsian framework. At this point, however, we arrive at the most serious difficulty with the Pogge–Beitz proposal: what is the bargain all about? The Rawlsian social contract takes place in Humean circumstances of justice, and it is a bargain for mutual advantage. Pogge has focused on the requirement of fairness that is built into Rawls's Veil of Ignorance and simply omitted Rawls's endorsement of Humean circumstances of justice as the starting point for the bargain. As Rawls insists, the requirement of equality among the parties is his analogue to the state of nature in classical social contract doctrine, so if that is omitted we have a major departure from the contract tradition.

We have already seen that when the bargain is envisaged as taking place among nations, it cannot be cast in this form unless we omit not only non-liberal states, but also pretty much everyone except the G8. If we imagine the bargain as taking place among individual persons, things are indeed different: for the individual persons of the world are at least morally equal, and in some ways they – all those who are not disabled, that is! – might be argued to be roughly equal in basic economic productivity and life chances, before the contingencies of life begin to affect them. But when is that? Surely not at any time after birth, for every child is born into a world that begins to affect its life chances directly and dramatically, through differential nutrition, differential cognitive stimulation, differential exposure to kindness or violence, and so on. As we have seen, life expectancy at birth in the poorest nations is half what it is in Sweden; this aggregate figure derives from all kinds of differences at the level of individual lives.

Are individuals equal in life chances before birth? Surely not. Whatever account we give of the fetus, we must say that by the time a human being is born, differences in maternal nutrition, health care, bodily integrity, and emotional well-being, not to mention HIV status, have already affected its life chances. For that matter, even getting the chance to be born is not a matter with respect to which there is rough equality: the staggering rise in sex-selective abortion in many developing countries means that females conceived in some parts of the world are grossly unequal in life chances both to boys in that same part of the world and to girls and boys in other parts of the world.

Unfortunately, then, the inequalities between nations that make the two-stage bargain exclude some nations in order to conform to the Humean circumstances of justice are translated into inequalities between persons in basic life-chances. There is no time when a human or even a potential human is alive that such inequalities do not obtain.

Pogge and Beitz abhor such inequalities in basic life chances. To cope with them, providing a philosophical rationale for an ambitious commitment to global redistribution, is the whole point of their project. But what I am trying to bring out is that this commitment is not so easily reconciled with the Rawlsian framework, even in the improved non-Rawlsian way in which they use it. It is all very well to say that the Original Position should be applied at the global level; as I have said, that idea does dramatize some important issues of fairness. But once we go into things in more detail, we find that the global bargain they propose actually requires a departure of major proportions from the Rawlsian framework. For it requires abandoning the Humean circumstances of justice as setting the stage for the bargain, and including from the start all who are currently unequal in power. Above all, it requires admitting from the start that the point of the bargain is not, and cannot be, mutual advantage among "rough equals." It must be human fellowship, and human respect, in a more expansive sense.

SOCIAL COOPERATION: THE PRIORITY OF ENTITLEMENTS

Because we live in a world in which it is simply not true that cooperating with others on fair terms will be advantageous to all, we must boldly insist that this account of social cooperation, even in its moralized Kantian form, is not the one we need to guide us. We have, and use ideas of cooperation that are much richer than this. These richer ideas already inhabit the pre-contractarian natural law tradition, as my epigraph from

Grotius makes clear. With Grotius, we ought to think of ourselves as people who want to live with others. A central part of our own good, each and every one of us, is to produce, and live in, a world that is morally decent, a world in which all human beings have what they need to live a life with human dignity.

The capabilities approach is an outcome-oriented approach. It says that a world in which people have all the capabilities on the list is a minimally just and decent world. Domestically, it interprets the purpose of social cooperation as that of establishing principles and institutions that guarantee that all human beings have the capabilities on the list, or can effectively claim them if they do not. It thus has a close relationship to institutional and constitutional design, and the capabilities on my list are understood as informal recommendations to nations that are making or amending their constitutions.

In the international case, how should the approach proceed? Some theories, such as Rawls, begin with the design of a fair procedure. My capabilities approach begins with outcomes: with a list of entitlements that have to be secured to citizens, if the society in question is a minimally just one. Especially in the current world, where institutions and their relations are constantly in flux, I believe it is wise to begin with human entitlements as our goal. We think what people are entitled to receive, and, even before we can say in detail who may have the duties, we conclude that there are such duties, and that we have a collective obligation to make sure people get what they are due.

We think about human dignity and what it requires. My approach suggests that we ought to do this in an Aristotelian/Marxian way, thinking about the prerequisites for living a life that is fully human rather than subhuman, a life worthy of the dignity of the human being. We include in this idea the idea of the human being as a being with, in Marx's phrase, "rich human need," which includes the need to live cooperatively with others. We insist that a fundamental part of the good of each and every human being will be to cooperate together for the fulfillment of human needs and the realization of fully human lives. We now argue that this fully human life requires many things from the world: adequate nutrition, education of the faculties, protection of bodily integrity, liberty for speech and religious self-expression – and so forth. If this is so, then we all have entitlements based on justice to a minimum of each of these central goods. So far, things are very definite: the idea of what human beings need for fully human living is an intuitive idea, realized in many human rights documents.

But if human beings have such entitlements, then we are all under a collective obligation to provide the people of the world with what they need. Thus the first answer to the question, "Who has the duties?" is that we all do. Humanity is under a collective obligation to find ways of living and cooperating together so that all human beings have decent lives. Now, after getting clear on that, we begin to think about how to bring that about. The focus on capabilities reminds us that we will need to make special efforts to address the unequal needs of those who begin from a position of social disadvantage. Moreover, a focus on capabilities, although closely allied with the human rights approach, adds an important clarification to the idea of human rights: for it informs us that our goal is not merely "negative liberty" or absence of interfering state action – one very common understanding of the notion of rights – but, instead, the full ability of people to be and to choose these very important things. Thus all capabilities have an economic aspect: even the freedom of speech requires education, adequate nutrition, etc.

Although the approach remains focused on the person as goal, and is committed to securing the basic goods of life for each, it is respectful of cultural difference in several ways: in the role carved out for nations in implementing and more concretely specifying the list; in the prominence, on this list, of the major liberties of speech and conscience; and in the idea that capability, not functioning, is the appropriate political goal – once an opportunity is given to people, they may choose what to do with it.

GLOBALIZING THE CAPABILITIES APPROACH: THE ROLE OF INSTITUTIONS

So far, the capabilities approach has announced some ambitious goals for the world, and some general principles regarding pluralism and national sovereignty. Obviously, however, a great deal more remains to be said about precisely how the approach can be used to generate political principles for today's world. To some extent, this job is a practical job, a job for economists, political scientists, diplomats, and policy-makers. Philosophy is good at normative reasoning and at laying out general structures of thought. In a rapidly changing world, however, any very concrete prescriptions for implementation need to be made in partnership with other disciplines.

To say this is not at all to say that philosophy is not urgently practical. Ideas shape the way policy-makers do their work. That is why, from its very inception, the capabilities approach contested the idea of development as economic growth, and insisted on the idea of "human development." That is why it seems crucial, now, to call into question the idea of mutual advantage as the goal of social cooperation. The capabilities approach is not remote and impractical, but urgently practical, when it urges us to rethink our ideas of social cooperation. For we can see that many short-sighted policies in development and international financial policy flow from such ideas (see Soros, 2002).

We can certainly go somewhat further than this, in speaking about realizing the capabilities in our world. We must, indeed, confront the question of how to allocate the duties of promoting the capabilities, in a world that contains nations, economic agreements and agencies, other international agreements and agencies, corporations, and individual people. To say that "we all" have the duties is all very well, and true. But it would be good if we could go further, saying something about the proper allocation of duties between individuals and institutions, and among institutions of various kinds.

Institutions are made by people, and it is ultimately people who should be seen as having moral duties to promote human capabilities. Nonetheless, there are three reasons why we should think of the duties as assigned, derivatively, to institutional structures. First of all, there are *collective action problems*. Think of a nation. If we say that the citizens have duties to maintain the system of property rights, the tax structure, the system of criminal justice, and so forth, we are in one sense saying something true and important. There are no living beings in the state other than its people; there is no magical superperson who will shoulder the work. Nonetheless, if each person tries to choose individually, massive confusion would ensue. It is far better to create a decent institutional structure and then to regard individuals as delegating their ethical responsibility to that structure. Much the same is true in the international sphere.

Second, there are issues of *fairness*. If I care a lot about the poor in my country, and give a lot of my personal money to support their needs, I am thus impoverishing myself and my family, relatively to those who begin in the same place but who do nothing for the poor. Any system of voluntary philanthropy has this problem. As long as others are not made to pay their fair share, whatever that is, the ones who do pay both have to do more (if the problem is to be solved) and have to incur a relative disadvantage that they would not incur if the system imposed a proportional burden on everyone (see Murphy, 2001).

Finally, there is a more subtle issue about the personal life. In Utilitarianism, given that all moral responsibility is understood as personal responsibility to maximize total or average welfare, there is a large question about what becomes of the person and the sense that a person has a life. People are just engines of maximization. More or less all of their energy has to be devoted to calculating the right thing to do, and then doing it. They will have to choose the careers that maximize total or average well-being, the friendships, the political commitments. The sense that there is anything that is really them or their own is difficult to maintain.[8] This worry is really a set of closely related worries: about personal integrity, about agency, about friendship and family, about the sources of the meaning of life, and about the nature of political agency.

We do not need to elaborate all of these concerns further here in order to see that there is a great deal in them – and from the perspective of the capabilities approach itself. The capabilities approach aims at giving people the necessary conditions of a life with human dignity. It would be a self-defeating theory indeed if the injunction to promote human capabilities devoured people's lives, removing personal projects and space to such an extent that nobody at all had the chance to lead a dignified life.

A good solution to this problem is to assign the responsibility for promoting others' well-being (capabilities) to institutions, giving individuals broad discretion about how to use their lives apart from that (see Nagel, 1991). Institutions impose on all, in a fair way, the duty to support the capabilities of all, up to a minimum threshold. Beyond that, people are free to use their money, time, and other resources as their own conception of the good dictates. Ethical norms internal to each religious or ethical comprehensive doctrine will determine how far each person is ethically responsible for doing more than what is institutionally required. But the political task of supporting the capabilities threshold itself is delegated to institutions.

In the domestic case, we can easily say quite a lot about what institutions bear the burden of supporting the capabilities of the nation's citizens: the structure of institutions laid out in the nation's constitution, together with the set of entitlements prescribed in the constitution itself. This structure will include legislature, courts, administration and at least some administrative agencies, laws defining the institution of the family and allocating privileges to its members, the system of taxation and welfare, the overall structure of the economic system, the criminal justice system, etc.

When we move to the global plane, however, nothing is clear. If a world state were desirable, we could at least describe its structure. But it is far from desirable. Unlike domestic basic structures, a world state would be very unlikely to have a decent level of accountability to its citizens. It is too vast an undertaking, and differences of culture and language make communication too difficult. The world state is also dangerous: if it should become unjust there is no recourse to external aid. Moreover, even if those problems could be overcome, there is a deep moral problem with the idea of a world state, uniform in its institutions. National sovereignty, I argued, has moral importance, as a way people have of asserting their right to give themselves laws.

If these arguments are good, the institutional structure at the global level ought to remain thin and decentralized. Part of it will consist, quite simply, of the domestic basic structures, to which we shall assign responsibilities for redistributing some of their wealth to other nations. Part of it will consist of multinational corporations, to whom we shall assign certain responsibilities for promoting human capabilities in the nations in which they do business. Part of it will consist of global economic policies, agencies, and agreements, including the World Bank, the International Monetary Fund (IMF), various trade agreements, and so forth. Part will consist of other international bodies, such as the United Nations, the International Labor Organization, the World Court and the new world criminal court, and of international agreements in many areas, such as human rights, labor, environment. Part of it will consist of nongovernmental organizations, ranging from the large and multinational to the small and local.

The form this structure has assumed up until now is the result of history, rather than of deliberate normative reflection. There is thus an odd fit between normative political philosophy and the details of a set of institutions as oddly assorted as this. It is also clear that the allocation of responsibility among different parts of the global structure must remain provisional, and subject to change and rethinking. Notice, as well, that the allocation is an ethical allocation: there is no coercive structure over the whole to enforce on any given part a definite set of tasks. Nonetheless, we can articulate some principles for a world order of this kind, which can at least help us think about how capabilities can be promoted in a world of inequalities.

TEN PRINCIPLES FOR THE GLOBAL STRUCTURE

1. *Over-determination of responsibility: the domestic never escapes it.* Most nations, well and honestly run, can promote many or even most of the human capabilities up to some reasonable threshold level. I have

said that if justice requires the mitigation of global inequality, justice is not satisfied even if poor nations can promote the capabilities internally. Nonetheless, we can begin by insisting that they do all that is in their power. If the fulfillment of capabilities is over-determined, so much the better.

2. *National sovereignty should be respected, within the constraints of promoting human capabilities.* In talking about justification and implementation I have already outlined the ideas behind this principle. In general, coercive intervention is justified in only a limited range of circumstances. But persuasion and persuasive use of funding are always a good thing. This brings me to my next principle:

3. *Prosperous nations have a responsibility to give a substantial portion of their GDP to poorer nations.* The prosperous nations of the world have the responsibility of supporting the human capabilities of their own citizens, as Principle 1 asserts. But they also have additional responsibilities. They can reasonably be expected to give a great deal more than they currently give to assist poorer nations: the figure of two percent of GDP, while arbitrary, is a good sign of what might be morally adequate.

Less clear is the form such aid ought to take: should it be given in the first instance to governments, or also to non-governmental organizations? This must be left for contextual determination: the general principle would be not to undermine national sovereignty if the recipient nation is democratic, but at the same time to give aid in an efficient way, and a way that shows respect for the capabilities on the list.

4. *Multinational corporations have responsibilities for promoting human capabilities in the regions in which they operate.* The understanding of what a corporation is for, up until now, has been dominated by the profit motive. This understanding has not prevented corporations from devoting quite a lot of money to charity domestically, but there is no generally accepted standard of moral responsibility. The new global order must have a clear public understanding that part of doing business decently in a region is to devote a substantial amount of one's profits to promoting education and good environmental conditions. There are good efficiency arguments for this: corporations do better with a stable, well-educated work force. Education also promotes political engagement, crucial for the health of a democracy; and corporations do well under conditions of political

stability. Nonetheless, those arguments should be subsidiary to a general public understanding that such support is what decency requires. At the same time, corporations should undertake to promote good labor conditions, going beyond what local laws require.

5. *The main structures of the global economic system must be designed to be fair to poor and developing countries.* As we have said, the fact that many nations can feed all their people does not mean that it is fair for some countries to have additional burdens placed in their way. Exactly what this principle involves is a matter that economists debate, and will long continue debating. But there is pretty general agreement that the ways in which the IMF and various global trade agreements have been operating are insufficiently informed by careful ethical reflection about these issues.

6. *We should cultivate a thin, decentralized, and yet forceful global public sphere.* A world state is not, we argued, an appropriate aspiration. But there is no reason why a thin system of global governance, with at least some coercive powers, should not be compatible with the sovereignty and freedom of individual nations. This system should include a world criminal court of the sort currently proposed, to deal with grave human-rights violations; a set of world environmental regulations, with enforcement mechanisms, plus a tax on the industrial nations of the North to support the development of pollution controls in the South; a set of global trade regulations that would try to harness the juggernaut of globalization to a set of moral goals for human development, as set forth in the capabilities list; a set of global labor standards, for both the formal and the informal sector, together with sanctions for companies that do not obey them; some limited forms of global taxation that would effect transfers of wealth from richer to poorer nations (such as the global resource tax suggested by Thomas Pogge); and, finally, a wide range of international accords and treaties that can be incorporated into the nations' systems of law through judicial and legislative action.[9]

7. *All institutions and individuals should focus on the problems of the disadvantaged in each nation and region.* We have observed that national sovereignty, while morally important, risks insulating from criticism and change the situation of women and other disadvantaged groups within each nation. The situation of people (whoever they are, at any given time) whose quality of life is especially low, as measured by the capabilities list, should therefore be a persistent

focus of attention for the world community as a whole. Although coercive sanctions will be appropriate in only some cases, our ability to justify a richer set of norms should lead to tireless efforts of persuasion, political mobilization, and selective funding.

8. *Care for the ill, the elderly, and the disabled should be a prominent focus of the world community.* A growing problem in today's world, as the population ages and as more and more people are living with HIV/AIDS, is the need to care for people in a condition of dependency. The state, the workplace, and the family must all change so that needs for care are met without crippling the well-being and the aspirations of women.

9. *The family should be treated as a sphere that is precious but not "private."* The world community should protect the individual liberties of people, which includes their right to choose to marry and form a family, and various further rights associated with that. But the protection of the human capabilities of family members is always paramount. The millions of girl children who die of neglect and lack of essential food and care are not dying because the state has persecuted them; they are dying because their parents do not want another female mouth to feed (and another dowry to pay), and the state has not done enough to protect female lives.

10. *All institutions and individuals have a responsibility to support education, as key to the empowerment of currently disadvantaged people.* Education is a key to all the human capabilities (see Nussbaum, 2004). It is also among the resources that is most unequally distributed around the world. Domestic governments can do much more in more or less all cases to promote education in each nation; but corporations, non-governmental organizations (funded by individual contributions, foreign aid from governments, etc.), and the global public sphere (in international documents and fora) can do a great deal more than they now do to promote universal primary and secondary education everywhere.

There is no natural place to stop this list of principles. One might have had a list of twenty principles, rather than ten. Nonetheless, the principles, together with the theoretical analysis that supports them, are at least a sign of what the capabilities approach can offer, as we move from goals and entitlements to the construction of a decent global society. If our world is to be a decent world in the future, we must acknowledge right now that we are citizens of one interdependent world, held together by mutual fellowship as well as the pursuit of mutual advantage, by compassion as well as self-interest, by a love of human dignity in all people, even when there is nothing we have to gain from cooperating with them. Or rather, even when what we have to gain is the biggest thing of all: participation in a just and morally decent world.

1 All data in this paragraph are from *Human Development Report 2002*, pp. 141–44. Data are from 2000. Sierra Leone ranks last overall among the 173 countries in the Human Development Index.
2 Kant says, rightly, that "Law of Nations" is a misnomer: it ought to be "Law of States" (in his Latin, *ius publicum civitatum*).
3 See also "Idea for a Universal History," where Kant speaks of the "barbarous freedom of established states" (Kant, 1970, p. 49); "Theory and Practice," where he speaks of a "state of international right, based upon enforceable public laws to which each state must submit (by analogy with a state of civil or political right among individual men)" (Kant, 1970, p. 92); "Perpetual Peace," where he speaks of the "lawless condition of pure warfare" between states, and continues, "Just like individual men, they must renounce their savage and lawless freedom, adapt themselves to public coercive laws" (Kant, 1970, p. 105).
4 For this language, see Rawls (1993b, pp. 144–45): "the political conception is a module, an essential constituent part, that in different ways fits into and can be supported by various reasonable comprehensive doctrines that endure in the society regulated by it."
5 See Rawls (1999a, p. 65 n.2): "this liberty of conscience may not be as extensive nor as equal for all members of society: for instance, one religion may legally predominate in the state government, while other religions, though tolerated, may be denied the right to hold certain positions."
6 See Rawls (1999a, p. 71): ". . . all persons in a decent hierarchical society are not regarded as free and equal citizens, nor as separate individuals deserving equal representation (according to the maxim: one citizen, one vote). . ."
7 In his formulation, none, since the society is assumed to be closed.
8 In one form, this family of objections is eloquently pressed by Bernard Williams (1973, pp. 77–150).
9 In several cases, for example, the norms of sex equality in CEDAW have been held to be binding on nations that have ratified it, in a way that has affected the outcome of legal disputes, and also generated new legislation.

CHAPTER 14

Tolerating injustice

Jon Mandle

The charge that liberalism undermines itself is a familiar one. Robert Frost's famous quip captures the thought: "A liberal is a man too broad-minded to take his own side in a quarrel." Since liberalism is committed to toleration, the threat is persistent and real: how can liberals claim to tolerate diverse ethical beliefs while at the same time affirm their own principles? The matter is complex, but liberal theory can and must distinguish between the kinds of diversity that are to be tolerated and those that are not. Political liberalism takes a first step toward answering this challenge by distinguishing the right (that is, matters of justice) from the good (that is, matters concerning the content of a good life). This is more than an arbitrary conceptual distinction within the realm of the ethical. It is based on political liberalism's substantive commitment that while a broad range of doctrines of the good life are to be tolerated, its own principles of justice are correct. Furthermore, unlike other components of a comprehensive ethical doctrine, for liberals the basic principles of social justice may be coercively enforced through state power if necessary. For Rawls, following Weber, "political power is always coercive power backed by the government's use of sanctions, for government alone has the authority to use force in upholding its laws" (Rawls, 1996, p. 136. See also Rawls, 1999b, p. 207).

Rawls insists that debates about constitutional essentials and matters of basic social justice should be conducted within the limits of public reason in part because they will be coercively enforced in the face of a diversity of reasonable comprehensive doctrines (Rawls, 1996, p. 214. See also Rawls, 1999c). We should aim, therefore, to provide a justification of the design of the basic structure of society that could be accepted by all reasonable individuals. But Rawls is aware that not all individuals will *in fact* accept such a justification. Some people simply are unreasonable. We must treat them justly, of course, but we must also recognize that we are unlikely to be able to offer a justification that they will find acceptable. In the more extreme cases, Rawls says, "the problem is to contain them so that they do not undermine the unity and justice of society" (Rawls, 1996, p. xix). Rawls's account shows that, in Stephen Macedo's words, political liberalism is (or can be) "tough-minded" and "resolute in facing up to the fact that no version of liberalism can make everyone happy" (Macedo, 1995, p. 470).

When Rawls turns to matters of international justice, however, his account looks noticeably less tough-minded, and it may appear as though he is pursuing a vain attempt precisely to make everyone happy. Specifically, Rawls argues that liberal democratic societies should recognize certain "decent hierarchical societies" "as equal participating members in good standing of the Society of Peoples" (Rawls, 1999a, p. 59). He insists on toleration for these societies, despite the fact that they are not democratic and do not embrace liberal principles of justice even as an ideal. Rawls's position is that a society committed to liberal principles of justice ought to tolerate certain forms of injustice in other societies that it would not accept within its own society. It is important to emphasize, however, that even this toleration has limits, so it is not right to say that Rawls aims to make *everyone* happy. Members of the Society of Peoples will *not* tolerate "outlaw states" that systematically violate basic human rights or are expansionary: "An outlaw state that violates these rights is to be condemned and in grave cases may be subjected to forceful sanctions and even to intervention" (Rawls, 1999a, p. 81). We will discuss below what distinguishes decent hierarchical societies from outlaw states, but the essential point is that Rawls insists that a just society should tolerate certain kinds of injustice internationally that it would not accept domestically.

Why should a society committed to liberal principles of justice and willing to enforce them domestically refrain from doing so internationally? One possible answer emphasizes that even if one believes that the same principles of justice ought to apply to both domestic and foreign societies, the circumstances of application differ between the two. For example, there may be a greater likelihood of error in determining what justice requires in foreign countries than in one's own. Furthermore, efforts to bring about changes in foreign countries may generate resentment and become counter-productive, or at a minimum have harmful, though unintended, consequences. The ethos of a society is crucial for the stability of just institutions, but this is something that may be difficult to change, especially for outsiders. Charles Beitz, following this line of thinking, claims, "It seems likely that the main objections to a general permission to intervene in the cause of justice are practical rather than theoretical in the sense that they hold such intervention, in practice, to be difficult to calculate and control" (Beitz, 1979, p. 83). But Rawls emphasizes that he believes the grounds for toleration are deeper than such practical considerations:

It is important to emphasize that the reasons for not imposing sanctions [on decent hierarchical societies] do not boil down solely to the prevention of possible error and miscalculation in dealing with a foreign people. The danger of error, miscalculation, and also arrogance on the part of those who propose sanctions must, of course, be taken into account; yet decent hierarchical societies do have certain institutional features that deserve respect, even if their institutions as a whole are not sufficiently reasonable from the point of view of political liberalism or liberalism generally. (Rawls, 1999a, pp. 83–84)

For Rawls, the toleration of decent hierarchical societies is not merely a matter of instrumental concerns about the effectiveness of the imposition of institutions on another country. So, why does Rawls support the toleration of at least certain kinds of injustice in the international realm? The answer is not clear. I will describe the most common interpretation and agree with critics that this provides an inadequate defense of Rawls's position before offering an alternative account.

By far the most widespread interpretation of Rawls's *The Law of Peoples* emphasizes the following analogy: just as in the domestic case we aim at identifying principles of justice that are acceptable to individuals holding a wide range of doctrines of the good, in the international case we aim at identifying principles of justice that are acceptable to peoples holding a wide range of conceptions of justice. In the former case, we aim at creating an overlapping consensus of reasonable comprehensive doctrines; in the latter, we aim at an overlapping consensus of conceptions of justice. Rawls himself suggests a similar analogy (Rawls, 1999a, pp. 17–19). But critics are right that as it stands, this analogy fails to provide the needed defense. If liberal principles of justice are the correct response to the presence of a diversity of reasonable comprehensive doctrines in the domestic case, why are not those same principles equally the correct response to the fact of reasonable diversity of comprehensive doctrines in the international case?

It is worth recalling the contrast between a true overlapping consensus and a mere *modus vivendi* (See Rawls, 1996, especially pp. 144–54). In the case of an overlapping consensus, each individual holding a reasonable comprehensive doctrine views the principles of justice as *correct*, not involving any compromise of his or her fundamental ethical commitments.

In the case of a *modus vivendi* on the other hand, practical necessity requires that one temper one's ideal conception of justice in the interest of reaching agreement with others who hold a conflicting conception. But it is only an overlapping consensus, Rawls believes, that can achieve stability for the right reasons in both the domestic and international cases (Rawls, 1999a, p. 45). Actual circumstances might dictate that a *modus vivendi* is all that one can realistically achieve, but an overlapping consensus remains Rawls's ideal. The most common reading of *The Law of Peoples* in effect treats the toleration of decent hierarchical societies as a form of *modus vivendi*. Practical necessity may require that liberal societies refrain from imposing liberal principles of justice on other societies, but there is no deeper reason for toleration, and the compromise must be recognized for what it is. As Thomas McCarthy asks, "Why should [a liberal, democratic people] surrender their basic *political* principles for the sake of reaching agreement with peoples who do not share them?" (McCarthy, 1997, p. 209. See also Pogge, 1994b, especially p. 216, and Moellendorf, 2002, pp. 14–15). Or, as Kok-Chor Tan has written, Rawls's *Law of Peoples* "is inspired more by the need to *accommodate* representatives of [decent hierarchical societies], to ensure that his law of peoples can be endorsed by some nonliberal states as well, than by the goal of achieving stability for the right reasons" (Tan, 2000, p. 31). It is not surprising, then, that Tan, along with many of Rawls's critics, believes that Rawls's toleration of decent hierarchical societies is "blatantly inconsistent" (Tan, 2000, p. 31).

Rawls fails to explain adequately why the toleration of decent hierarchical societies is not simply a (perhaps necessary) compromise. Indeed, some things he says suggest exactly this view (see for example 1999a, p. 61). To begin to develop an adequate account, it is worth emphasizing that Rawls's toleration of decent hierarchical peoples in no way implies that he believes them to be *just*. On the contrary, he thinks that they are not just, nor are they reasonable: they fail to treat individuals as free and equal. Rawls does not withdraw his endorsement of liberal principles of justice. He is as explicit as he can be: "To repeat, I am not saying that a decent hierarchical society is as reasonable and just as a liberal society" (Rawls, 1999a, p. 83). What he is questioning is the *enforcement* of his principles of justice by one society on another. Here is the view that he rejects: "nonliberal societies fail to treat persons . . . as truly free and equal, and *therefore* . . . nonliberal societies are always properly subject to some form of sanction – political, economic, or even military – depending on the case" (Rawls, 1999a, p. 60). It is the "*therefore*" that

Rawls emphasizes and objects to. Rawls's position is that a society that embraces liberal principles of justice will refrain from imposing those principles on others, despite its belief that they are correct. Indeed, this toleration, Rawls claims, follows from a commitment to those very principles.

We now need to look more carefully at the criteria for a society to count as "decent" and therefore to be included as a member in good standing in the Society of Peoples. These are the nonliberal societies that liberal societies may criticize but would not subject to coercion, even in the interest of justice. First of all, a decent hierarchical society "does not have aggressive aims, and it recognizes that it must gain its legitimate ends through diplomacy and trade and other ways of peace" (Rawls, 1999a, p. 64). This seems unobjectionable. A liberal democratic society will have no reason *of principle* for tolerating a society that is aggressive, expansionary, and militaristic. (Practical considerations may, of course, be another matter.) Rawls's remaining three criteria concern domestic institutional arrangements, and I will focus on these:

(a) The first part is that a decent hierarchical people's system of law, in accordance with its common good idea of justice . . . secures for all members of the people what have come to be called human rights . . .
   Among the human rights are the right to life (to the means of subsistence and security); to liberty (to freedom from slavery, serfdom, and forced occupation, and to a sufficient measure of liberty of conscience to ensure freedom of religion and thought); to property (personal property); and to formal equality as expressed by the rules of natural justice (that is, that similar cases be treated similarly). . .
(b) The second part is that a decent people's system of law must be such as to impose *bona fide* moral duties and obligations (distinct from human rights) on all persons within the people's territory . . .
(c) Finally, the third part . . . is that there must be a sincere and not unreasonable belief on the part of judges and other officials who administer the legal system that the law is indeed guided by a common good idea of justice . . . This sincere and reasonable belief on the part of judges and officials must be shown in their good faith and willingness to defend publicly society's injunctions as justified by law. (Rawls, 1999a, pp. 65-67)

All three of these criteria concern legal and political institutions. That is, Rawls believes that a society qualifies for inclusion in the Society of Peoples and therefore is to be tolerated, if it is non-expansionary and its *political structure* meets these three conditions.

It may be surprising that Rawls's focus appears to be exclusively on the political structure of a society. After all, when he develops principles of domestic justice, they are to govern the basic structure of society as a whole, that is "a society's main political, social, and economic institutions, and how they fit together into one unified system of social cooperation from one generation to the next" (Rawls, 1996, p. 11). Political institutions, although only one part of the basic structure, play a unique role in it. It is through its political institutions that a society makes and imposes explicit, collective, and binding decisions on itself. Although the political structures of a society do not exhaust the basic structure, it is through the political institutions that the people collectively and deliberately shape the basic structure of their society. Laws rarely represent the will of every individual in a society. Nonetheless, *when legitimate,* they represent the will of the citizens as a corporate body. Legitimate law, that is, represents the collective decision of the society. On the reading I will now develop, the three criteria listed above should be read as conditions on legitimate law. In other words, if a society has a system of legitimate law and it is not expansionary, then it counts as decent and is entitled to full toleration.[1]

The constitution of a society, let us say, is the system of publicly recognized rules for making and applying (ordinary) laws. A constitution in this sense may be written or unwritten; some parts may be explicit, while other parts implicit (see Freeman, 1992). In the ideal, a constitution ought to produce laws that ensure justice. (There may be other desiderata as well, such as expressing the self-conception of citizens.) But no constitutional procedure can be guaranteed always to produce such an ideal outcome, and there will often be disagreement about whether an ordinary law is just and desirable. We need criteria, therefore, that define when the constitution is good enough to produce valid and binding law, even if those laws are not ideal. This is what a *legitimate* system of law does. When the political structure is legitimate in this sense, citizens may disagree with a particular law, but in general they will properly recognize it as binding on them, and the society may enforce such a law. This, I take it, is what Rawls means when he says, in the second criterion above, that the system of law "impose[s] *bona fide* moral duties and obligations . . . on all persons within the . . . territory." In some discussions, "legitimacy" is a weaker notion, implying only the right of the state to enforce its laws, not an obligation or duty on the part of citizens to obedience. Although I will use the stronger notion, since Rawls apparently endorses it, it will turn out that the argument for toleration of decent societies does not depend on it.

Rawls does not tell us precisely when a system of law is legitimate and imposes *bona fide* moral duties and obligations, but we can tease out three elements in his account. First, the system of law must be generally recognized to be binding by the citizens of that society. This is implicit in Rawls's claim that decent peoples are well-ordered (Rawls, 1999a, p. 4). In addition to receiving widespread support, a system of law must satisfy both a substantive and a procedural requirement. The substantive requirement is, as stated in Rawls's first criterion, that the legal order respects and protects basic human rights. The procedural element is that the law is made and enforced in a way that can properly be said to reflect the will of the people, according to their "common good" conception of justice. Let us say, then, that in addition to a *system of law* being legitimate, a *particular law* is legitimate, even if not fully just, when it does not violate any fundamental human rights and is the product of a legitimate procedure.

Assume that the procedural requirement is satisfied, for example, by a majoritarian, democratic procedure. Such a majoritarian procedure, by itself, affords no guarantee of protection to those not in the majority. It is surely unreasonable to demand compliance from individuals who have their most fundamental rights violated, who are enslaved or denied the rule of law, for example, even if this reflects the wishes of the majority. There is room for debate concerning which specific rights are to count as fundamental in this sense, and it is significant that Rawls does not claim his list to be exhaustive. I will not here go into any details, except to point out that a right to democratic political institutions is absent. In recent years, there has been growing debate about whether there is such a fundamental human right. In the framework developed here, this question concerns whether the procedural requirement on legitimacy requires democracy.

Rawls's answer is that legitimacy does not require democracy, understood in the sense of one person, one vote.[2] I hasten to add that Rawls can at the same time maintain that *justice* does require democracy. Furthermore, he explicitly leaves open the possibility that, as an empirical matter of fact, "full democratic and liberal rights are necessary to prevent violations of human rights" (Rawls, 1999a, p. 75, n.16). Thus, Rawls emphasizes that "The Law of Peoples does not presuppose the existence of actual decent hierarchical peoples . . ." (Rawls, 1999a, p. 75). The claim here is merely that it is conceptually possible for a non-democratic system of law (that has widespread support and respects and protects basic human rights) to impose *bone fide* moral duties, and therefore be legitimate. A just and liberal society aims at institutions of political justice that treat all citizens as free and equal. That is its idea of the common good. But other societies may hold a common good conception of justice that endorses a more substantive common aim. Consistent with respect for basic human rights, this common aim serves to identify what, from a political point of view, count as the fundamental interests of members of the society (see Rawls, 1999a, pp. 34, 71, n. 10).

Consider, for example, a society that holds a common good conception of justice structured around a particular religion. Such a society might take steps to promote certain religious practices and restrict high governmental positions to members of that religion. In important ways, it will not treat all citizens as free and equal. Still, if it is truly organizing itself around a common good conception of justice and is not simply an arbitrary exercise of power, it must recognize and take into account the good (as it understands it) of each citizen. As an immediate implication of this, it must respect the basic human rights of all of its members. If it fails to do this, it could not plausibly be understood as affirming a common good conception of justice. Indeed, it could not be understood as a system of social cooperation: when basic human rights "are regularly violated, we have command by force, a slave system, and no cooperation of any kind" (Rawls, 1999a, p. 68). This means, for example, that it must recognize basic liberty of conscience and tolerate a diversity of religious practices.

Furthermore, there must be institutional mechanisms by which individuals can challenge the received and dominant interpretation of the common good. Rawls's model of a decent hierarchical society, for example, provides for "a family of representative bodies whose role in the hierarchy is to take part in an established procedure of consultation and to look after what the people's common good idea of justice regards as the important interests of all members of the people" (Rawls, 1999b, p. 71). The operation of such a consultational mechanism requires a significant measure of free political speech. But still more is required, since "Dissent is respected in the sense that a reply is due that spells out how the government thinks it can both reasonably interpret its policies in line with its common good idea of justice and impose duties and obligations on all members of society" (Rawls, 1999a, p. 78; cf. p. 72). If these conditions are not met, we have not a system of legitimate law, but an arbitrary exercise of power, and as Rawls states, "Laws supported merely by force are grounds for rebellion and resistance" (Rawls, 1999a, p. 66; cf. p. 88). What is crucial is that although liberal democracy is not necessary for legitimacy, there must be institutional mechanisms through which individuals are able to challenge and influence their society's interpretation of its common good.

When legitimate, the legal structure of a society imposes *bone fide* moral duties and obligations on the people within its territory. Principal among these is a general duty to obey the law. Although Rawls holds that there is such a general (defeasible) duty, this is a hotly contested topic in political theory. After discussing grounds for this duty, I will show below that the argument for toleration of decent (legitimate) societies actually depends on a weaker and less controversial duty. Although Rawls has consistently held that there is a general (defeasible) duty to obey laws that are the product of legitimate procedures, his understanding of the grounds for this duty has changed. In a paper first published in 1964, "Legal Obligation and the Duty of Fair Play," he argued that "our moral obligation to obey the law is a special case of the duty of fair play" (Rawls, 1999d, p. 128).[3] In *A Theory of Justice*, Rawls continues to endorse the duty of fair play, now called "the principle of fairness." Indeed, he argues that the principle of fairness can "account for all [moral] requirements that are obligations as distinct from natural duties" (Rawls, 1999b, p. 96). The key feature of obligations, as opposed to natural duties, is that "they arise as a result of our voluntary acts" (Rawls, 1999b, p. 97). But in *A Theory of Justice*, Rawls argues that there is no voluntary act that all citizens undertake that could generate an obligation to obey the law (see Rawls, 1999b, p. 296).[4] Therefore, he concludes: "There is, I believe, no political obligation, strictly speaking, for citizens generally" (Rawls, 1999b, p. 98). In contrast to obligations, however, natural duties "apply to us without regard to our voluntary acts" (Rawls, 1999b, p. 98). One such duty is the duty of justice that "requires us to support and to comply with just institutions that exist and apply to us . . .Thus if the basic structure of society is just, or as just as it is reasonable to expect in the circumstances, everyone has a natural duty to do his part in the existing scheme" (Rawls, 1999b, p. 99). In other words, when the basic structure of one's society is sufficiently just, there is a duty to comply with its laws.

It remains controversial whether the natural duty of justice can ground the normative requirement that citizens of sufficiently just societies obey the law. Critics charge that the natural duty of justice cannot establish adequately when an institution is supposed to "apply to us" in the relevant sense. A. John Simmons gives a clear statement of this objection when he writes that "it is hard to see how such a duty could account for one being bound to one particular set of political institutions in any special way" (Simmons, 1979, p. 155). The duty of justice requires us to promote just institutions "wherever they may be and to whomever they apply" (Simmons, 1979, p. 154). Jeremy Waldron, in reply, has defended the duty of justice, and attempted to show how it can generate a particular commitment to a particular political order (see Waldron, 1993).

Fortunately, for our purposes we need not resolve this dispute because we are concerned not with the duty to obey the legitimate law of a particular society, but the duty not to use force to interfere with *any* legitimate political institutions. If, as Rawls and Waldron believe, some form of the duty of justice can adequately establish a particular connection between a citizen and the laws of her society, then it can also ground the requirement that a citizen not use coercive force to change the legitimate institutions of her society. Recall that a legitimate political order has institutional mechanisms that allow individuals to influence the laws of her society. The prohibition on using force to interfere with legitimate institutions of law, like the duty to obey the law, is defeasible. In some extreme circumstances, it may be appropriate to attempt to change or resist an unjust law through the use of force rather than through the legitimate institutional mechanisms already in place. But typically, such militancy will only be appropriate when the law violates basic human rights and therefore puts the legitimacy of the law into doubt. Now if a citizen ought not to interfere with a legitimate political institution of her society, it seems clear that no foreigner should do so either. As Waldron puts it, focusing on one aspect of the legal system: "if the criminal justice system of a country is fair, everyone everywhere has a duty not to obstruct it, whether they owe any particular allegiance to that system and live under its laws or not" (Waldron, 1993, p. 10). The point holds beyond the criminal justice system and applies to political and legal institutions generally.

On the other hand, if, as Simmons believes, the duty of justice cannot adequately tie an individual to the laws of her society, it still can establish a general duty not to interfere with any legitimate institutions. Indeed, it would seem to follow even more directly, since we are here talking about a general duty not to interfere with any legitimate political structure. It might be said in reply that citizens have institutional avenues available to them to register their opposition but that foreigners are typically excluded from these.[5] This is true, but it does not follow that foreigners may resort to force. If we think of legitimate law as the expression of the will of a people, it is not inappropriate that foreigners be excluded. Unlike the citizens, they are not bound by those laws, after all. So, although it may be controversial whether the duty of justice can adequately connect a citizen to *her own* system of laws and ground the moral requirement that citizens obey those laws, it can ground the *general* prohibition on interfering with legitimate laws and legitimate institutions of law. In other words, individuals and societies ought to refrain from using force to attempt to make other legitimate societies more just.

We are now in a position to tie together the various strands and briefly reconstruct Rawls's argument for the toleration of decent societies. Rawls's *Law of Peoples* is an attempt to "work out the ideals and principles of the *foreign policy* of a reasonably just *liberal* people" (Rawls, 1999b, p. 10). Assuming that we have already identified and satisfied to an acceptable degree the principles of domestic justice, *The Law of Peoples* proceeds in two stages. First, it considers which principles should be used to regulate the relations among liberal democratic peoples. Rawls considers this by introducing a "second original position" that is designed to model "fair conditions under which the parties, this time the rational representatives of liberal peoples, are to specify the Law of Peoples, guided by appropriate reasons" (Rawls, 1999b, p. 32). The key, here, is that we are looking for fair principles with which to regulate the relations among liberal democratic societies. There is no effort to accommodate the existence of nonliberal societies. It is only at the second stage that the relationship to decent (nonliberal) peoples is considered.

So, at the first stage, which principles would liberal peoples endorse to govern toleration with respect to one another? Since liberal peoples are motivated by a concern for justice, and since they all satisfy this requirement to a reasonable degree, it seems clear that they would agree to tolerate one another. However, it is possible for a reasonably just constitutional democracy to become less so. Given the parties' commitment to justice, they would be concerned to prevent this possibility. Consider, for example, the possibility of an external invasion by an aggressive and expansionary outlaw state. This obviously could pose a substantial threat to the justice of a democratic society, and so the parties would want to endorse principles to resist such an attack. For that reason, Rawls argues that the parties would endorse a "right to self-defense but no right to instigate war for reasons other than self-defense" (Rawls, 1999a, p. 37). Furthermore, to strengthen their ability to resist such threats, it is easy to imagine that they would form defensive military alliances and agree that an attack on one member of the Society of Peoples would authorize all to use military force in its defense.

But now consider the fact that, Rawls's arguments for stability notwithstanding, it is possible for the justice of a society to be undermined internally, without external invasion. This could happen gradually, as citizens become less vigilant in the defense of their rights, or more spectacularly, through a *coup d'état*. Would the parties endorse principles authorizing the use of force to prevent such a deterioration of justice? One possible answer is that the parties would adopt a principle that prohibits the other members of the Society of Peoples from using force to attempt to restore the justice of a society when it is undermined internally. In effect, this would be to endorse the traditional notion of absolute domestic sovereignty. Given that the parties are motivated by a concern for justice, however, they would reject this. They would endorse principles that would allow them to take steps to curb at least the worst violations of human rights, wherever they occur. As I have stressed, there may be practical concerns about the effectiveness of foreign intervention, but these cannot be grounds for *toleration* of regimes that systematically violate basic human rights.

On the other hand, I believe that the parties would also reject a principle that authorizes the use of force against *all* deviations from the ideal requirements of justice. This is for several reasons. First of all, although the parties represent societies that are reasonably just, they are not necessarily ideally so (Rawls, 1999a, p. 24). If they authorized the use of force for any divergence from ideal justice, there would be, as a practical matter, no society immune from external pressure. Second, there is likely to be reasonable disagreement about which principles of justice are the most appropriate ones. Rawls believes that a family of liberal political principles are reasonable, even if not equally so (Rawls, 1999a, p. 14). Third, there is likely to be disagreement about which specific policies would satisfy the principles of justice. But most important is the reason discussed above. When a political structure is legitimate, even if not fully just, in addition to respecting basic human rights and imposing *bone fide* moral obligations and duties on its citizens, it retains internal institutional mechanisms through which citizens can advocate that it become more just and democratic. If the political structure is good enough that members of that society ought not use force to change it or its laws, the parties will agree that foreigners ought not do so either. Legitimacy, therefore, is a sufficient condition for foreigners to refrain from using force to change the basic structure of a society in the name of justice.[6]

Assume, then, that liberal democratic peoples would endorse a principle prohibiting the use of force in the name of justice unless the injustice was severe enough to undermine the legitimacy of the society. We can now proceed to the second stage of the argument and ask whether decent hierarchical societies would endorse those very same principles. Rawls argues that a non-democratic, hierarchical society that was nonetheless legitimate *could* do so. (He does not argue that such a society necessarily would.) Recall that in addition to the three criteria associated with its political structure, the first criterion of a decent society is that it "does not have aggressive aims, and it recognizes that it must gain its legitimate ends through diplomacy and trade and other ways of peace" (Rawls, 1999a, p. 64). This is simply part of the definition of decency. A society that had a legitimate but non-democratic political order, but was aggressive and militaristic, surely would not adopt the principles of the Society of Peoples, but neither would it count as decent. A decent society, in other words, will tolerate liberal democracies, and liberal democracies will tolerate it in turn because it is legitimate. That is, a decent society can become a fully equal member of the Society of Peoples.

Some of Rawls's critics give the impression that his argument for toleration of some forms of injustice shows a weakened commitment to the principles of domestic justice. I have argued that Rawls is correct in saying that it shows no such thing. In the case of a domestic overlapping consensus, individuals holding reasonable comprehensive doctrines have good moral reasons to tolerate one another. Yet, individuals committed to a particular comprehensive doctrine may believe that those who hold a different comprehensive doctrine hold a false and possibly immoral (though not unreasonable) view. They may think it would be better if everyone held the comprehensive doctrine that they take to be the true one. And they may say so and explain why they believe that. Similarly, in the international case, toleration of decent hierarchical societies does not imply that they are just. Furthermore, although there is apparently widespread confusion on this point, Rawls is explicit that the Law of Peoples does not prohibit liberal democracies from advocating their principles of justice and criticizing others:

Critical objections, based either on political liberalism, or on comprehensive doctrines, both religious and nonreligious, will continue concerning this and all other matters. Raising these objections is the right of liberal peoples and is fully consistent with the liberties and integrity of decent hierarchical societies. (Rawls, 1999a, p. 84)

Toleration concerns restraints on the use of force, not a compromise on the ideals one advocates. Liberal peoples may believe it would be best if all societies espoused liberal democratic principles and so, while refraining from the use of force with respect to decent peoples, they may encourage them to become more democratic and just. This presumably is what Rawls means when he says, "Liberal peoples must try to encourage decent peoples and not frustrate their vitality by *coercively* insisting that all societies be liberal" (Rawls, 1999a, p. 62, my emphasis; cf. p. 61). It is unclear, however, why Rawls thinks that "it is not reasonable for a liberal people to adopt as part of its own foreign policy the granting of subsidies to other peoples as incentives to become more liberal" (Rawls, 1999a, p. 85). Surely there is nothing wrong with a liberal people providing assistance to a society that has expressed the desire to become more democratic. If that is right, there seems to be no objection in principle to a liberal people announcing a standing offer to assist peoples seeking to become more democratic (see Freeman, 2003, pp. 46, 60, n. 84). What is crucial is that the liberal people not neglect or threaten (even implicitly) to deny their other international obligations and duties. This would make their "assistance" objectionably coercive.

As Rawls's critics rightly point out, there is an important dis-analogy between toleration of reasonable comprehensive doctrines in the domestic case and toleration of decent hierarchical societies in the international case: in the domestic case all reasonable comprehensive doctrines are committed to liberal political principles, while decent hierarchical societies are not. Critics charge, therefore, that it is possible to see how we can ground the toleration of reasonable comprehensive doctrines in political principles of justice, but that we cannot ground toleration of decent hierarchical societies in the very principles that those societies reject. I have argued that we can. In fact, this phenomenon is closely related to the more familiar idea of legitimate law itself. Philosophers have long recognized that political institutions that allow a society to make a collective, authoritative, and binding decision make a crucial contribution to the cause of justice. I cannot here present a case why it is important for justice to have a legitimate system of law, so I will simply have to leave this as an undefended assumption in Rawls's account.

Assume, then, that institutions of law are crucially important to the cause of justice. If this is so, then justice will require accepting certain substantive injustices, because no arrangement of political institutions can guarantee all and only just laws. Some political institutions are better than others, however, and the ones that are good enough are legitimate. That is, the cause of justice is served, in general, by abiding by the results of legitimate constitutional procedures, even when one judges those results to be (substantively) unjust. Conversely, the cause of justice is weakened if the results of such legitimate political institutions are resisted by force. And if that is the case, then the cause of justice is also weakened by resisting the institutions themselves by force. This holds for citizens and non-citizens alike. But citizens are not trapped by the injustices of a political structure once it meets the threshold of legitimacy. Although the use of force is antithetical to the cause of justice in such cases, recall that a legitimate political structure will have legitimate procedures that allow for correction in the name of justice. There is room for disagreement concerning the specific conditions of legitimacy. But however that standard is specified, one can advocate the use of force against such legitimate institutions only by denying the great importance to justice of legitimate (though imperfect) political institutions. Understood in this way, the toleration of decent societies does not involve any compromise of liberal principles of justice, but rather results from that very commitment.

NOTES

I would like to thank Josh Cohen for discussions that helped me to clarify the core ideas of this essay. I would also like to thank Alyssa Bernstein for sharing her unpublished paper, which I found to be very helpful as I was developing my thoughts on Rawls's views. Finally, I also thank Jay Mandle, Joan Mandle, Darrel Moellendorf, and Thomas Pogge for suggestions and comments on earlier drafts of this essay.

1 Several authors have noted the importance of the concept of legitimacy in Rawls's more recent work. See Estlund (1996), Dreben (2003), Tesón (1995), Wenar (2002), and Bernstein (unpublished).
2 For this understanding of democracy, see, for example, Rawls (1999a, pp. 71, 73).
3 He defines the principle of fair play on p. 122; compare Rawls (1999b, p. 96).
4 For a defense of the principle of fairness as a basis for political obligations, see Klosko (1992).
5 Although not necessarily. It is easy to imagine an institutional mechanism that allows resident aliens to vote or that requires the consultation with foreign countries likely to be adversely affected by a proposed environmental policy, for example. I leave cases such as these aside, including the status of resident aliens.
6 It is certainly not a necessary condition, however. There may be many good reasons not to use force against a society that lacks legitimacy. It is also worth noting that I have said nothing about the kind of force that might be appropriate.

CHAPTER 15

Cosmopolitan hope

Catriona McKinnon

> The problems of the world cannot possibly be solved by skeptics or
> cynics whose horizons are limited by the obvious realities. We need
> men who can dream of things that never were and ask, why not?
>
> (attributed to John F. Kennedy)

> . . . the world is not in itself inhospitable to political justice and its
> good. Our social world might have been different and there is hope
> for those at another time and place.
>
> (Rawls, 2001, p. 38)

INTRODUCTION

The term 'cosmopolitanism' denotes various interconnected projects. Many arguments in the literature raise doubts about the relevance of national and state boundaries to questions of justice: these questions connect with questions about the scope, assignment, and nature of cosmopolitan duties of justice. Cutting across these debates are discussions about the content of principles of global justice, raising questions about the universality of the values realized by these principles. And then there are various detailed questions about the nature of the institutions fit to deliver global justice.

These strands of cosmopolitan thought are important and flourishing. However, none of them directly addresses an objection to cosmopolitanism common outside of academic circles, which is that although the cosmopolitan ideal is acceptable in theory, it will never be realized in practice: cosmopolitans who hope for the realization of this ideal are well-meaning but deluded people who lack a proper grasp of how the realities of human nature and social interaction limit what is achievable in political practice. The objection is that even if the moral arguments for cosmopolitanism work, hope for a cosmopolitan future is naive and misguided. I shall refer to this as the "hard-nosed" objection.

The hard-nosed objection can be made in response to any ideal-oriented political project. Although my concern here is with cosmopolitanism, it will help to fix our thoughts to consider the objection as expressed against communism by Erwin Goldstine in Philip Roth's novel *I Married a Communist*.

a person with an average intelligence cannot take this story, this fairy tale of Communism, and swallow it. "We will do something that will be wonderful . . ." But we know what our brother is, don't we? He's a shit. And we know what our friend is, don't we? He's a semi-shit. And *we* are semi-shits. So how can it be wonderful? Not even cynicism, not even skepticism, just ordinary powers of human observation tell us *that is not possible.* (Roth, 1999, p. 95)

Substitute "cosmopolitanism" for "communism" in this passage and we have the objection I shall address. Despite Goldstine's claims to the contrary, the hard-nosed objection is a subtle form of skepticism about cosmopolitan justice. What the hard-nosed objector is skeptical about is not the moral requirement to seek global justice that lies at the heart of cosmopolitanism. The hard-nosed objector accepts (or, at least, does not reject) this requirement and instead questions – often in knowing, world weary tones – whether it is reasonable to hope that the state of affairs aimed at by this requirement will be realized.

There are two ways to understand this objection. First, that the cosmopolitan objective is not a *legitimate* object of hope; and second, that cosmopolitan hope, even if legitimate, is *unsound. Pace* the objector, I shall argue that cosmopolitan hope is both legitimate and sound; that is, I shall argue that cosmopolitan hope is consistent with and permitted by the cosmopolitan requirement. This is sufficient to rebut the hard-nosed objection. However, I shall also sketch two arguments for the stronger thesis that retaining commitment to the cosmopolitan ideal *requires* cosmopolitan hope, which means that the hard-nosed objection cannot be made at all. Let me begin by laying out the cosmopolitan ideal, and the moral requirement that accompanies it.

THE COSMOPOLITAN IDEAL

The ideal I take to be common to all forms of cosmopolitanism is this:

The cosmopolitan ideal: A world in which some fundamental principles of justice govern relations between all persons in all places.

The moral requirement that accompanies the cosmopolitan ideal, and which is common to all forms of cosmopolitanism, is this:

The cosmopolitan requirement: any commitment to some fundamental principles of justice at the domestic level ought to be extended so as to generate principles of justice with cosmopolitan scope.[1]

The objective of cosmopolitan hope is the achievement of the cosmopolitan ideal of global justice through action fit to satisfy the demands of the cosmopolitan requirement. What cosmopolitans hope for is the extension of commitments to justice at the domestic level (however these commitments are generated, and whatever their content) to the global level so as to create a world governed by principles of global justice. The hard-nosed objector aims to prise apart acceptance of the cosmopolitan requirement (which she endorses, or at least does not reject) and commitment to – as evinced in hope for – the cosmopolitan ideal: the hard-nosed objector accepts the demands of the cosmopolitan requirement but rejects hope for the cosmopolitan ideal as naive and misguided. The hard-nosed objector is not an outright skeptic about all aspects of cosmopolitanism: she allows that we have the obligations stated in the cosmopolitan requirement, but thinks that these obligations can and ought to be defended as such without false hope for the world of global justice constitutive of the cosmopolitan ideal. The hard-nosed objector is not a skeptic about the cosmopolitan obligations that we owe to one another, or the cosmopolitan rights that we hold against one another. Rather, the focus of the hard-nosed objector's skepticism is the prospects for the creation of a cosmopolitan world order through the performance of the obligations laid down by the cosmopolitan requirement.

The form of cosmopolitan hope I shall defend can now be stated. Cosmopolitan hope is hope for the realization of the cosmopolitan ideal: the objective of cosmopolitan hope is a world in which some fundamental principles of justice governing relations between individuals and groups at the domestic level also govern such relations at the global level. To hope for the cosmopolitan ideal is to hope that persons extend their commitment to some fundamental principles of justice at the domestic level to the global level, as demanded by the cosmopolitan requirement. The hard-nosed objection is that hope for the cosmopolitan ideal, and the concomitant hope for the extension of commitment demanded by the cosmopolitan requirement, is naive because it fails to take seriously facts about the world which make the achievement of this state through action fit to satisfy the requirement impossible or unlikely, even though the requirement itself is legitimate. In that case, cosmopolitan hope is either illegitimate (because the cosmopolitan objective is not a fit object of hope), or unsound (because one or more components of cosmopolitan hope must be rejected). By way of addressing the first version of the hard-nosed objection I shall give a general account of the nature of hope.

Cosmopolitan hope is hope for a specific objective as laid out in the cosmopolitan ideal. Let me outline in general terms what it is to have a specific hope before considering whether the cosmopolitan ideal yields a legitimate objective for specific hope.[2]

Specific hope is hope aimed at an objective which exists in the future, is believed to be good by the hoper, and is desired by the hoper in virtue of this belief. Furthermore, hope generates a disposition to act so as to make the realization of hope's objective more probable whenever possible, all else being equal. Without this disposition, a hoper lacks the practical commitment to her objective that is characteristic of hope: we would think it odd to describe a person as hoping for an objective if she fails to act so as to realize the objective when presented with a real opportunity to do so.

The motivation to pursue an objective that issues from hope must be distinguished from motivational states with different provenances. The motivation to pursue hope's objective consists of a desire for the objective in virtue of the hoper's belief that the objective is good. In contrast, a motivation to pursue an objective which does not issue from hope (if it is to be characterized in terms of belief and desire at all) can consist of a desire for the objective in spite of the agent's belief that the objective is bad. For example, if I desire a glass of wine and I believe that there is a bottle on the shelf, I will be motivated to open the bottle and pour a glass, all else being equal; and I may be so motivated despite my belief that drinking wine will do me harm. However, with respect to hope, it must be the case that I desire what I hope for because I believe it to be good: we do not hope for objectives we believe to be bad (even if we are nevertheless motivated to pursue them).

A further component of specific hope is a belief about the future in which its objective exists. This belief can be characterized in two ways: (1) that the objective is possible; (2) that the objective is probable. The success of the hard-nosed objection to cosmopolitan hope (on the first interpretation of it) turns on which of these descriptions of the belief about the future in which hope's objective exists is accurate.

On the first "possibility" interpretation, specific hope involves the belief that the objective of hope is both logically and physically possible. Commitment to the logical possibility of hope's objective provides a minimal constraint on the content of the belief about the future in which hope's objective exists: all it rules out is hope for an objective which contains a formal contradiction (for example, hope that I both pass and fail the exam).

Commitment to the physical possibility of hope's objective is a more demanding constraint. What I mean by the claim that an objective is "physically possible" is that, given what we know about the world and the agents inhabiting it, that objective could exist in the world.[3] Thus, commitment to this constraint ensures that the hoper believes that her objective could be realized in the world she inhabits. This constraint means that the hoper believes that the future in which a hoped for objective exists is *her* future. Without this constraint a person could counterintuitively be said to hope for an objective she believes to be logically possible, but which she believes could not be realized in the actual world. To illustrate, consider a person who believes that it would be a good thing to live forever, desires this for herself in virtue of this belief, and is disposed to do things she believes will increase the odds of her living forever, whenever possible, even though she knows that, *qua* human, she cannot live forever. On the account of hope just suggested, this person is not accurately described as hoping to live forever. Although the proposition toward which her attitudes of belief and desire are directed – "that I should live forever" – involve no logical contradiction, the state described by this proposition – that of eternal life – is not physically possible, given human biology. Rather than describing this person as hoping for everlasting life, we would describe her as wishing for or fantasizing about it.

On the second "probability" interpretation, specific hope involves not only the belief that the objective of hope is possible, but furthermore the belief that it is probable. This interpretation should be rejected on the grounds that it has the unwelcome implication that hope collapses either into blind faith, or into optimism, and there is good reason to think that hope is distinct from both these attitudes toward future objectives. Let me explain.

There are two ways in which the judgement that hope's objective is probable could be supported. First, by reference to the hoper's belief that she has evidence to support this probability judgement, and second, by reference to a non-evidence related belief held by the hoper (for example, a belief in divine providence). If the hoper's judgement that her objective is probable is supported by an evidence-related belief, then her hope takes the form of optimism (Boden, 1966). The optimist believes that the future is likely to bring to pass those things she desires and believes to be good; the optimist believes, let us say, that the probability of the objectives she desires is 0.5 or more. The optimist's reason for believing this is that she believes she has evidence that it is probable that her desires will be fulfilled. The evidence that the optimist marshals to support her judgements about the future sometimes turns out to be nothing more than a projection of her own good will on to the world: optimists are often nothing but wishful thinkers. However, that is besides the point. The optimist believes that she has evidence for judgements about the future, regardless of whether the evidence she believes herself to have is good evidence (or evidence at all): in virtue of the evidence she believes that she has, the optimist thinks that the future is laid out in a way that is likely to satisfy her desires for the objectives about which she is optimistic. In contrast, if the hoper's judgement that her objective is probable is supported by a non-evidence related belief, then her hope takes the form of blind faith. Here, the hoper judges that the probability of her objective is 0.5 or more, and supports this judgement by reference to, for example, her belief in the existence of a benevolent god.

Neither of these characterizations of hope is satisfactory, as can be seen by considering the following example. Imagine a mother whose teenage daughter has been missing for six months who retains hope that one day her daughter will return. The mother does not think that the return of her daughter is probable, which is not to say that she thinks it is improbable either. Rather, she makes no judgements about its probability. That is what makes her situation so painful: she simply does not know. The mother does not make predictions about what the future contains in her hoping: she does not "pocket the future in advance" (Stratton-Lake, 1990, p. 129). It might be that she keeps open the possibility of her daughter's return without calculating the odds because she has no evidence which enables her to make this calculation, and she is agnostic about the existence of a benevolent god. However, the point is that her failure to make probability judgements about her daughter's return does not prevent her from hoping for it. That the mother makes no judgements about the probability of her daughter's return, but is accurately described as hoping for her daughter's return, militates against any account of hope which makes judgements of the probability of hope's objectives a necessary component of hope, whether supported by evidence-related beliefs or not.[4]

Refraining from judging the probability of an objective is, I think, characteristic of all forms of specific hope: specific hope is characterized by a radical uncertainty with respect to its objectives, which shows that it is a mistake to characterize it in terms of probability judgements about these objectives. Of course, specific hope can be – and often is – accompanied by blind faith or optimistic judgements about the probability of hope's objective. But these judgements are not components of hope.

This fact about hope explains why pessimism with respect to an objective differs from hopelessness with respect to that objective. Pessimism with respect to a specific objective, like optimism, is either premised on the pessimist's belief that she has evidence to support her belief that the objective she is pessimistic about is improbable, or on a non-evidence related belief (perhaps the pessimist is just a misery guts, or believes in the existence of a malevolent god). In contrast, a loss of hope with respect to an objective does not depend on judgements about the objective's improbability; indeed, it is a feature of specific hope that it often becomes more intense the less probable the objective is believed by the hoper to be. In that case, pessimism about an objective and hope for that objective are consistent: hope can be retained even in the bleakest of circumstances. A loss of specific hope only attends the hoper's judgement that her objective is impossible, or contra-certain. Upon making such a judgement the hoper despairs of realizing her objective.

Given this account of specific hope it is clear that the cosmopolitan ideal yields a legitimate objective for specific hope. The cosmopolitan objective exists in the future, and is believed to be good and possible by cosmopolitans who desire it in virtue of their belief that it is good, and yields a disposition in them to act so as to make the realization of the cosmopolitan objective more likely, all else being equal. Furthermore, and importantly, it is not the case that those who hope for the cosmopolitan objective must be optimistic about this objective.[5] The upshot of the discussion in this section is that hard-nosed objectors who claim that cosmopolitan hope is misguided because the cosmopolitan ideal is *unlikely* to be realized make a misplaced objection. Cosmopolitans can be, and often are, deeply pessimistic about the prospects for realizing the cosmopolitan ideal, and yet continue to hope for it. To reach these cosmopolitans the hard-nosed objector must claim that although cosmopolitan hope is legitimate insofar as it yields an objective which can be hoped for, such hope is not sound.

IS COSMOPOLITAN HOPE SOUND?

Specific hope has four fundamental components.

1. a belief that hope's objective is possible;
2. a belief that hope's objective is good;
3. a desire for hope's objective in virtue of the belief that it is good;
4. a disposition to act so as to make hope's objective more probable (all else being equal) yielded by (1) – (3).

There are conditions related to each of these components according to which a specific hope can be judged to be sound. The first condition relates to the belief that the objective of hope is good: a hard-nosed objector might claim that this provides a component of sound hope if and only if this belief is true. So, let us turn to the ways in which a belief about the goodness of any hope's objectives could be false.

There are some objectives of hope – malformed objectives – which, we think, ought not to be hoped for. Some hopes are plain spiteful and malicious: hope for an innocent person to come to some harm. Others might be well-grounded but still nefarious in content: hope for an old enemy to contract a fatal disease, or to die poor and lonely. Still others are personal and born of unhappiness: hope to be run over by a bus, or killed in a plane crash. We think that a person with such hopes would be better off without them. This intuitive judgement can be understood in at least three ways:

  i. that the hope's objective is *morally objectionable*
  ii. that the hoper would *be a better person* without these hopes
  iii. that the hoper would *do better* without these hopes

The first interpretation (i) imports moral and ethical values into the judgements of malformed objectives. The second interpretation (ii) translates these judgements of the objective into judgements of the person who hopes for the objective. The third interpretation (iii) treats malformed objectives as instrumental impediments to the achievement of the hoper's other goals and aims; here, hope's objectives are judged by criteria of instrumental rationality. The three interpretations are consistent if it is the case that a person does better only when she is better – that is, if instrumental success in achieving goals and aims matters only when those goals and aims are morally or ethically good – and if the moral quality of a person can be judged by the moral quality of what she hopes for.

Before considering how these criticisms might apply to cosmopolitan hope it is worth noting that criticisms which focus on the dispositional component of hope in (4) collapse into one or another of the criticisms of the goodness of hope's objectives as laid out in (i)–(iii). In criticism of the disposition to act so as to make the cosmopolitan objective probable (4), it might be claimed

a. that this disposition harms the hoper, or
b. that this disposition harms others

If (a) is claimed then only (ii) or (iii) above can be intended: the harm that the disposition causes the hoper can only be moral harm, or harm to the hoper's capacities to pursue whatever other ends she has. If (b) is claimed, then what we are offered is an interpretation of (i) above. So, in dismissing criticisms of the first component of cosmopolitan hope as they appear in (i), (ii), and (iii) I shall also be dismissing criticisms of the fourth component of cosmopolitan hope (and I will not return to these criticisms later).

Is the cosmopolitan objective malformed in any of these ways? With respect to (iii), it is hard to see how hope for the cosmopolitan ideal must impede any cosmopolitan hoper's pursuit of their other aims. Of course, we can dream up an example of an obsessed cosmopolitan who spends day and night trying to convince people to extend their commitment to basic rights beyond their domestic context by trying to show how reasoning about rights in the domestic context must transfer to the global context. But what is wrong here has nothing to do with the content of the hoper's objective, and everything to do with the manner in which it is pursued. If the hard-nosed objection to the soundness of cosmopolitan hope relates to the moral quality of the cosmopolitan objective, then it must be understood via the claims in (i) and/or (ii).

To object as in (i) that the cosmopolitan objective is malformed according to moral criteria requires an argument to show that there is something morally objectionable about a situation in which people extend their commitment to principles of justice in a local context to a global context, whatever these principles are, so as to create a cosmopolitan world of global justice. If we are of a virtue ethics bent, this claim can be interpreted so as to yield the putative hard nosed judgement informed by (ii) that a person who hopes for the cosmopolitan objective would be a better person without this hope.

The problem with both of these interpretations is simply that they are not available to the hard-nosed objector. As I made clear in my introduction, the hard-nosed objector does not question the legitimacy of the cosmopolitan moral requirement; to return to Erwin Goldstine, his claim is that he and humanity are "shits" or "semi-shits," and that this prevents them from realizing a "wonderful" political state. What the hard-nosed objector doubts is whether hope for the cosmopolitan ideal to be realized through action fit to satisfy the requirement is well placed, whereas the objection under consideration addresses the moral quality of the objective of cosmopolitan hope. Given that the hard-nosed objector accepts that the cosmopolitan requirement is a legitimate moral requirement, she cannot object to cosmopolitan hope by questioning the morality of its objective as aimed at by the requirement.

The next possibility for interpretation of the hard-nosed objection is that it relates to the belief that the cosmopolitan objective is logically and physically possible. Criteria for the soundness of this component relate to the truth of the belief: a hard-nosed objector might insist that this belief must be true in order for the hope to be sound.

To believe that an objective is physically possible is to believe that it is logically possible and that it could be realized in the actual world. So, to show that belief in the possibility of the cosmopolitan objective is false requires showing either that it contains or entails a logical contradiction, or that it could not exist in the actual world. If either of these things can be established, then the hard-nosed objector can reject cosmopolitan hope on the grounds that it involves a false belief. It is clear that the cosmopolitan objective does not contain or entail a logical contradiction. In that case, the hard-nosed objector must show that the cosmopolitan objective could not be realized in the actual world, despite its achievement in other possible worlds which differ from this one. How might this case be argued?

Here, hard-nosed objectors tend to invite reflection on history and human nature. Surely, they argue, any honest and sober reflection on the course of human history shows that the belief that human beings as they are could overcome all the enmities and hatreds that divide them in order to extend their local commitment to justice so as to achieve the cosmopolitan ideal is false (remember Erwin Goldstine). Regardless of what is true in other possible worlds, in this one the record of history shows that it is not possible for people to transform their reasoning about justice in the way stated by the cosmopolitan objective.

There are at least three reflections which should lead us to be suspicious of such arguments. First, although it is true that human history is bathed in blood and hatred, it is also true that great progress has been made with respect to the extension of the scope of principles of justice so as to include groups of people who were hitherto oppressed or despised. In many places slavery has been abolished, women have the vote, homosexuality is not a crime, and religion can be practiced freely. Of course, it might be objected that these inclusions do not really represent progress, but we can safely ignore this response. Second, even if such progress had not been made there would still not be grounds for asserting the physical impossibility of the cosmopolitan objective. Human beings are malleable: their past practices do not determine their future ones. Finally, cosmopolitans can accept that human history makes realization of the cosmopolitan ideal overwhelmingly unlikely, but as we saw in the section on "Hope," pessimism with respect to the prospects for an objective is quite consistent with hope for that objective.

The final form that an objection to the soundness of cosmopolitan hope might take relates to the desire for its objective in virtue of the belief that the objective is good.[6] A *prima facie* attractive way to think about criteria of soundness according to which the desire for any hope's objective is to be judged relates to the extent to which it harmonizes with the proper purposes and functioning of human beings: the desire component of cosmopolitan hope is sound if and only if this desire promotes – or is at least consistent with – the proper purposes of human beings.

A hard-nosed objection taking this form would have to show that desiring the cosmopolitan objective conflicts with proper human purposes, *even when* the content of the objective is not morally objectionable (so as to avoid the collapse of this objection into the one considered earlier which relates to the moral quality of hope's objective). The cosmopolitan objective is a state in which persons extend their commitment to some fundamental local principles of justice to the global level. It might be objected that any person who desires this objective has a conception of humanity as possessed of, and capable of exercising, their reason in the same way, so as to extend their local commitments to principles of justice in order to come to accept the same global principles of justice. It could be argued that this is in conflict with the proper purposes and functioning of a human being because part of what it is for any person to exercise her reason correctly is for her to accept that others may legitimately exercise their reason in a different way. So, the hard-nosed objector might claim that to desire the cosmopolitan objective is to desire something which must be rejected by the hoper when she exercises her reason correctly. If we think that the correct use of reason is part of any account of proper human functioning and purposes, then a desire for the cosmopolitan objective is unsound.

One way in which this objection can be made in more detail is with a version of Rawls's "burdens of judgement" argument for acceptance of the permanence of reasonable pluralism.[7] Rawls argues that part of what it is for a person to exercise her reason correctly with respect to questions of justice is for her to accept that everyone's reason operates under "burdens of judgement." The burdens of judgement are particularly weighty with respect to political matters (such as those addressed by cosmopolitanism), thinks Rawls, "in view of the very great complexity of the questions raised, the often impressionistic nature of the evidence, and the severity of the conflicts they commonly address" (Rawls, 2001, p. 36. See also Rawls, 1993b, pp. 54–57). The existence of these burdens means that we should not expect the free exercise of reason by all persons to lead each of them to reach the same conclusions on moral, religious, and philosophical questions as they bear on their political judgements: they might, but this would be a result of coincidence rather than as a result of the conclusions they come to share having been uniquely determined by reason. Rawls's argument is that the correct exercise of reason by a person will lead her to accept that the correct exercise of reason by others need not deliver agreement between them on various important questions. Making the hard-nosed objection in these terms, the argument is that the desire for the cosmopolitan objective conflicts with the demands of reason. The burdens of judgement make it unreasonable to expect that all persons should employ the same method of reasoning to reach agreement on global principles of justice. If we think it is an important part of proper human functioning that reason is exercised correctly, then desire for the cosmopolitan objective makes cosmopolitan hope unsound.

This version of the objection makes an illicit move. It is not necessary for realization of the cosmopolitan objective through satisfaction of the cosmopolitan requirement that all persons employ *the same* method of reasoning to support global principles of justice. Rather, the cosmopolitan requirement states that each person ought to extend commitments to local principles of justice to justify the same principles at the global level, whatever the reasoning they use to support this commitment. It is consistent with realization of the cosmopolitan ideal through this requirement that there is a plurality of methods of reasoning about global justice, and desire for the cosmopolitan objective carries no more of a requirement for uniformity than the ideal that is realized when the objective is achieved. Given that the cosmopolitan requirement governs the relationship between reasoning about justice in local and global contexts, if reasoning in local contexts is diverse, then the cosmopolitan requirement does not demand uniformity of reasoning to support global principles. All it demands is the extension in each local context of reasoning-generated commitments to local principles of justice to the global level. In that case, there can be as many paths to global principles of justice as there are local contexts.

IS COSMOPOLITAN HOPE REQUIRED?

The argument thus far has shown that cosmopolitan hope is consistent with, and thus permitted by, commitment to the cosmopolitan requirement: the section entitled "Hope" established the legitimacy of the cosmopolitan ideal as an objective of hope, and the next section that cosmopolitan hope is sound. However, in response to the hard-nosed objector we may want to make the stronger claim that cosmopolitan hope is furthermore required given commitment to the cosmopolitan requirement. I shall indicate two ways in which this stronger conclusion could be established.

The first argument invokes the Humean principle "'ought' implies 'can.'" This principle states that it must be possible to perform the actions, or create the state of affairs, demanded by any moral requirements expressible in an "ought" statement. If the Humean principle is true then hard-nosed acceptance of the cosmopolitan requirement straightforwardly requires acceptance that what it aims at is possible (as argued in "Hope"). However, hard-nosed acceptance of the cosmopolitan requirement as a *moral* requirement also involves acceptance that what it aims at is good. If we ought to desire what is good, and be disposed to bring it about wherever possible, then anyone who accepts the cosmopolitan requirement ought to hope for the realization of the cosmopolitan ideal, because the requirement aims at this ideal. In virtue of accepting the cosmopolitan requirement the hard-nosed objector is committed to hope for the cosmopolitan ideal.

The second argument is Kantian. The hard-nosed objector endorses the cosmopolitan requirement, which demands the extension of local commitments to justice to the global level. The hard-nosed objection aims to prise apart commitment to this requirement from hope for the cosmopolitan ideal wherein the extension creates a world of global justice: one hard-nosed objection (considered in "Is cosmopolitan hope sound?") is that hope for this ideal is misguided given facts about the world and human beings which make the ideal impossible. However, we might claim that it is not facts about the world or human nature that make cosmopolitan hope misguided, but rather the hard-nosed conception of the cosmopolitan ideal as impossible *itself* that undermines cosmopolitan hope, and that commitment to the cosmopolitan requirement requires the abandonment of this hard-nosed attitude to the cosmopolitan ideal through the cultivation of cosmopolitan hope.

Consider an analogy.[8] A person stands at the edge of a crevasse and is committed to continuing forward. In order to be able to jump across she has to believe that she *can* make the jump and, importantly, this belief alters the probability of making a successful jump: if she cannot talk herself into this state of belief then her ability to make the jump will be impaired and she is less likely to be successful than if she believes that she can do it. Making the jump *as if* she can reach the other side increases the likelihood that she will in fact reach the other side. We might claim that the hard-nosed objector is in the same position as the ravine jumper with respect to the cosmopolitan ideal. Whereas the ravine jumper is committed to continuing forward, the objector is committed to extending her commitments to justice in the way demanded by the cosmopolitan requirement. The ravine jumper who doubts her ability to make the jump thereby lessens her chances of successfully making the jump; the objector who questions possibility of the cosmopolitan ideal thereby impairs her capacity to act so as to satisfy the cosmopolitan requirement. The requirement demands of each person that she extend her commitment to justice at the local level to the global level: if I believe, in a hard-nosed way, that the ideal to be realized by satisfaction of this requirement by all persons is impossible then my own capacity to act so as to satisfy this requirement will be damaged. By being hard-nosed with respect to the cosmopolitan ideal, the objector deprives herself of the motivation to act in the way demanded by the cosmopolitan requirement: what is the point of such action, given that the ideal toward which the requirement points is ultimately quixotic? In virtue of the practical demands made by the cosmopolitan requirement, a hard-nosed objector genuinely committed to it must not divest herself of the motivation to pursue it by judging it to be impossible: she must act as if the objective is possible, which is tantamount to cherishing specific hope for it.[9]

CONCLUSION

To recapitulate, the hard-nosed objection to cosmopolitan hope is that although the cosmopolitan requirement is legitimate, hope for the cosmopolitan ideal is misplaced. I have considered different ways in which the hard-nosed objection might be understood. First, that the cosmopolitan ideal is highly improbable, and so not a fit object of hope. In response, I argued that hope does not involve judgements of the probability of hope's objectives, in which case this criticism misses its target. Second, I considered various hard-nosed ways of attacking the four components of cosmopolitan hope, and I argued that none of them establishes that such hope is unsound. Furthermore, I suggested that the commitment to the cosmopolitan requirement on the part of the hard-nosed objector requires cosmopolitan hope. If this stronger thesis is true then the objection not only fails to show that hope for the cosmopolitan ideal ought to be abandoned, but is furthermore internally inconsistent: commitment to the cosmopolitan requirement makes cosmopolitan hope a duty.

In conclusion, the discussion here has both a political and a philosophical focus. The political focus is on the nature and demands of cosmopolitanism. The (more oblique) philosophical focus is on the relationship between moral requirements, moral ideals, and moral motivation. The philosophical contention to which the arguments here contribute is that acceptance of any moral requirement demands commitment to a future ideal state of affairs in which all persons act so as to satisfy that requirement. To characterize the commitment to an ideal that acceptance of a moral requirement carries in terms of hope is to characterize it as a practical commitment. When I accept a moral requirement I must commit to more than just the thought that it would be nice if that requirement were satisfied in all cases: I must commit to action to bring about that state of affairs, and this commitment rules out a conception of that future state of affairs as impossible. In relation to hard-nosed people, the challenge is this: either abandon commitment to the cosmopolitan requirement, or cultivate hope for a future world of global justice.

NOTES

I would like to thank Jeremy Moss for his helpful comments. I would also like to thank audiences who discussed this essay with me at the Birkbeck Philosophy Society and the York Political Theory Workshop; in particular, Sue Mendus and Matt Matravers.
1 This formulation owes much to Simon Caney's statement of the "principal cosmopolitan claim" (Caney, 2001b, p. 977).
2 For a good general account of different forms of hope, and useful specific accounts of how the concept of hope figures in the work of Immanuel Kant, Ernst Bloch, and Gabriel Marcel, see Godfrey (1987).
3 For more on the senses of possibility appealed to here see the entry on "possibility" in Honderich (1995, pp. 706-07).

4 A qualification is necessary here. In order for the mother to keep alive hope for her daughter's return it must be the case that she does not judge her daughter's return to be contra-certain or certain. The judgement that her daughter's return is contra-certain – that is, has a probability of 0 – is inconsistent with the belief that her daughter's return is physically possible. And the judgement that her daughter's return is certain – that is, has a probability of 1 – is characteristic not of hope for an objective, but rather of expectation or anticipation. In that case, judgements about the probability of hope's objectives are constitutive of hope, but only to the extent that the probability of the objective is not judged to be 0 or 1. (I shall suppress this qualification in the subsequent discussion.)

5 See, for example, Moellendorf (2002).

6 There are real problems raised by the question of whether a belief in the goodness of an objective can generate a desire for it, or whether the motivation to pursue a good objective requires an extant desire for the objective believed to be good. But this is a problem for anyone interested in the relationship between commitment to a moral ideal or principle and the motivation to act so as to realize that ideal or satisfy that principle. I make no comment on this tangled web here.

7 I do not attribute the following argument to Rawls.

8 Thanks are due to Sue Mendus for discussion on this point.

9 Kant makes a similar point when he claims the following with respect to the "irresistible veto" that "There shall be no war": "even if the fulfillment of this pacific intention were forever to remain a pious hope, we should still not be deceiving ourselves if we made it our maxim to work unceasingly towards it, for it is our duty to do so" (Kant, [1970], p. 174).

Bibliography

Ackerman, B., and Alstott, A. (1999). *The Stakeholder Society.* Yale University Press: New Haven, Conn.

Anderson, E. (1999). What is the point of equality? *Ethics,* 109, pp. 287–337.

Appiah, A. (1996). Cosmopolitan patriots. In M. Nussbaum (ed.), *For Love of Country.* Beacon Press: Boston, Mass.

Arendt, H. (1961). The crisis in culture. In H. Arendt, *Between Past and Future: Six Exercises in Political Thought.* Meridian: New York.

Barry, B. (1982). Humanity and justice in global perspective. In J. R. Pennock and J. W. Chapman (eds.), *Ethics, Economics and the Law, Nomos XXIV.* New York University Press: New York.

(1989). *Theories of Justice.* Harvester Wheatsheaf: London.

(1995). *Justice as Impartiality.* Clarendon Press: Oxford.

(1998a). International society from a cosmopolitan perspective. In Mapel and Nardin (eds.) (1998).

(1998b). Something in the disputation not unpleasant. In P. Kelly (ed.), *Impartiality, Neutrality and Justice: Re-thinking Brian Barry's Justice as Impartiality.* Edinburgh University Press: Edinburgh.

(1999). Statism and nationalism: a cosmopolitan critique. In I. Shapiro and L. Brilmayer (eds.), *Global Justice.* New York University Press: New York.

(2001). *Culture and Equality.* Harvard University Press: Cambridge, Mass.

Beitz, C. (1975). Justice and international relations. *Philosophy and Public Affairs,* 4, pp. 288–95.

(1979 [2nd edn, 1999]). *Political Theory and International Relations.* Princeton University Press: Princeton.

(1983). Cosmopolitan ideals and national sentiment, *Journal of Philosophy,* 80, pp. 591–600.

(1994). Cosmopolitan liberalism and the states system. In Brown (ed.) (1994).

(1998). Philosophy of international relations. In *Routledge Encyclopaedia of Philosophy.* Routledge: London, pp. 826–33.

(1999). Social and cosmopolitan liberalism. *International Affairs,* 75, pp. 531–45.

Benhabib, S. (1992). *Situating the Self.* Polity Press: Cambridge.

Bernstein, A. (unpublished). A cosmopolitan law of peoples.

Blake, M. (2002). Distributive justice, state coercion, and autonomy. *Philosophy and Public Affairs*, 30, pp. 257–96.

Boden, M. (1966). Optimism. *Philosophy*, 51, pp. 291–303.

Böhme, G. (2001). *Ethics in Context*. Polity Press: Cambridge.

Bok, S. (1996). *From Part to Whole*. In J. Cohen (ed.), *For Love of Country*. Beacon Press: Boston.

Brighouse, H. (1996). Egalitarianism and equal availability of political influence. *Journal of Political Philosophy*, 4.

(1998). Against nationalism. In J. Couture, K. Nielsen, and M. Seymour (eds.), *Rethinking Nationalism*. Calgary University Press: Calgary, Alberta.

Brock, G. (2002). Liberal nationalism vs. cosmopolitanism: locating the disputes. *Public Affairs Quarterly*, 16, pp. 307–27.

Brown, C. (ed.) (1994). *Political Restructuring in Europe: Ethical Perspectives*. Routledge: London.

Buchanan A (2000a). The internal legitimacy of humanitarian intervention. *Journal of Political Philosophy*, 7, pp. 71–87.

(2000b). Rawls's Law of Peoples, *Ethics*, 110, pp. 697–721.

Cabrera, L. (2004). *Political Theory of Global Justice: A Cosmopolitan Case for the World State*. Routledge: London.

Caney S (2001a). Cosmopolitan justice and equalizing opportunities. In T. Pogge (ed.), *Global Justice*. Blackwell: Oxford.

(2001b). International distributive justice. *Political Studies*. 49, pp. 974–97.

Chen, S. and Ravallion, M. (2001). How did the world's poorest fare in the 1990s? *Review of Income and Wealth*, 47, pp. 283–300.

Cohen G. A. (1993). Equality of what? On welfare, good and capabilities. In M. Nussbaum and A. Sen (eds.), *Quality of Life*. Oxford University Press: Oxford.

(1994). Incentives, inequality and community. In S. Darwall (ed.), *Equal Freedom*. University of Michigan Press: Ann Arbor.

Cohen, J. (1989). Deliberation and democratic legitimacy. In A. Hamlin and P. Pettit (eds.), *The Good Polity*. Blackwell: Oxford.

Cohen, J. (ed.) (1996). *For Love of Country: Debating the Limits of Patriotism*. Beacon Press: Boston.

Cohen, M. (1985). Moral skepticism and international relations. In C. Beitz *et al.* (eds.), *International Ethics: A Philosophy and Public Affairs Reader*, Princeton University Press: Princeton.

Copp, D. (1992). The right to an adequate standard of living: autonomy and the basic needs. *Social Philosophy and Policy*, 9, pp. 231–61.

(1995). *Morality, Normativity, and Society*. Oxford University Press: New York.

(1998). Equality, justice, and the basic needs. In G. Brock (ed.), *Necessary Goods*. Rowman and Littlefield: Oxford and Lanham, MA, pp. 113–33.

(1999). The idea of a legitimate state. *Philosophy and Public Affairs*, 28, pp. 3–45.

(2000). Capitalism versus democracy: the marketing of votes and the marketing of political power. In J. D. Bishop (ed.), *Ethics and Capitalism*. University of Toronto Press, Toronto.

Couture, J. (1999). Are cosmopolitans better equipped to face globalization than liberal nationalists? *Imprints*, 3, pp. 156–67.

(2001). Cosmopolitan democracy and liberal nationalism. In N. Miscevic (ed.), *Nationalism and Ethnic Conflict*. Open Court: Chicago and Lasalle, Illinois.

Couture, J. and Nielsen, K. (1998). Liberal nationalism both cosmopolitan and rooted. In J. Couture, K. Nielsen, and M. Seymour (eds.), *Rethinking Nationalism*. University of Calgary Press: Calgary, Alberta.

Dagger, R. (1985). Rights, boundaries and the bonds of community. *American Political Science Review*, 79, pp. 436–47.

Dahl, R. A. (1989). *Democracy and its Critics*. Yale University Press: New Haven.

Dent, N. (1988). *Rousseau: An Introduction to his Psychological, Social, and Political Theory*. Blackwell: Oxford.

Dreben, B. (2003). On Rawls and political liberalism. In Freeman (ed.) (2003).

Dowding, K., De Wispelaere, J., and White, S. (eds.) (2003). *The Ethics of Stakeholding*. Palgrave: London.

Dworkin, R. (1981a). Is there a right to pornography? *Oxford Journal of Legal Studies*, 1, pp. 177–212.

(1981b). What is equality? Part 2: Equality of resources. *Philosophy and Public Affairs*, 10, pp. 283–345.

(1986). *Law's Empire*. Fontana: London.

Easterly, W. (2000). The effects of IMF and World Bank programs on poverty. World Bank Oct. 31. Accessed from:http://www.imf.org/external/pubs/ft/staffp/2000/00-00/e.pdf.

Elster, J. (1992). *Local Justice*. Russell Sage Foundation: New York.

Estlund, D. (1996). The survival of egalitarian justice in John Rawls' "Political Liberalism." *Journal of Political Philosophy*, 4.

Fletcher, G. (1994). Get serious. *Boston Review*. October/November, p. 30.

Fleurbaey, M. (1995). Equality and responsibility. *European Economic Review*, 39, pp. 683–89.

Fourier, C. (1972). *The Social Destiny of Man*. Gordon Press: New York.

Frankfurt, H. (1987). Equality as a moral ideal. *Ethics*, 98, pp. 21–43.

Freeman, S. (1992). Original meaning, democratic interpretation, and the constitution. *Philosophy and Public Affairs*, 21.

(2003). Introduction: John Rawls – An overview. In Freeman (ed.) (2003).

(2005). The Law of Peoples, social cooperation, human rights, and distributive justice. *Social Philosophy and Policy*, forthcoming.

Freeman, S. (ed.) (2003). *The Cambridge Companion to Rawls*. Cambridge University Press: Cambridge.

Friedman, M. (1985). *What are Friends For?* Cornell University Press: Ithaca, N.Y.

Gadamer, H. (1975). *Truth and Method*. Sheed and Ward: London.

Gellner, E. (1971). *Thought and Change*. Weidenfeld & Nicolson: London.

Giddens, A. (1984). *The Constitution of Society*. Polity Press: Cambridge

Godfrey, J. (1987). *A Philosophy of Human Hope*. Martinus Nijhoff Publishers: Dordrecht.

Goodin, R. (1988). What is so special about our fellow countrymen? *Ethics*, 98, pp. 663–87.

(1992). *Green Political Theory.* Polity Press: Cambridge.

Griffin, J. (1986). *Well-Being.* Oxford University Press: Oxford.

Habermas, J. (1973). Wahrheitstheorien. In H. Fahrenbach (ed.), *Wirchlichkeit und Reflexion.* Neske: Pfüllingen.

(1988). *Theory and Practice.* Polity Press: Cambridge.

(1996). *Between Facts and Norms: Contributions to a Discourse Theory of Law and Democracy.* Polity Press: Cambridge.

Hamlin, A. and Pettit, P. (eds.) (1989). *The Good Polity.* Blackwell: Oxford.

Hampshire, S. (1989). *Innocence and Experience.* Harvard University Press: Cambridge, Mass.

Held, D. (1995). *Democracy and the Global Order: From the Modern State to Cosmopolitan Governance.* Polity Press: Cambridge.

(1996). *Models of Democracy.* Second edn. Polity Press: Cambridge.

(2002). Law of states, law of peoples. *Legal Theory*, 8, 2, pp. 1–44.

(2004). *Global Covenant: The Social Democratic Alternative to the Washington Consensus.* Polity Press: Cambridge.

(2006). *Cosmopolitanism: A Defence.* Polity Press: Cambridge.

Held, D. (ed.) (1991). *Political Theory Today.* Polity Press: Cambridge.

Held, D., McGrew, A., Goldblatt, D., Perraton, J. (1999). *Global Transformations: Politics, Economics and Culture.* Polity Press: Cambridge.

Hill, T. (1973). Servility and self-respect, *Monist*, 57, pp. 87–104. Also in Hill, T. (1991). *Autonomy and Self-Respect.* Cambridge University Press: Cambridge.

(1987). The importance of autonomy. In E. Kittay and D. Meyers (eds.), *Women and Moral Theory.* Roman and Allanheld: Towata, NJ.

Honderich, T. (ed.) (1995). *The Oxford Companion to Philosophy.* Oxford University Press: Oxford.

Horstmann, A. (1976). Kosmopolit, Kosmopolitismus. In *Historisches Worterbuch der Philosphie.* Band 4, Schwabe: Basel, pp. 1156–68.

International Labour Organization. (ILO) (2002). *A Future Without Child Labour.* Accessed from http://www.ilo.org/dyn/declaris/declarationweb.indexpage.

International Panel of Eminent Personalities (2000). *Rwanda: The Preventable Genocide.* Accessed from www.visiontv.ca/RememberRwanda/Report.pdf.

Jones, C. (1999). *Global Justice.* Oxford University Press: Oxford.

Kant, I. (1970). *Kant's Political Writings.* Edited by Reiss H. Cambridge University Press: Cambridge.

Kelly, E. (2000). Personal concern. *The Canadian Journal of Philosophy*, 30, pp. 115–36.

Kelly, P. (ed.) (1998). *Impartiality, Neutrality and Justice: Re-Reading Brian Barry's Justice as Impartiality.* Edinburgh University Press: Edinburgh.

Keohane, R. (2002). *Power and Governance in a Partially Globalized World.* Routledge: New York and London.

Keohane, R. with Nye, J. (Jr.) (2000a). Introduction to Joseph S. Nye and John D. Donahue (eds.), *Governance in a Globalizing World.* Washington: Brookings.

Keohane, R. and Nye, J. (Jr.) (2000b). *Power and Interdependence.* 3rd edn. Addison Wesley Longman: Boston.

Klosko, G. (1992). *The Principle of Fairness and Political Obligation.* Rowman and Littlefield: Lanham, Md.

Kollontai, A. (1992). *Love of Worker Bees,* C. Porter (ed.) Academy: Chicago.

Kuper, A. (2000). Rawlsian global justice: beyond *The Law of Peoples* to a cosmopolitan law of persons. *Political Theory,* 28, pp. 640–74.

Kymlicka, W. (1990). Two theories of justice, *Inquiry,* 33, pp. 99–119.

(1995). *Multicultural Citizenship.* Oxford University Press: Oxford.

(2001). *Politics in the Vernacular.* Oxford University Press: Oxford.

(2002). *Contemporary Political Philosophy.* 2nd edn. Oxford University Press: Oxford.

Lam, R. and Wantchekon, L. (1999). *Dictatorships as a Political Dutch Disease.* Accessed from www.library.yale.edu/socsci/egcdp795.pdf.

Locke, J. (1960). An essay concerning the true original, extent, and end of civil government. In P. Laslett (ed.), *John Locke: Two Treatises of Government.* Cambridge University Press: Cambridge.

(1967). *Two Treatises of Government,* ed. P. Laslett. 2nd edn. Cambridge University Press: Cambridge.

Loury, G. (2002). *The Anatomy of Racial Inequality.* Harvard University Press: Cambridge, Mass.

MacCormick, D. N. (1981). *Legal Right and Social Democracy.* Oxford University Press: Oxford.

Macedo, S. (1995). Liberal civic education and religious fundamentalism: the case of God v. John Rawls? *Ethics,* 105, pp. 468–96.

MacIntyre, A (1984). Is patriotism a virtue? *The Lindley Lectures.* University of Kansas Press: Kansas City.

Mack, E. (1995). The self-ownership proviso: a new and improved Lockean proviso. *Social Philosophy and Policy,* 12, pp. 186–218.

Mackie, J. (1977). *Ethics: Inventing Right and Wrong.* Penguin: Harmondsworth, Middlesex.

Mapel, D. and Nardin, T. (eds.) (1998). *International Society: Diverse Ethical Perspectives.* Princeton University Press: Princeton, NJ.

Marshall, T. (1973). *Class, Citizenship and the Welfare State.* Greenwood Press: Westport, Conn.

McCarthy, T. (1991) *Ideals and Illusions.* MIT Press: Cambridge, Mass.

(1997). On the idea of a reasonable Law of Peoples. In J. Bohman and M. Lutz-Bachmann (eds.), *Perpetual Peace: Essays on Kant's Cosmopolitan Ideal.* MIT Press: Cambridge, Mass.

(1999). On reconciling cosmopolitan unity and national diversity. *Public Culture,* 11, pp. 175–208.

McMahan, J. (1997). The limits of national partiality. In R. McKim and J. McMahan (eds.), *The Morality of Nationalism.* Oxford University Press: Oxford.

Milanovic, B. (2002). True world income distribution, 1988 and 1993: first calculation based on household surveys alone. *The Economic Journal*, 112, pp. 51–92. Accessed from www.blackwellpublishers.co.uk/specialarticles/ecoj50673.pdf.

Miller, D. (1988). The ethical significance of nationality. *Ethics*, 98, pp. 647–62.

(1989). *Market, State and Community: Theoretical Foundations of Market Socialism*. Clarendon Press: Oxford.

(1995). *On Nationality*. Oxford University Press: Oxford.

(1998). The limits of cosmopolitan justice. In Mapel and Nardin (eds.) (1998).

(2000). *Citizenship and National Identity*. Polity Press: Cambridge.

Miller, R. (1992). *Moral Differences*. Princeton University Press: Princeton.

(2004). Cosmopolitanism and its limits. *International Journal of Politics and Ethics*, 3.

Moellendorf, D. (2002). *Cosmopolitan Justice*. Westview Press: Boulder, Colo.

Moravscic, A. (1997). Taking preferences seriously: a liberal theory of international politics, *International Organization*, 51, pp. 513–54.

Morgenthau, H. (1952). *In Defense of the National Interest*. Alfred A. Knopf: New York.

(1985). *Politics Among Nations: The Struggle for Power and Peace*. (6th edn.). Revised by Thompson K. Knopf: New York.

Murphy, L. (1993). The demands of beneficence, *Philosophy and Public Affairs*, 22, pp. 267–92.

(2001). *Moral Demands in Non-Ideal Theory*. Cambridge University Press: New York.

Nagel, T. (1977). Poverty and food: why charity is not enough. In P. Brown and H. Shue (eds.), *Food Policy: The Responsibility of the United States in the Life and Death Choices*. The Free Press: New York.

(1991). *Equality and Partiality*. Oxford University Press: New York.

Nielsen, K. (1996–97). Cultural nationalism, neither ethnic nor civic. *Philosophical Forum*, 28, pp. 42–52.

(1988). World government, security, and global justice. In S. Luper-Foy (ed.), *Problems of International Justice*. Westview Press: Boulder and London.

(1996). *Naturalism without Foundations*. Prometheus Books: Amherst, N.Y.

(2003). *Globalization and Justice*. Humanity Press: Amherst, NY.

Nozick, R. (1974). *Anarchy, State and Utopia*. Blackwell: Oxford.

Nussbaum, M. (1996). Patriotism and cosmopolitanism. In Cohen (ed.) (1996).

(1997a). *Cultivating Humanity*. Harvard University Press: Cambridge, Mass.

(1997b). Kant and cosmopolitanism. In J. Bohman and M. Lutz-Bachmann (eds.), *Perpetual Peace: Essays on Kant's Cosmopolitan Ideal*. MIT Press: Cambridge, Mass.

(2000). Duties of material aid: Cicero's problematic legacy, *Journal of Political Philosophy*, 8, pp. 176–206.

(2004). Women's Education: a global challenge, *Signs*, 29, pp. 325–56.

Okin, S. (1989). *Justice, Gender and the Family*. Basic Books: New York.

O'Neill, O. (1990). Enlightenment as autonomy: Kant's vindication of reason. In L. Jordanova and P. Hulme (eds.), *The Enlightenment and its Shadows.* Routledge: London.

——— (1991). Transnational justice. In Held (ed.) (1991).

——— (1992). Magic associations and imperfect people. In B. Barry and R. Goodin (eds.) *Free Movement.* Harvester Wheatsheaf: Hemel Hempstead.

——— (2000). *Bounds of Justice.* Cambridge University Press: Cambridge.

Parfit, D. (1995). Equality or priority. Lindley Lecture, University of Kansas: Lawrence, Kans.

Pogge, T. (1989). *Realizing Rawls.* Cornell University Press: Ithaca, NY.

——— (1994a). Cosmopolitanism and sovereignty. In Brown (ed.) (1994).

——— (1994b). An egalitarian law of peoples. *Philosophy and Public Affairs,* 23, pp. 195–224.

——— (1998a). Human rights and human responsibilities. In C. Cronin and Pablo de Grieff (eds.), *Transnational Politics and Deliberative Democracy.* MIT Press: Cambridge, Mass.

——— (1998b). The Bounds of Nationalism. In J. Couture, K. Nielsen, and M. Seymour (eds.), *Rethinking Nationalism.* Calgary University Press: Calgary, Alberta.

——— (2002). *World Poverty and Human Rights: Cosmopolitan Responsibilities and Reforms.* Polity Press: Cambridge.

——— (2004). The incoherence between Rawls's theories of justice, *Fordham Law Review,* 72/5, pp. 1739–59.

Rawls, J. (1971). *A Theory of Justice.* Harvard University Press: Cambridge, Mass.

——— (1972). *A Theory of Justice.* Oxford University Press: Oxford.

——— (1985). Justice as fairness: political not metaphysical, *Philosophy of Public Affairs,* 14(3).

——— (1993a). The Law of Peoples, *Critical Inquiry,* 20, pp. 36–68.

——— (1993b). *Political Liberalism.* Columbia: New York.

——— (1996). *Political Liberalism.* Revised edn. Columbia University Press: New York.

——— (1999a). *The Law of Peoples.* Harvard University Press: Cambridge, Mass.

——— (1999b). *A Theory of Justice.* 2nd edn. Harvard University Press: Cambridge, Mass.

——— (1999c). The idea of public reason revisited. In Rawls (1999a).

——— (1999d). Legal obligation and the duty of fair play. In S. Freeman (ed.) *J. Rawls: Collected Papers.* Harvard University Press: Cambridge, Mass.

——— (2001). *Justice as Fairness: A Restatement.* Harvard University Press: Cambridge, Mass.

Raz, J. (1986). *The Morality of Freedom.* Oxford University Press: Oxford.

Risse, T., Ropp, S., and Sikkink, K. (eds.) (1999). *The Power of Human Rights: International Norms and Domestic Change.* Cambridge University Press: Cambridge.

Risse, Mathias (2003) Do we harm the global poor? Presentation at *Author Meets Critics* session at the Eastern Division Meeting of the American

Philosophical Association, 30 December 2003. Also available at: http://ksghome.harvard.edu/~.mrisse.academic.ksg/papers_Philosophy.htm.

Roemer, J. E. (1996). *Theories of Distributive Justice*. Harvard University Press: Cambridge, Mass.

Roth, P. (1999). *I Married a Communist*. Vintage: London.

Sandel, M. (1996). *Democracy's Discontent*. Harvard University Press: Cambridge, Mass.

Scanlon, T. (1982). Contractualism and utilitarianism. In Sen and Williams (eds.) (1982).

(1998). *What We Owe to Each Other*. Harvard University Press: Cambridge, Mass.

Scheffler, S. (1997). Relationships and responsibilities, *Philosophy and Public Affairs*, 26, pp. 189–209.

(1999). Conceptions of cosmopolitanism. *Utilitas*, 11, pp. 255–76.

(2001). *Boundaries and Allegiances*. Oxford University Press: Oxford.

Schlereth, T. (1977). *The Cosmopolitan Ideal in Enlightenment Thought*. University of Notre Dame Press: Notre Dame.

Schmidt, J. (1998). Civility, enlightenment and society: conceptual confusions and Kantian remedies, *American Political Science Review*, 92, pp. 419–227.

Schwarzenbach, S. (1996). On civic friendship, *Ethics*, 107, pp. 97–128.

Sen, A. (1983). Poor, relatively speaking. *Oxford Economic Papers*, 35, pp. 153–69.

(1987). *The Standard of Living*, The Tanner Lectures, Cambridge, 1985. Edited by Geoffrey Hawthorn. Cambridge University Press: Cambridge.

(1992). *Inequality Re-Examined*. Oxford University Press: Oxford.

(1999) *Development as Freedom*. Oxford University Press: Oxford.

(2002). Justice across borders. In P. De Grieff and C. Cronin (eds.), *Global Justice, Transnational Politics*. MIT Press: Boston.

Sen, A. and Williams, B. (eds.) (1982). *Utilitarianism and Beyond*. Cambridge University Press: Cambridge.

Seymour, M. (1998). Introduction: questioning the ethnic-civic dichotomy. In J. Couture, K. Nielsen, and M. Seymour (eds.), *Rethinking Nationalism*. University of Calgary Press: Calgary, Alberta.

Shue, H. (1980). *Basic Rights*. Princeton University Press: Princeton.

(1983). The burdens of justice. *Journal of Philosophy*, 80, pp. 604–06.

(1988). Mediating duties, *Ethics*, 98, pp. 687–704.

Simmons, A. J. (1979). *Moral Principles and Political Obligations*. Princeton University Press: Princeton.

Singer, P. (1972). Famine, affluence and morality, *Philosophy and Public Affairs*, 1, pp. 229–43.

(2002). *One World*. Yale University Press: New Haven.

Sit, V. F. (2001). Globalization, foreign direct investment, and urbanization in developing countries. In S. Yusuf, S. Evenett, and W. Wu (eds.), *Facets of Globalization: International and Local Dimensions of Development*. World Bank Discussion Paper No. 415. World Bank: Washington, DC.

Slaughter, A. (1993). International law in a world of liberal states. International law and international relations theory: a dual agenda, *American Journal of International Law*, 6, pp. 503–38.

Slote, M. (1990). *Goods and Virtues*. Clarendon Press: Oxford.

Soros, G. (2002). *The New Republic*. August.

Steiner, H. (1994). *An Essay on Rights*. Blackwell: Oxford and Cambridge, Mass.

(2003). Compatriot priority and justice among thieves. In A. Reeve and A. Williams (eds.), *Real Libertarianism Assessed: Political Theory after Van Parijs*. Palgrave: London and New York.

Sterba, J. P. (1978). New libertarianism, *American Philosophical Quarterly*, 15.

Stratton-Lake, P. (1990). The Future of Reason: Kant's Conception of the Finitude of Thinking, PhD thesis, University of Essex.

Swift, A. (2003). *How Not to Be a Hypocrite*. Routledge: London.

Sypnowich, C. (2003). Equality: from Marxism to Liberalism (and Back Again), *Political Studies Review*, 1, pp. 333–43.

Tamir, Y. (1993). *Liberal Nationalism*. Princeton University Press: Princeton.

Tan, K. (1998) Liberal toleration in the law of peoples, *Ethics*, 108, pp. 276–95.

(2000). *Toleration, Diversity, and Global Justice*. University of Pennsylvania Press: Philadelphia.

(2002). Liberal nationalism and cosmopolitan justice, *Ethical Theory and Moral Practice*, 5, pp. 431–61.

(2004a). Commentary on Kai Nielsen's *Globalization and Justice*. APA Pacific Division Meeting, Pasadena, California, 29 March 2004.

(2004b). Justice and personal pursuits, *Journal of Philosophy*, 101, pp. 331–62.

(2004c). *Justice Without Borders*. Cambridge University Press: Cambridge.

(2005). Cosmopolitanism, impartiality and patriotic partiality. *Canadian Journal of Philosophy*.

Tesón, F. (1995). The Rawlsian theory of international law, *Ethics and International Affairs*, 9.

Thomson, J. (1971). A defense of abortion, *Philosophy and Public Affairs*, 1, pp. 47–66.

Tideman, N. (1991). Commons and commonwealths. In R. Andelson (ed.), *Commons without Tragedy*. Shepheard-Walwyn: London.

Tully, J. (1995). *Strange Multiplicity: Constitutionalism in an Age of Diversity*. Cambridge University Press: Cambridge.

United Nations Conference on Trade and Development (UNCTAD) (1999). Industrial countries must work harder for development if globalization is to deliver on its promises. Accessed from: http://www.unctad.org/Templates/webflyer.asp?docid=3082&intItemID=2021&lang=1.

United Nations Development Programme (UNDP) (1998). *Human Development Report 1998*. Oxford University Press: New York.

(1999). *Human Development Report 1999*. Oxford University Press: New York.

(2002a). *Human Development Balance Sheet*. Accessed from: http://hdr.und.org/reports/global/2002/en/pdf/HDR%20PR_balance.pdf.

(2002b). *Human Development Report*. Accessed from: http://hdr.undp.org/reports/global/1999/en/pdf/chapterone.pdf.

(2003). *Human Development Report 2003*. Oxford University Press: New York.

(2004). *Human Development Report 2004*. UNDP: New York.

Unger, P. (1999). *Living High and Letting Die: Our Illusion of Innocence*. Oxford University Press: Oxford.

UNICEF (2000). *The State of the World's Children*. Accessed from: http://www.unicef.org/sowcoo/.

Van Parijs, P. (1995). *Real Freedom for All*. Oxford University Press: Oxford.

Waldron, J. (1988). *The Right to Private Property*. Oxford University Press: Oxford.

(1993). Special ties and natural duties. *Philosophy and Public Affairs*. 22.

(1992). Minority cultures and the cosmopolitan alternative. *University of Michigan Journal of Law Reform*, 25, pp. 751–92.

(1999). Minority cultures and the cosmopolitan alternative. In W. Kymlicka (ed.). *The Rights of Minority Cultures*. Oxford University Press: Oxford.

Walzer, M. (1983). *Spheres of Justice: A Defence of Pluralism and Equality*. Martin Robertson: Oxford.

Wantchekon, L. (1999). *Why Do Resource Dependent Countries Have Authoritarian Governments?* Accessed from www.yale.edu/leitner/pdf/1999-11.pdf.

Weale, A. (1998). From contracts to pluralism? In Kelly (ed.) (1998).

Wenar, L. (2002). The legitimacy of peoples. In P. De Grieff and C. Cronin (eds.), *Global Justice and Transnational Politics*. MIT Press: Cambridge, Mass.

Williams, B. (1973). A critique of utilitarianism. In J. Smart and B. Williams (eds.), *Utilitarianism: For and Against*. Cambridge University Press: Cambridge.

World Bank (1994). Special program of assistance launching the third phase. World Bank: Washington. Cited in D. Sahn, P. Dorosh, and S. Younger (eds.) (1997), *Structural Adjustment Reconsidered*. Cambridge University Press: Cambridge.

Index

agency 12–13, 41–42, 47
Anderson, E. 78–80
Appiah, A. 57
Arendt, H. 24
associative duties 133–146, 150–151, 158
autonomy 20, 24, 41–42, 46, 63, 77

Barry, B. 14, 17, 18, 19, 21, 22, 51, 184, 186
Beitz, C. 153, 164, 173, 207–209, 219
Benhabib, S. 21
Blake, M. 87
Boden, M. 239
Brighouse, H. 59
Brock, G. 169

Caney, S. 24
capabilities 78–80, 85, 197, 210–214
    and primary goods 61–67
Cohen, G. A. 65
consent 13
corruption 104
cosmopolitan hope 239
    defined 236–237
cosmopolitanism 2–4, 10–11, 56–58, 133–146, 164,
        180, 183–185, 234, 235–236
    weak 3, 17
    strong 3, 17
    rooted 7
    thick 16, 17
    thin 16, 17
    layered 18
    etymology of 56
    ethical versus aesthetic 56–58
    and equal respect 133–146
    and utopianism 235–248
cultural diversity 16

decent hierarchical societies 202, 204, 220,
        222–223
democracy 5, 21
democratic citizenship 5, 78–80, 82, 83–84

and democratic equality 79–83, 85–86
democratic community 137, 146
    and inequality 83–84
democratic equality 83–84
difference principle 46, 60
duties 45, 93–95, 133, 148,
        150, 158, 211
    associative duties 133–146, 150–151, 158
Dworkin, R. 31

Easterly, W. 155
education 217
egalitarianism 22, 55, 61–67, 75–76, 151, 166
    and community 67
    and democratic equality 85–86
    and luck 70, 75–76, 78–80
Elster, J. 171
entitlement theory 97
equal moral concern 25, 127, 128
equal moral worth 5, 12
equal opportunities 41
equal respect 128, 131–133, 151, 152, 183

family 17, 28, 76, 88–89, 114, 137,
        190–191, 217
female genital mutilation 123
Fleurbaey, M. 42
friendship 175–177
Frost, R. 219

Gadamer, H. 22
Gellner, E. 29
general will 16
global basic structure 4, 6–7, 47–48, 51,
        100–101, 102–105, 149, 151–155, 165, 211–214,
        214–218
    and reforms 105–108, 211–214
    and patriotic partiality 165–178
global fund 36
global inequality 55, 72, 127, 130, 131, 166,
        169–170, 196, 203–204, 208–209

global redistribution 34–36, 39–41, 55, 72–74,
    75–90, 93–105, 155–161, 164, 169,
    196, 207, 215, 234, 235–248
global resources dividend 105–107, 165–166
global state 48–50
Goodin, R. 15, 44, 127, 143, 157
Griffin, J. 63
Grotius, Hugo 198, 206, 215

Habermas, J. 18, 21, 25
Hampshire, S. 120
health care 105–106
Hill, T. 132
hope 237–247
    cosmopolitan hope 239
    specific hope 240
human flourishing 61–67, 69–72, 113
    and charity 67
    and closeness 69
    and freedom 66
    and self-determination 69–72
    and global redistribution 72–74
human nature 234, 242–243, 243–244
human rights 112, 113, 117, 123–124,
    207, 211, 220, 230
Hume, D. 29, 198, 203, 208, 246

immigration 193–194, 201
impartiality 20, 21, 133, 165, 168, 181
individualism 12
inequality 55, 72, 127, 130, 131, 166, 169–170,
    196, 203–204, 208–209
international law 110

Kant, I. 11, 25, 51, 131–133, 199, 246–247
Kelly, E. 22
Keohane, R. 154
Kuper, R. 19
Kymlicka, W. 55, 168, 185

legitimacy 24, 26, 224–225, 225–229
liberalism 28, 30, 31, 35, 116, 219–233,
    and nationalism 28–30, 164–165, 169, 185–194
    and reason 30
libertarianism 94, 95, 101, 106
liberties 41–42
localism 71, 143, 171–172, 184
Lockean proviso 34, 46–47
Locke, J. 33, 34, 35, 95, 96, 98–99, 100, 106
luck and egalitarianism 78–80, 149

MacCormick, D. N. 29
Marshall, T. 20
Marx, K. 210
McCarthy, T. 16, 18, 222

Miller, D. 17, 18, 167–171, 185
Miller, R. 152
Moellendorf, D. 46, 47, 51, 222
moral imperialism 121
moral pluralism 120, 173
    and redistribution 173
Morgenthau, H. 110, 119–122
Murphy, L. 44–43

Nagel, T. 51, 96
nation 1, 212
national interest 110, 122, 124
national membership 55, 164
    and redistribution 167–174
    value of 174–178, 187–188
nationalism 1, 28, 32, 185
    and liberalism 28–30, 164–165,
        169, 185–194
natural law 199
needs 5, 7, 14, 39–53, 63, 128, 210–211
    basic needs principle 43
    and duties 45
    and sufficiency 46
    of compatriots 131
neutrality 19
    ethical and political 19
Nozick, R. 31, 43–44, 46–47, 96
Nussbaum, M. 17, 164, 184
Nye, J. 154

O'Neill, O. 22, 23, 28, 29, 149
Obligatory Exclusivity Thesis 110–111
open borders 193–194

parental nurturance 137, *see also* family
particularism 127, 180, 182–183
    and universalism 128, 180, 182–183
    and patriotic partiality (bias) 129
patriotic bias, *see* patriotic partiality
patriotic partiality 55, 127, 129, 131–133, 155–161,
    164, 165–178, 180, 184–185, 215
    and equal respect 131–133
    defended 133
    and democratic community 137
    and social trust 134–137
    strong and weak 186–187
    and parental partiality 190–191
Patten, A. 101, 102, 103
Permissible Exclusivity Thesis 6–7, 111–112,
    112–122, 122–125,
    justifications of 112–122
    and realism 119–122
    and human rights 112, 113
    and liberalism 116
personal responsibility 13

Pogge, T. 19, 59, 164, 165–166, 173, 194,
207–209, 222
political community 10, 14, 80
poverty 92–93, 96, 137, 145
poverty traps 78, 102–105
property rights 31, 98–99

radical inequality 96, 97, 100
Rawls, J. 1–2, 17, 21, 31, 40, 43, 46, 51, 52–53,
58–61, 68, 70–71, 75, 81, 87, 95, 132, 152,
170, 180, 197–218, 219–233, 245
and the burdens of judgment 245
and decent hierarchical peoples 202, 204, 220,
222–223, 230
and legitimacy 224–225, 225–229, 230
and primary goods 46, 60, 61–67
and reflective equilibrium 180–183
and stability 76–78
and two stage bargain 199–201, 201–202
realism (in international relations) 119–122
fiduciary 113–114
Hobbesian 114–116, 117–118, 119
recognition 78
rights 30–32
as universal 35
see also property rights; human rights
Roth, P. 235

Satz, D. 99, 101
Scanlon, T. 22, 132
Scheffler, S. 17, 137, 174, 175
secession 34
self-determination 21, 55, 69–72, 167–168
self-ownership 32
self-respect 77, 78, 129

Sen, A. 14, 46, 84, 197, *see also* capabilities
Shue, H. 95, 156, 172
Simmons, A. 227, 228–229
Singer, P. 95
social contract theory 197–218
social exclusion 63
social trust 134–137, 142, 146
sovereignty 21, 191–193, 215, 230
special relationships 17, 137
stability 76–78
State of Nature 45, 50, 96, 198
states 10, 158
stoics 10, 21, 183
Stratton-Lake, P. 246–247
subordination of women 84, 123
subsidiarity 14
sufficiency 92–93
sustainability 15

Tamir, Y. 165
Tan, K. 60, 71, 184–185, 186–190,
193, 222
Thomson, J. 133–146

Unger, P. 95
universalism 128, 180, 182–183
utilitarianism 197
utopianism 122, 235–248
and human nature 242–243

Van Parijs, P. 38

Waldron, J. 37, 57, 208–209
Walzer, M. 18, 51
Weale, A. 19